Christology in Conflict

For Sandra with love and thanks

Christology in Conflict

*The Identity of a Saviour in
Rahner and Barth*

BRUCE MARSHALL

Basil Blackwell

Copyright © Bruce D. Marshall 1987

First published 1987

Basil Blackwell Ltd
108 Cowley Road, Oxford, OX4 1JF, UK

Basil Blackwell Inc.
432 Park Avenue South, Suite 1503
New York, NY 10016, USA

British Library Cataloguing in Publication Data

Marshall, Bruce
   Christology in conflict: the identity of
   a saviour in Rahner and Barth.
   1. Jesus Christ
   I. Title
   232   BT202
   ISBN 0-631-15465-5

Library of Congress Cataloging in Publication Data

Marshall, Bruce, 1955–
   Christology in conflict.
   Revision of the author's thesis (Ph. D.)—
   Yale University presented under title:
   Particular identity and method in Christology.
   Bibliography: p.
   Includes index.
   1. Jesus Christ—History of doctrines—20th century.
2. Rahner, Karl, 1904—Contributions in Christology.
3. Barth, Karl, 1886—1968—Contributions in Christology.
I. Title.
BT198.M387   1987   232'.092'2   87-6592
ISBN 0-631-15465-5

Typeset in 11 on 12½ pt Baskerville
by Alan Sutton Publishing, Gloucester
Printed in Great Britain by T.J. Press Ltd, Padstow

Contents

Contents

Preface

The problem with which this book deals has been pervasive in Christian theology since the Enlightenment: how can universal and ultimate significance be ascribed coherently to Jesus of Nazareth, a particular person? The theological conflict over this question is by no means peculiar to Karl Rahner and Karl Barth: many other theologians have taken sides on the issue, if not often as powerfully as have these two. Conversely, there is more to each of their theologies than this conflict (including, I suspect, important areas where they would be allies rather than opponents). This problem overlaps with other recurrent issues in modern theology, especially in the areas of Christology, hermeneutics and theological method. For example, the developing argument in America between revisionist and postliberal theologies is closely bound up with this problem, but that argument covers a much broader front. At the same time, however, the question of how a universal saviour can have a particular identity has its own logic and cannot be resolved simply by an appeal to general 'revisionist' or 'postliberal' principles. This distinctive question and the conflict to which it has given rise need as far as possible to be clarified and assessed on their own terms. That is what I have attempted to do.

A few remarks are necessary regarding the translations and citations in the text. The major works of Rahner and Barth are for the most part available in uniform English translations. Because these standard translations are readily accessible and are the means by which most English speakers (myself included) come to know Rahner and Barth, I have used them wherever possible. However, they are not always reliable or precise and for that reason I have frequently made my own translation from the

German original, as well as doing this for those texts which are not available in translation. In order to make the notes useful both to those who have access to the German texts and those who do not, I have given references to both the German and the English editions. If the German edition is cited first, the translation is my own; if the English edition is cited first, I have followed the standard translation. Thus the citation, *SzT*, vol. 8, p. 44; *TI*, vol. 9, p. 29, gives both German and English references for a passage quoted from Rahner, and indicates that the translation is my own (the abbreviations are explained in the notes). For the citations of Thomas Aquinas the matter is simpler – all the translations are my own.

An earlier version of this study was my doctoral dissertation at Yale University. This makes it especially fitting to thank those who have been my teachers. There are two to whom I owe a special debt. George Lindbeck has been for me a continuing example of the way generosity of spirit and critical perception can coincide. He read all of these chapters with care and enabled me to see how I could improve them in both ways. For me, as for many others, Hans Frei has been an unending source of good ideas, and has helped me to bring those ideas to fruition in such a way that they are genuinely my own. David Kelsey and Gene Outka read the original dissertation and made a number of helpful suggestions. Several friends who were my colleagues in the theology programme at Yale commented perceptively on parts of this study in various stages of its preparation and have been my companions in many happy hours of theological conversation: Kathryn Tanner, Mark Horst, Paul McGlasson and Ronald Feenstra. To Edmund Perry of Northwestern University I also owe special thanks, since without his timely help I might never have taken up the study of theology.

Dean Keith Anderson of St Olaf College provided a grant to aid in the preparation of the typescript. The labour of producing the typescript was done with cheerful energy by Jay Norton, senior student at the College. Stephan Chambers, Julia Mosse and the editorial staff of Basil Blackwell have made the distance from Northfield to Oxford seem trifling.

My gratitude to my parents and to my wife in connection with this book is of a rather different kind. My mother and father willingly provided for the education of their four children, at great personal sacrifice and with no strings attached. My wife Sandra willingly assumed far more than her share of our common responsibilities and graciously bore with my absence (not to mention, on occasion, my presence) while this study was being written. To them go my deepest thanks.

Bruce D. Marshall
Northfield, Minnesota

1

Introduction: The Historical Shape
of the Problem

My interest in this book is to analyse and assess two quite
different methods or strategies, peculiar to modern theology, for
showing how Jesus Christ, the particular person whose identity is
depicted in the Gospel stories, can be ultimately meaningful or
significant. I am not primarily concerned with the specific way
Jesus' significance is characterized, although I will have occasion
to examine several characterizations of it in some detail. Rather,
I shall try to discover whether one of these two divergent
strategies, which seek to show how the redeeming significance
Christians ascribe to Jesus can be meaningful or intelligible, is
more consistent with a conviction they both share – that he
alone, as a particular person, can have this function and
significance. Since one of these strategies, unquestionably the
more prevalent of the two in modern theology, has had a rich and
varied history since the late seventeenth century, it may be useful
to give some indication of the historical background and development of the issue to which I will be directing my attention.

In order to trace, however briefly, the origin of the problem
with which this book is concerned, I must begin with what seems
to have been a distinctive feature of life in the West during the
millennium or so when, for the great majority, Christianity was
the native and global context of action, affection and belief.
Beginning in the early Middle Ages, it seems to have been taken
quite for granted, in popular as well as learned or 'high' culture,
that the function of that which is 'ultimately significant' or 'most
important' in human life belonged uniquely and solely to Jesus
Christ, the particular person whose story is told in the Bible.
This is not merely to say that Jesus of Nazareth was assumed,
where Christianity had been assimilated at all, to be the Lord,

saviour, redeemer and so forth. That fact alone does not capture the comprehensiveness of the assumption. Not only is this exalted status ascribed to Jesus as a matter of course, but it is assumed that *whatever* is appropriately characterized as 'ultimately meaningful' or 'ultimately significant' is to be referred to him. Materially, this means that the Biblical story as a whole centres on him, the concepts and doctrines which may issue from engagement with that story (for example 'creation', 'sin', 'redemption') are all tied to him in some way, and the dispositions and actions which are congruent with that story and its conceptual redescription (such as 'faith', 'hope', and 'love') each look to him in their own manner. This is not to say, of course, that there was any unanimity about just how the Bible should be read in detail, or about just what doctrinal formulations and life prescriptions were truly coherent with the figure depicted in the Gospels. People sometimes fought and died over these matters, and even when they only argued there was an enormous diversity of views. But Catholics and heretics, mystics and scholastics, learned and unlearned, and, later, Protestants of all kinds, were at one in the assumption that whatever is ultimately meaningful or significant, and therefore 'redemption' and a 'redeemer', is indissolubly bound up with the particular person, Jesus Christ. Indeed, the mutually necessary relation of Jesus' particular identity with whatever has the function of ultimate meaningfulness or significance was taken to be an entirely fit and nonproblematic one. A great deal of attention was given to precisely *how* Jesus has or fulfils this function, but *that* it belongs to him alone was so obvious that there was no need to draw explicit attention to the fact.

The point of these remarks is not simply to exercise a capacity for colossal generalization but to establish a point of contrast with what was to come. For towards the end of the seventeenth century, as had not been the case in over a millennium, the inextricable tie of all that is ultimately meaningful to Jesus Christ as a particular person ceased to be completely obvious in Western culture. There had, of course, always been isolated individuals outside the cultural mainstream who in one way or another had denied it. But, as the first stage of English Deism indicates perhaps most clearly, there was beginning to develop in the late seventeenth century a culturally supportable place where it was possible and sensical to draw explicit attention to this assumption, and thus also explicitly to reject it.

In England and slightly later in France, the denial of this long-dominant and obvious conviction initially had a place only in high culture, where for the most part it remained, with steadily growing influence, throughout the eighteenth century. The heart of the Deists's denial of the traditional assumption lies simply in their willingness to argue that the opposite is true. That which has the function of ultimate meaningfulness or significance, they argued, should be readily available to everyone. For just this reason it cannot be inextricably and necessarily tied to a particular person, or more generally to the particular data of a supernatural revelation, since these are inevitably not accessible to all. For the problem with which I am concerned, however, the decisive and truly formative development occurs when the novel Deist assumption is taken over, virtually as a matter of course, by writers with an explicit Christian and theological interest. Such writers clearly retain something like the traditional Christian assumption that whatever is ultimately meaningful is uniquely and unsurpassably realized in the particular person, Jesus Christ. At the same time, they find compelling the Deist contention that whatever is ultimately meaningful must in at least some form be available to everyone and therefore must admit of being expressed in logically general terms.

By accepting both assumptions and striving to work out a compromise between them, these writers were attempting to mediate between two perceived alternatives which were alike unacceptable for them. In the English situation of the late seventeenth and early eighteenth centuries, the alternatives were Deism, which had no use for the particularity of Jesus, and Puritanism, for which the ultimate meaningfulness of Jesus as a particular person was woven into a doctrinal scheme in which double predestination and original sin were, so it appeared, indispensable explicative elements. The mediating aim was thus to show that the meaningfulness of redemption, a redeemer and revelation was indeed established by the coherence of such notions with general and implicitly universal criteria of religious and moral meaningfulness (as the Deists had maintained), but that redemption and its cognates remain uniquely and perfectly realized in Jesus Christ as a particular person (as the Puritans had maintained). During this period, perhaps the clearest English example of this procedure is the concluding section of Locke's *The Reasonableness of Christianity*.[1]

However, it was not in England or France but in Germany that this reversal of the traditional assumption, as it has been briefly outlined, was accomplished in a way that had a deep and lasting impact on theology. The German Enlightenment shared with that in England and France the new conviction that whatever has the function of ultimate meaningfulness or significance must in some form be available to or participated in by all, and so must necessarily have the status of something general rather than something particular. But the Germans articulated this assumption, so characteristic of nascent secularity and modernity, in a distinctive way. Quite unlike parallel movements in France and England, the Enlightenment in Germany did not assert itself by rejecting Christianity outright. Rather, the emergence in German high culture of this characteristically modern assumption about 'that which is ultimately meaningful' was consistently informed by an urge to find a culturally significant place (aesthetic, moral, metaphysical, or sometimes all three) for a radically revised Christianity. Primarily, this meant reinterpreting what was taken to be the heart of traditional Christianity – the belief that Jesus of Nazareth is the unique historical redeemer – in such a way that some tangible connection with the Christian notion of redemption remained but without any indissoluble bond to Jesus himself. More precisely, beginning with Lessing and Herder and culminating with Hegel and Marx, German writers of this period sought increasingly comprehensive ways of either making the idea of redemption symbolically significant, or else making the generalized idea of a unique redeemer itself indispensable.

In a famous epigram, Lessing stated pungently and with fruitful ambiguity the basic conviction which would guide not only the Enlightenment but also (albeit in significantly altered form) Idealism and Romanticism, in their radical reinterpretation of the Christian ideas of redemption and a redeemer: 'Accidental truths of history can never become the proof of necessary truths of reason.'[2] A little later, in his 'The Education of the Human Race', Lessing sketched a view of quasi-providential human historical development which can appropriately be characterized or symbolized as 'redemption', and in which Christian doctrines like the

Trinity and 'the Son's satisfaction', while irrational and senseless in what Lessing took to be their manifest meaning, may yet have a latent and usable rational meaning.[3] However, Lessing indicates, the various 'positive religions', especially Christianity with its global claims about the import of Jesus Christ as a particular person, are only aids on the way to the realization of this latent meaning, and may all be equally valuable for that purpose.[4]

It fell to Kant, however, to develop the Enlightenment assumption expressed in Lessing's epigram into a systematic reinterpretation of the idea of a unique redeemer which wholly dispensed with any appeal to Jesus of Nazareth. In Kant's *Religion Within the Limits of Reason Alone*, the unique redeemer is an ideal of perfection, a moral archetype for which we need no 'empirical example', since the archetype, in Kant's words, 'is to be sought nowhere but in our own reason'.[5] With Hegel the matter is somewhat more complicated since he wants to find some role for Jesus, however ambiguous, in the process of redemption. Finally though, for Hegel the reconciliation of the absolute with its natural and historical objectification must be grasped conceptually rather than representationally and hence must be shorn of the limitations of particularity. Even for Marx, 'that which is ultimately significant' is a historical process of alienation and reconciliation which in some respects bears a striking resemblance to the Christian belief in redemption (especially to the Hegelian construal of that belief). But any attempt to tie this process to Jesus of Nazareth is not only unnecessary (as, in different ways, Lessing and Kant had held), but a damaging obstacle which must be overcome.

Along these lines, German high culture from roughly the mid-eighteenth to the mid-nineteenth century saw an enormously powerful series of developments in which the function of 'that which is ultimately significant' in human life and culture was repeatedly claimed for some radically revised version of the Christian belief in redemption (even if, as with Marx, this came to involve an explicit rejection of Christianity). Throughout this development, it was assumed that whatever is ultimately meaningful and valuable, however conceived, must be the kind of thing which admits of characterization in general terms, and in this way be accessible in some form to all persons. For the radical revisionists, this assumption could only be maintained if that which is

ultimately meaningful and significant, while it may express the
true but latent meaning of Christianity, bears no essential and
necessary connection to Jesus as a particular person.

Even more readily than in England, much Protestant theology
in Germany found the new assumption about the fundamentally
general character of 'that which is ultimately meaningful' not only
congenial, but virtually self-evident. Yet against the radical
revisionists, with whom they shared this assumption, they usually
supposed that it was consistent with the Christian conviction that
all things ultimately meaningful are indissolubly bound up with
Jesus of Nazareth. Indeed, perhaps largely because they were
faced with alternatives that found meaning in Christianity by
explicitly cutting the tie of its concepts and doctrines to the
person of Jesus, theologians in Germany who strove for the
'mediating' position asserted this conviction with sometimes
astonishing vigour and inventiveness, far outstripping that of the
ultimately unsuccessful Christian high-culture response to Deism
in England. To be sure, there are Neologians and Rationalists
(like Semler the Biblical critic and Wegscheider the dogmatician)
for whom, under the influence of the new assumption, the bond of
what is morally and religiously meaningful in Christianity to
Jesus as a particular person is attenuated to the point of triviality;
what he provides is for the most part available elsewhere, even if
not in such pure form.[6] But in Schleiermacher the new assumption and the Christian conviction are stated and combined with
exceptional power.

On the one hand, the meaningfulness and significance of the
ideas of redemption and a redeemer depend for Schleiermacher
upon the coherence of these ideas with the notion of a universal,
immediate consciousness of God, coupled with that of the full
realization of this consciousness in the other forms of human
experience. More precisely, the 'redemption' of which Christians
speak is meaningful and intelligible because it can be conceived
as the relative domination of the universal God-consciousness (or
'feeling of absolute dependence') in all experience. Similarly, the
idea of a 'redeemer' is capable of being 'ultimately significant' for
Schleiermacher (as it had been, in a very different way, for Kant)
because it can be conceived as an 'archetype' (*Urbild*); the
redeemer is the one whose God-consciousness completely
dominates all of his or her experience, and is thus conceived as

the ideal perfection of the basic condition of which all persons are at least implicitly aware as their own.[7] In both cases, 'the dominance of the God-consciousness in experience' serves as a ground or criterion, not for the truth, but precisely for meaningfulness and intelligibility, of the Christian belief in redemption and a redeemer; the latter can be shown to cohere in a unique way with this criterion. For my purposes, the crucial feature of this criterion, a feature which it shares with the different criteria proposed by the radical revisionists, is its logical type: it is a general criterion which characterizes 'the kind of thing' which can be ultimately meaningful or significant, and so quite intentionally involves no logically necessary reference to Jesus as a particular person, or indeed to any Christian *specificum*.

On the other hand, Schleiermacher forcefully asserts the conviction that the ideas of redemption and a redeemer, and thus 'that which is ultimately significant', have in fact been uniquely and unsurpassably realized precisely in Jesus as a particular person, and only in him. The Christian religion is distinguished 'by the fact that in it everything is related to the redemption accomplished by Jesus of Nazareth', who himself 'is distinguished from all others as Redeemer alone and for all'.[8] It is this conviction which Schleiermacher will strive to honour and to explicate in his entire theology; he will do so, as I have indicated, by following a method or strategy in which the meaningfulness of that conviction is justified by its coherence with a general criterion.

In the theological generations that followed Schleiermacher and Hegel, the mediating strategy which Schleiermacher had so powerfully articulated was virtually taken for granted in German theology; however it might be executed, this was assumed to be the right way to proceed in theology, and especially in Christology. There were, of course, important exceptions to this generalization. D. F. Strauss in particular was a thorn in the side of his contemporaries, on account of his sometimes caustic denial, from within the theological guild, that a meaningful notion of redemption could be indissolubly bound to Jesus as a particular person. For the most part, however, the mediating strategy which I have outlined was the order of the day and it was worked out in a wide variety of ways. Some, under the influence of Hegel, sought to include the assumption of reference to Jesus within a meaningful notion of redemption by speculative means (Biedermann, for example). A great many others, influenced primarily by Schleier-macher, sought in various ways to do the same thing without relying upon a comprehensive speculative instrument (for example, Nitzsch and Schweizer, who followed Schleiermacher closely, and Rothe, who did not).[9] Still others sought to articulate the same connection in a self-consciously conservative and confessional mode (such as J. C. K. Hofmann). Subsequent shifts in the reigning theological conceptuality proved to be quite compatible with the mediating strategy. Ritschl and his school argued that theology did not have to follow either Schleiermacher or Hegel, but still maintained that the meaningfulness of redemption and a redeemer must be accessible on the basis of its coherence with general criteria. The so-called dialectical and neo-orthodox theology which originated in the early 1920s is only an apparent exception to this trend. These writers drastically altered the typical characterizations of 'that which is ultimately significant' from those which had usually prevailed in nineteenth-century theology. It was now not some form of divine presence in immediate experience or cultural aspiration which grounded the meaningfulness of the distinctively Christian belief in redemption, but some form of universally felt divine absence from immediate experience and cultural aspiration. As before, the criterion or ground for the meaningfulness of redemption and a redeemer remains logically general and implicitly universal in character. In our own day, the preference for conceiving the criterion of 'ultimate significance' in negative or paradoxical ways has largely faded; Karl Rahner is typical in proposing, as we shall see, a distinctly positive criterion of 'ultimate significance' as a basis for executing the mediating strategy.

The point of departure for this book is specifically the logic of this mediating position, the historical context of which I have tried briefly to indicate.[10] While the logic of the position will occupy some length in subsequent chapters, it is well to be clear about the basic shape of the argument at the outset. The aim of this mediating argument has been, and continues to be, to find a way between perceived alternatives which seem equally unacceptable. On the one side is an inflexible and ungenerous kind of orthodoxy, which grounds the meaningfulness of redemption through Jesus Christ (or perhaps of some cognate characterization of Jesus' ultimate significance) simply in an appeal to divine or Biblical authority, and perhaps also by locating it in a supposedly fixed matrix of dogma. On the other side there are various worldviews which, while they may in some cases not only be sympathetic to Christianity but be genuninely theological as well, yet reject any necessary connection of 'that which is ultimately significant' to Jesus Christ. As I have indicated, the project of mediating between these alternatives suggests a distinctive method or strategy for Christology, especially systematic or dogmatic Christology. That method will distinguish, in practice if not always explicitly, between two main tasks or questions in Christology. One task is to show how the kinds of significance Christians ascribe to Jesus Christ can be universally meaningful and accessible on the strength of their coherence with logically general criteria, which indicate what kind of thing can count as 'ultimately meaningful' (such criteria often taking the form of a pre-thematic experience or structure putatively common to all persons). The complementary task is to explicate (rather than to establish or prove) the basic conviction that Jesus Christ is the particular person to whom alone these various kinds of significance actually belong. This is often done by indicating some way in which dominant features of Jesus' particular life seem to fit with the material significance, presumed to be meaningful on other grounds, which Christians ascribe to him. These two tasks are taken to be consistent with one another and mutually necessary. Together, so the mediating argument goes, these two tasks constitute the proper method or procedure by which the meaningfulness and intelligibility of the Christian belief in redemption and a redeemer can be maintained in the modern world, without sacrificing or subverting the indissoluble bond of that belief to Jesus Christ as a particular person. The aim and logic of this mediating method in Christology are aptly summarized in a remark by Hans Frei, commenting on the relative constancy of this procedure, despite repeated shifts of conceptuality, since the days of Locke. Most proponents of this mediating Christology, Frei observes,

> have disavowed that they were out to 'prove' the truth of Christianity, chiefly the assertion that Jesus Christ is the Redeemer – the claim with which (as it seemed to them) all

other Christian doctrines must harmonize. But they have all agreed that in one way or another the religious *meaningfulness* (as distinct from demonstration of the truth) of the claim could, indeed must, be perspicuous through its relation to other accounts of general human experience.[11]

The aim of this study, it can be said, is two-fold. In the first place, I will try to see whether this distinctive christological *method* is actually consistent with the *assumption* upon which its proponents ordinarily insist, the assumption being that however we characterize 'that which is ultimately significant', the latter is necessarily bound up with Jesus Christ as a particular person. To this end, I will take a detailed look at a highly influential recent attempt consistently to combine the distinctive method and the specific assumption to which I have drawn attention: the Christology of Karl Rahner. Rahner is an especially good test case for the consistency of the typical mediating strategy. Perhaps even more than Schleiermacher, he articulates and applies this christological method or procedure with exceptional circumspection, and is also quite clear about his basic doctrinal commitments. Especially important among the latter is the indispensability of Jesus Christ as a particular person for any theologically admissible account of 'that which is ultimately meaningful', or, to use Rahner's term, of that which is *heilsbedeutsam* ('significant for salvation'). Thus Rahner gives a careful account of how what he calls 'an absolute saviour' can be meaningful and accessible on the basis of a general criterion, and also vigorously maintains the conviction that only Jesus Christ can in fact be the 'absolute saviour'. Chapters 2 and 3 are devoted to analysing and assessing the consistency of Rahner's christological method with this christological conviction.

The second aim of this study is suggested by my assessment of Rahner's procedure. If, as I shall argue, the distinctive christological strategy characteristic of mediating theology is finally unsuccessful, not because of any failure in execution (for Rahner executes it brilliantly), but because intrinsic logical barriers keep it from being executed consistently, then contemporary Christology seems faced with an explicit choice about its basic aims. It can, as did the radical revisionists in Enlightenment Germany, deliberately jettison the conviction that whatever is 'ultimately significant' can in a meaningful way be definitively tied to Jesus Christ as a particular person. Or it can find ways of articulating the conviction that Jesus Christ uniquely has the function of 'that which is ultimately significant' in which the meaningfulness of this conviction does not depend upon an appeal to general, putatively universal criteria, but which do not on that account attempt to ground the meaningfulness of the conviction in an appeal to sheer divine authority. In chapter 4 I will try to outline such a procedure, as it is evinced in Karl Barth's theology of reconciliation (although this strategy could be executed very differently from the way Barth himself works it out). In chapter 5, I will consider the special problems which arise, given the procedure found in Barth, with regard to the assumption (shared by Rahner) that the 'immediate presence' or 'incarnation' of God in Jesus Christ is in some form indispensable to further characterizations of his ultimate significance. At this point, it will be useful to introduce a few considerations from the Christology of Thomas Aquinas, which bear in an illuminating way on this specific nest of issues.

Throughout this study, it should be pointed out, the procedure exemplified by Barth will be called 'the first way', and that exemplified by Rahner will be called 'the second way'. The rhetorical usefulness of these bland designations will be apparent when they are introduced in the next chapter. But there is a more substantive reason for my preferring 'the second way' to a more suggestive term such as 'mediating Christology'. As I have indicated, the christological procedure which I will call 'the second way', distinguished by its appeal to general criteria of meaningfulness, usually has been taken for granted by theologians wanting to find a middle way between the perceived alternatives of an orthodoxy which rests solely on an appeal to divine or Biblical authority, and a position which cuts the tie to Jesus altogether. But Barth, following a radically different christological procedure ('the first way', as I shall call it), also wants clearly to avoid both of these positions. As will be seen, moreover, Barth seeks not so much to mediate between these two views as to set the issue of the relation between Jesus' particularity and his significance on a basically different footing. I will therefore mark the distinction between these two christological methods, which are my main concern, in relatively neutral fashion.

One other note – a cautionary one – is in order before I turn to Rahner. This concerns the use of the phrase 'Jesus Christ as a particular person'. What I mean by the phrase, especially by the notion of 'a particular person', will be discussed in some detail later on.[12] But with regard to the way in which we have access to or acquaintance with this particular person, the phrase will be taken to have the broad sense of 'the one who is identified on the basis of the Gospel narratives'. This means that for the purposes here, it is an entirely open question precisely how Jesus can be successfully identified 'on the basis of' these narratives and, more specifically, what role historical criticism might play in this identification. This is simply because the *way* Jesus is identified would seem to have no decisive effect on the logic of the issue with which we are concerned. One could, for example, hold that historical criticism is the sole yardstick for what can count as an identifying description of Jesus, and also maintain that whatever significance is ascribed to Jesus, as identified in this manner, is itself ultimately meaningful on account of its coherence with general criteria. Or, to put the point more broadly, it would be possible to follow either one of the two christological strategies which are our main concern either with relatively little reliance on historical criticism for the identification of Jesus Christ in his particuliarity (as do Rahner and especially Barth), or with extensive reliance on historical criticism for that purpose (as do contemporary writers like Pannenberg on the Protestant side, and Schillebeeckx and Küng on the Catholic side), without affecting the logic of the method in question.[13] This implies that no amount of rigour or success in achieving a purely historical identification of Jesus is sufficient by itself to ensure that he is logically indispensable in a christological account of 'that which is ultimately significant', as both strategies assume he must be. I will not argue this point any further but will assume along the lines just indicated that the way in which Jesus Christ is identified in his particularity, and the basis upon which the significance ascribed to him is taken to be meaningful and intelligible, are logically distinct issues which vary independently of one another.[14] My concern here is solely with the latter issue, that is, with indicating what kind of christological method consistently maintains the assumption that Jesus Christ, however we succeed in identifying and naming him, is alone the definitive bearer of 'that which is ultimately significant'.

NOTES

1   Cf. chapter 2, n. 29.
2   Gotthold Lessing, 'On the Proof of the Spirit and of Power', in *Lessing's Theological Writings*, ed. and tr. Henry Chadwick, (Stanford, CA: 1972), p. 53.
3   Cf. 'The Education of the Human Race', nos 73–5 in *Lessing's Theological Writings*, pp. 94–5.
4   On the penultimate usefulness of Christianity, cf. 'The Education of the Human Race', no. 77 in *Lessing's Theological Writings*, p. 95. On the basically equal value of all 'positive' religions, cf. 'the parable of the rings' in Lessing's play, *Nathan the Wise*, Act III, Scene 7.
5   Immanuel Kant, *Religion Within the Limits of Reason Alone*, tr. Theodore M. Greene and Hoyt A. Hudson, (New York: 1960), p. 57.
6   So, for example, Emanuel Hirsch summarizes Semler's view of the indispensable reference to Jesus as the 'conviction that Jesus is the teacher, benefactor and redeemer who exercises divine authority, and who teaches the general grace and love of God for our moral (that is, ethical–religious) benefit' in *Geschichte der neuern evangelischen Theologie*, 4th edn (5 vols, Gütersloh: 1968), vol. 4, p. 80.
7   Cf. Friedrich Schleiermacher, *The Christian Faith*, 2nd edn, tr. H. R. Mackintosh and J. S. Stewart (Philadelphia: 1976), §93, on the redeemer as *Urbild*.
8   Schleiermacher, *Christian Faith*, §11, prop., §11, 4.
9   This group explicitly saw itself as practising 'mediating theology' (*Vermittlungstheologie*), although, as I have outlined, the position existed well before the name.
10 It should be noted that the essentially christological mediating project with which I am concerned here is only one of several kinds of 'mediation' characteristic of modern theology. Attempts to mediate between 'Christianity and culture', and between 'theology and philosophy', for example, have also been steady preoccupations. While all these projects overlap in various ways, they are not identical, and all should not be equated with the specific issue upon which my attention will be focused.
11 Hans W. Frei, *The Eclipse of Biblical Narrative* (New Haven: 1974), p. 128.
12 Cf. especially chap. 2, pp. 42–7, and chap. 4, pp. 124–5.
13 Pannenberg, for example, while he strives for an identifying description of Jesus as a particular person which is justified at each point on historical grounds alone, follows basically the same strategy as Rahner (although in a different conceptual mode) when it comes to showing how the redeeming significance which he takes to be

appropriate to that description can actually be meaningful and intelligible. For an instance of this procedure in Pannenberg's case, cf. chap. 2, n. 29.

14 Rahner's Christology exemplifies this logical distinction with particular clarity; cf. chap. 2, especially pp. 47–53. I am also assuming, it should be mentioned, that 'Jesus' as identified on the basis of a historical reconstruction of the Gospel narratives, and 'Jesus' as identified through those narratives without an indispensable appeal to historical criticism, are the same logical and ascriptive subject. This is not self-evident, and is arguably not the case at all. But it is usually taken for granted by theologians for whom historical criticism has a necessary positive role in an identifying description of Jesus.

2

The Place of Jesus Christ in Rahner's Christology

In the following pages, I will attempt to clarify and assess the place of Jesus Christ as a particular person in Karl Rahner's Christology. More precisely, my aim is to discover whether the theological project which Rahner forcefully exemplifies can consistently account for the basic conviction, which he assumes is normative for Christian faith and theology, that the unique redeemer can only be Jesus as a particular person, distinct from all others. This question arises because Rahner's theology, and centrally his Christology, is like many others since the early eighteenth century in one distinctive respect: he supposes that in order to believe in Jesus Christ as the unique redeemer it is necessary to show how that belief is possible and credible, and to do so by an appeal to general criteria of religious and moral meaningfulness. Rahner carefully specifies the function of this demonstration of the possibility of belief in Jesus Christ, and he is under no illusion that it is the sole business of theology. Nevertheless, he insists that it is indispensable for any workable theology in our time. The fate of the particularity of Jesus in a theology and Christology preoccupied with, and guided by, this 'question of credibility' will thus be the dominant interest in the ensuing consideration of Rahner.

Due to the special nature of this interest, the following discussion, while detailed, will not be a complete treatment of Rahner's extraordinarily rich Christology, let alone of the wider aspects of his theology which I will occasionally introduce. Consequently, much that is perceptive and valuable in Rahner's Christology will receive scant attention here. His harmonization of 'the idea of an absolute saviour' with an evolutionary view of the world, his reconceptualization of the ideas of incarnation and hypostatic union in terms of an ontology in which being is symbolic self-expression, his deft resolution of a knot of problems surrounding the *scientia Christi* by appeal to a distinction between pre-thematic and thematized knowledge – to mention but a few major issues – will all be treated in passing, at best. By the same token, I will not be able to deal with a variety of critical questions that may arise in connection with these and other positions important to Rahner's Christology. Instead, I will persistently have to focus my attention upon those features of his Christology which cumulatively raise the question of how the particularity of Jesus Christ functions in that Christology as a whole, especially with regard to the characterizations of ultimate redeeming significance which are ascribed to Jesus. To begin with, I will have to indicate the way in which the structure of Rahner's Christology deliberately accommodates his desire to show how belief in Jesus Christ is possible and credible. Furthermore, I will have to specify just how much this demonstration of the possibility of belief should be taken to show.

RAHNER'S ARGUMENT *IN GLOBO*

Like all areas of theology, Christology for Rahner is basically divisible into two aspects, the transcendental and the categorial. In conjunction with a rich variety of associated concepts and descriptions, these two aspects together comprise 'the double structure of Christology'.[1] In order to grasp the full shape and significance of this comprehensive distinction specifically in Christology, the reasons he employs it and the questions he thinks it answers, one must look to see how Rahner actually uses it in that context. However, a brief characterization of the transcendental/categorial distinction in general will be a helpful preliminary to an analysis of its deployment in Rahner's Christology.

The 'transcendental' aspect of theology has three particularly important features. First of all, a transcendental procedure arises precisely in order to answer all questions of credibility and possibility; thus the transcendental aspect of theology seeks to show how various Christian beliefs and patterns of action are possible. 'A transcendental line of inquiry, regardless of the particular area of subject matter (*Gegenstandsbereich*) in which it is applied, is present when and to the extent that it raises the question of the conditions in which knowledge of a specific object (*Gegenstandes*) is possible in the knowing subject (*Subjekt*) himself.'[2] Rahner's way of explaining the first general feature of a transcendental theology already includes the second. A specifically transcendental inquiry in theology answers questions of possibility by locating conditions *in the human subject* which make a certain belief or action possible. Such a procedure seeks to say what it is about human beings that makes it possible for them to know God as he is attested in Scripture and the doctrines of the Church. In the transcendental aspect of theology, 'one . . . asks about the necessary conditions in the theological subject for the knowledge of each dogmatic object (*Gegenstand*), and one proves that there are such *a priori* conditions for the knowledge of this object.'[3] Third, transcendental theology in Rahner's hands implies a definite conception of the human subject. Since the point of any transcendental procedure is to locate the conditions in the human subject which make it possible for us to know specific, describable objects and have specific, describable experiences (here, 'dogmatic' objects and experiences), Rahner supposes that these conditions must make up a region in the human subject of a different order from that which they condition. This distinctive realm of human experience is conscious, but pre-thematic and pre-linguistic, even though it is susceptible of linguistic, conceptual elucidation. Precisely as conscious but pre-thematic, this 'transcendental experience' is (in its many and varied aspects) the universal, indispensable condition of the possibility of all our thematized, explicit, describable experiences. 'We shall call *transcendental experience* the subjective, unthematic, necessary and unfailing consciousness of the knowing subject that is co-present in every spiritual act of knowledge . . . This experience is called *transcendental* experience . . . because it consists precisely in the transcendence beyond any particular group of possible objects or categories.'[4]

By contrast with his occasional explicit sketches of the 'transcendental' aspect of theology, Rahner virtually never pauses to give a general characterization of the 'categorial' aspect. The basic import of what one could call 'categorial theology' is clear enough from what has been said about its contrast term.

'Categorial' simply means 'what can be put into categories', so the 'categorical aspect of theology' deals with 'dogmatic objects' in so far as they consist in, or are subject to, explicit linguistic description. More precisely (since for Rahner the transcendental too can, at least indirectly, be evoked in language), the 'categorial' is circumscribed in space and time; in this sense human words, the sacraments, the church and Scripture can all be called 'something categorial'.[5] Rahner is especially given to contrasting transcendental with 'historical', where 'historical' has the broad meaning of 'spatio-temporal', and so is equivalent to categorial.[6]

Despite the irreducible distinctness of the transcendental and categorial aspects of theology and their disparity in subject; matter (*a priori* experiential structures of the human subject; history, language and objects), the two belong together; indeed, they complement one another. Rahner typically puts his general remarks about this 'mutually conditioning' relationship in an anthropological vein: 'Man as subject and as person is a historical being in such a way that he is historical precisely *as* a transcendent subject; his subjective essence of unlimited transcendentality is mediated *historically* to him in his knowledge and in his free self-realization.'[7] Categorial realities can be apprehended by us only in so far as their basic structures are anticipated in our transcendental constitution, and at the same time we only grasp ourselves as the subjects of specifically transcendental experience by applying ourselves to the apprehension of historical, limited, objective realities.[8] As Rahner likes to put it, there is a 'circle between transcendental and categorial experience'.[9]

Ever since the extraordinary importance of Rahner's theology became apparent after the Second World War, much of the research on his work has focused on the details and justification of his general transcendental scheme, which I have just quite briefly outlined. Under the influence of Maréchal's critique of Kant, Rahner begins to work out his transcendental scheme in his first book, *Spirit in the World*, which strives to articulate a theory of knowledge that is at once transcendental and genuinely Thomistic.[10] In *Hearers of the Word* (*Hörer des Wortes*), his second book, Rahner further develops the scheme in the form of a general anthropology, which serves as the basis for a philosophy of religion structured by the idea of an *a priori* and transcendental human openness for a possible divine revelation.[11] Especially in

Roman Catholic theology, where his influence has been most strongly felt, intense interest has surrounded the plausibility of the transcendental scheme worked out in these early writings; the viability of Rahner's approach and of transcendental Thomism in general has been widely discussed on epistemological and general anthropological grounds, both of a theological and a more broadly philosophical sort.

My interest, by contrast, does not lie in Rahner's transcendental scheme *per se*, nor in assessing its epistemological and anthropological persuasiveness. These issues have been in the forefront of recent Rahner research, but for purposes here they can be left open. Indeed, for the sake of the ensuing argument I can grant the essentials of Rahner's transcendental scheme, specifically his claim that there are 'necessary conditions in the theological subject for the knowledge of each dogmatic object'. The theological problem with which I am concerned is the place of Jesus Christ as a particular person in a Christology structured by the need to show how universal criteria of meaningfulness can enable us to believe in him as the unique redeemer. This problem does not hinge upon the feasibility of Rahner's transcendental epistemology and anthropology as such but upon the feasibility of their application in a christological context, guided by the fundamental assumption of that need. In this sense, as will be seen, the problem to which I will attend arises precisely when one *accepts* the essentials of the transcendental scheme and puts them to a specific christological use. So I will not be further concerned with Rahner's transcendental scheme and its viability *in abstracto*, but with the way the scheme works in its christological application.

In order to appreciate the function of the specifically transcendental aspect of Rahner's Christology, and thereby its effect upon the status of the particularity of Jesus Christ, it is necessary to introduce a second comprehensive distinction. On Rahner's account, all theological objects, individually and as a whole, can be considered both from the perspective of fundamental theology and from the perspective of dogmatic theology. In essence, fundamental theology treats theological subject matter with respect to what makes it *credible*, while dogmatic theology treats this same subject matter with respect to the elucidation of its proper and complete *content*. Fundamental theology, as Rahner puts it, 'is the scientifically exact and methodical reflection on the reasons

(*Gründe*) existentially effective today for faith in the real event of
Christian revelation and its central contents'.[12] This task of
isolating the genuine, 'existentially effective' grounds for the
credibility of the content of Christian faith, as distinguished from
merely apparent or spurious grounds, falls primarily upon
'transcendental theology'. 'A "new fundamental theology" ought
to be to a great extent "transcendental", that is, it ought to reflect
on the conditions within the believing subject which make it
possible to realize the content of faith.'[13]

It is important to stress that for Rahner, fundamental theology
of this specifically transcendental kind is not merely an optional
project in theology, nor is it primarily conceived as an *apologia ad
extra*. On the contrary, a transcendental fundamental theology is a
necessary moment in Christian theology as a whole; in the first
instance, it is precisely the believer who, to whatever degree he or
she is reflectively capable, needs to clarify and secure the grounds
of his or her own faith. For, as Rahner emphasizes, only this
transcendental fundamental theology ensures that the 'central
contents of Christian revelation' can be distinguished from
something which is 'simply a mythological overlay on historical
events'.[14]

Now, given this general concept of fundamental theology, the
decisive question that fundamental theology has to put specifically to faith in Jesus Christ can best be stated using Rahner's
own terms. 'The "act" which seeks or explicitly finds Jesus
Christ', he emphasizes characteristically, 'is supposed to be
significant for salvation (*heilsbedeutsam sein soll*).'[15] In fundamental
theology, the decisive christological question then is, how can
Jesus Christ be *heilsbedeutsam*, significant for salvation? What are
the grounds upon which the belief is credible that Jesus Christ is
the unique historical redeemer, the one who alone has ultimate
significance for human life? Or, as Rahner puts it in one of his
earliest christological essays: 'What we have in mind is an
enquiry, more explicit than is usual, as to why man is capable of
faith in the Christ of Christian dogma.'[16] The characteristic place
and function of the particularity of Jesus in Rahner's Christology,
and the characteristic difficulties that arise here as well, originate
in the application of this notion of fundamental theology to faith
in Jesus Christ. That is, they originate in Rahner's basic convictions about how the belief that Jesus Christ is the unique

redeemer is to be rendered credible.

There seem to be two basically different and contrary ways in which the question, 'how can Jesus Christ be significant for salvation?', might be answered. One way would be to say that what makes Jesus Christ *heilsbedeutsam* is his own life, passion and death and resurrection, so that both the meaning and meaningfulness of 'that which is significant for salvation' are determined by and inseparable from his particularity. On this account, since Jesus is *heilsbedeutsam* precisely in virtue of the actions and events which make him a particular person, principally his death and resurrection, recognizing him as the particular person he is is the one logically indispensable condition of the possibility of knowing him to be *heilsbedeutsam*, that is, of faith in him as redeemer. This position need not shun the question of how faith in Jesus Christ as the unique redeemer is credible; but it insists that because of the way in which Jesus Christ is *heilsbedeutsam*, this question can in the final analysis only be answered by appeal to Jesus as a particular person, and hence by appeal to an identifying description of him. On this account, therefore, the 'credibility' question – the question of how faith in Jesus Christ is possible – cannot be answered by an appeal to general criteria of religious meaningfulness or significance for salvation. On the contrary, an adequate description of Jesus Christ is the logical basis of any answer to the question of how he can be significant for salvation; the task of theology in this respect is to elucidate conceptually the way in which significance for salvation is determined by and dependent on Jesus Christ as a particular person.[17]

A different way of answering this question of credibility would be to say that in order to show how Jesus Christ can be *heilsbedeutsam*, it must be possible to show how there can be *anything at all* which is *heilsbedeutsam*. That is, on this account one must show how it can be meaningful (*sinnvoll*) and intelligible (*verständlich*) to say that any reality is significant for salvation. Here, appeal to a description of Jesus Christ is taken to be insufficient as a basis for an explanation of how he can be *heilsbedeutsam*, although such a description is of course a necessary part of a complete account of Christian faith in Jesus as the unique redeemer. On the contrary, the general question of the credibility of that which is putatively *heilsbedeutsam* is separate and independent of the question of how the status of unique significance for salvation can be ascribed to

Jesus Christ as a particular person. Unless the possibility of something 'significant for salvation' can be shown to be credible, a belief like 'Jesus Christ is the unique saviour' will not be credible, even though a demonstration that there can be realities which are *heilsbedeutsam* does not alone fully account for the credibility of faith in Jesus Christ. Both questions must be answered in order to show how Jesus Christ can be significant for salvation; neither response by itself constitutes an adequate answer to the basic question of credibility.

For Rahner, one way to appreciate the need to raise this independent question about the credibility of a saving reality in general is simply to consider the notion of 'salvation'. In asking how Jesus can be *heilsbedeutsam*, one is asking about salvation. Now 'when I ask about salvation for myself, I am necessarily asking about myself in my totality, for this is precisely what the notion of salvation means.'[18] The first position I outlined would certainly agree that salvation affects us in our totality. However, Rahner takes it for granted that a description of a particular person cannot by itself affect me in 'my totality', but only in part. 'The reality of such salvific events [namely, those which engage the whole person] cannot be known simply *a posteriori*.'[19] On the contrary, an *a posteriori* description of Jesus as a particular person only raises the distinctive kind of question which characterizes this second approach: 'How can he [Jesus], the concrete one, in his historical-concrete reality which is not at all generally valid (*gar nicht allgemeingültigen*) be a norm for me?'[20] Thus, the very notion of salvation naturally and readily implies for Rahner that it is one thing to ask how a reality can be *heilsbedeutsam*, and another to ask how Jesus Christ can be such a reality.[21]

More broadly, Rahner has two different kinds of reasons for pursuing this second way of showing how faith in Jesus Christ can be credible. In one respect, like most who have taken this path since the early eighteenth century, he is following a basic, pre-systematic (and indeed pre-theological) conviction about how the Christian faith should be presented, especially to unbelievers or disenchanted believers. This conviction is so basic that the only reasons that can be given for it are secondary indications of how it makes sense to hold it, and Rahner rarely bothers explicitly with these. However, the logical genesis of Rahner's basic conviction, and hence of his commitment to the second way, is not difficult to trace. He holds three widespread assumptions which seem indisputable: (1) The Christian community has a responsibility to present the Christian message to the world in a credible way. (2) The Christian message is that Jesus Christ is the saviour of the world, that he is, in other words, *heilsbedeutsam*. (3) Modern people, precisely because of their modernity, find this message harder to believe than pre-modern people did.

Rahner is fundamentally convinced that the reason for this last difficulty is that the *kinds of things* Christians say and believe about Jesus Christ are incredible and inaccessible to modern people, presumably because of the way the Christian community has presented its message. 'All these difficulties of modern man can be traced to a common formal structure: theological statements are not formulated in such a way that man can see how what is meant in them is connected with his understanding of himself, as witnessed to in his own experience.'[22] Given this conviction about the essential problem people today have believing the Christian message, the best way to present the message credibly in the modern world is, it would seem, to show how the kinds of things the message says about Jesus can be believed by a modern person, that is, 'connected with his understanding of himself'.

It has already been shown what this basic conviction about the way the Christian message should be presented amounts to in an explicitly theological context: there must be a basic distinction between the credibility or meaningfulness of salvation and the enormous variety of things Christians say about it on the one hand, and the credibility of Jesus Christ as the saviour on the other. This conviction and distinction can be stated in logico-grammatical terms. The 'kinds of things' Christians say about salvation are taken by Rahner to constitute a class or genus of claims, the credibility of which must be established before they can be predicated of a particular subject. Or, more precisely, the credibility of this class of claims as such must be established in order for its attribution to a particular subject to result in a credible *proposition*. As I have already noted, Rahner's standard way of alluding to this basic conviction, which expresses itself in his pursuit of the second way, is to invoke the need to state Christian beliefs in a manner which avoids any appearance of 'mythology'. In the absence of an independent account of the credibility of the kinds of things Christians say about that which is *heilsbedeutsam,*

> the traditional theology runs the risk that the assertions of traditional theology will be deemed simply a mythological (in a pejorative sense) overlay on historical events, or that we shall have no criterion by means of which we are able to distinguish in the traditional Christology between a genuine reality of faith and an interpretation of it which no longer mediates the content of faith to us today.[23]

Rahner has a second kind of reason for dividing into two different questions the issue of how Jesus can be *heilsbedeutsam.* Unlike the first set of reasons, which in fact associates Rahner closely with the mainstream of modern Protestant theology, his other warrant for handling the issue in this way is bound up primarily with his vocation as a Catholic theologian. He is convinced that the teaching of the Church's *magisterium* on the universality of God's offer of salvation, properly understood, requires a Catholic theologian to follow what I have described as the second way of explaining the saving significance of Jesus Christ. Here he is a good deal more explicit than in his remarks about the need to avoid 'mythology'; the basic argument he thinks the *magisterium* requires is (in various forms) found frequently in his writings, especially in his discussions of 'anonymous Christianity': (1) 'The theological truth of the universal possibility of salvation,' Rahner supposes, 'may be taken without reserve to possess binding dogmatic force.'[24] God freely offers salvation to all persons as a real possibility for them, regardless of their particular social, cultural and historical situation. (2) In accordance with its own nature, this divinely offered salvation, wherever it is realized by persons, must be freely accepted and known as divine salvation. 'If, then, by virtue of God's universal and serious salvific will . . . salvation occurs even outside the explicit history of the Old and New Testaments, if it occurs everywhere in the history of the world and of salvation, then this history of salvation takes place by being accepted in freedom. But this is not possible without it being accepted as known.'[25] (3) 'The achievement by any man of his proper and definitive salvation is dependent upon Jesus Christ.'[26]

Taken together, the first two assumptions mean, Rahner supposes, that the reality of salvation can be adequately (if not completely) apprehended without reference to Jesus Christ. Consequently, the reality of salvation not only can, but must, be characterized independently of him. To use the terms I have already introduced, what constitutes a saving reality, one which is signficant for salvation (*heilsbedeutsam*), must be a distinct set of issues from what makes *Jesus Christ* significant for salvation. But the third assumption requires that an account must also be given of how this same salvation is uniquely and unsurpassably accomplished in Jesus Christ, an account, in other words, of the 'universal saving significance (*Heilsbedeutung*) of Jesus for all persons'.[27] In the context of the Roman Catholic Church's teaching on the universality of God's offer of salvation as Rahner reads it, both issues must be treated in order to give a proper theological explanation of the Christian confession of 'the historical Jesus as our Lord, the bringer of salvation in the absolute'.[28] So Rahner appeals to both an apologetic warrant, and what he takes to be a doctrinally mandated soteriological warrant, for his basic approach toward the question, 'how can Jesus Christ be significant for salvation?'

It will readily be appreciated how well-suited is Rahner's conception of transcendental theology to his basic convictions about the way the meaningfulness of salvation through Jesus Christ must be handled. Indeed, Rahner never expressly distinguishes, in this connection, between his transcendental *procedure* and his basic *approach*, although the latter could be worked out in a variety of non-transcendental ways.[29] Rather, he repeatedly insists that the logically distinct general question of how any reality can be *heilsbedeutsam* is to be answered precisely in terms of an elucidation of the transcendental conditions in the human subject which constitute our receptivity for a saving reality. This specifically transcendental discussion alone is, of course, insufficient to show how Jesus Christ can be significant for salvation; when the concept of 'a saving reality' has been worked out to the greatest possible extent, it is still necessary to introduce the categorial reality and description of Jesus as a particular person, and to show how it is that he comes to be regarded as such a 'saving reality'. So while transcendental theology 'does not entail a rationalistic and unhistorical reduction of man to the status of an abstract transcendental being', nevertheless it does mean 'that everything of significance for salvation is to be illuminated by referring it back to this transcendental being'.[30] Rahner's application of the transcendental/categorial distinction in Christology is his way of saying that a description of Jesus Christ in his particularity cannot possibly be the sufficient basis for explaining how he can be significant for salvation, and so is his way of saying that 'how can Jesus be *heilsbedeutsam*?' must be treated as implying two separate questions. 'The significance in terms of concrete human living (that is, as affecting the whole of man in his salvation) of historical facts is something which man is quite incapable of rendering intelligible without transcendental theology.'[31] In Rahner's hands that question peculiar to the second way, 'how can any reality be of saving significance?', becomes the more specific question of what the transcendental conditions in the subject are which make a saving reality possible for human beings. The second way becomes, in other words, a transcendental Christology.

The goal of this transcendental Christology is to show how Jesus Christ can be significant for salvation, that is, to establish that belief in Jesus Christ as the unique redeemer is meaningful and intelligible. I have already mentioned a basic assumption of this project, namely that a saving reality must be one which engages and affects human beings in their totality.[32] This means for Rahner that a saving reality must be one which seizes us in the depths of our transcendental experience; it cannot be simply a categorial reality 'known *a posteriori*', although it may have that aspect. But this is to say that saving realities must have the force of necessity for us, such that their acceptance or refusal ineluctably entails the ultimate consummation or loss of our humanity. 'Only that can belong to salvation, the lack of which violates (*verletzt*) the "essence" of man and so brings about the loss of salvation. For otherwise he could renounce his own "essence" without thereby losing salvation.'[33] This basic human relationship to possible saving realities, which on the one hand must be indispensable for us but on the other hand are not strictly speaking part of the human essence or definition, Rahner characterizes as a transcendental orientation or reference. If any realities are to be *heilsbedeutsam*, are 'to affect man as such', then 'he must discover that he is, of his very nature (*von sich aus*), oriented to them. In so far as he recognizes their bearing upon himself he engages in transcendental theology'.[34]

This orientation to a saving reality lies at the heart of our transcendental experience or subjectivity. It is ingredient in our 'transcendental constitution', and as such must be supposed to be universally present in human beings, even though many may not have explicit conceptual or 'thematized' knowledge of it.[35] The primary burden of a transcendental Christology is to uncover and characterize this universal, *a priori* orientation to a final and unsurpassable saving reality, to the kind of reality, in other words, which Jesus Christ is taken to be. The necessity of this particular theological project must not be underestimated, since it is precisely this transcendental orientation which in fact makes the Christian reality and message a *saving* reality and message for us, a reality which can 'affect man as such'. This is simply a christological instance of the general requirement that the grounds for believing the central contents of Christian faith be ascertained in a transcendental fundamental theology. Thus, a specifically transcendental Christology will, by attempting 'to point out (*nachzuweisen*) in the knowing subject an *a priori* reference to this object', make plain how a saving reality or object can be 'intelligible' (*verständlich*) and 'assimilable' (*assimilierbar*) for human beings.[36]

Notice that Rahner here makes no attempt to prove that there actually is such a transcendental orientation in human persons, or correlatively that there actually are saving realities. An attempt to prove either of these is not part of the goal of a transcendental Christology in Rahner's hands. Rather, he is arguing that *if* there are any saving realities, our relation to them will be radically structured by this transcendental orientation. A saving reality, if there is such a thing, will be significant and meaningful for us because we are oriented to it *von sich aus*, and hence capable of being affected and grasped by it in every aspect of our existence. This concept of a transcendental orientation towards a possible saving reality is the heart of Rahner's answer to the question which distinguishes the second way of accounting for Jesus' saving significance from the first – namely, how can any reality be *heilsbedeutsam*? As such, that concept is fundamental to achieving the overall goal of a transcendental Christology, which is to show how Jesus Christ himself can be *heilsbedeutsam*.

Since it constitutes the necessary general response to the question of how any reality can be *heilsbedeutsam*, the idea of a universal transcendental orientation to a saving reality or realities is indispensable to Rahner's attempt to give an account of how Jesus Christ can be of saving significance. However, this bare idea is by itself incapable of doing the job. While the notion of a transcendental orientation indicates why there can be any realities which are actually of saving significance, it provides no indication of what a saving reality might actually be like. Without some reasonably definite idea of a saving reality, of what we are oriented towards, it will be vacuous to say that Jesus Christ, or indeed any particular reality, is actually 'saving'. Rahner needs a middle term which can be informatively predicated of Jesus Christ and which at the same time is the kind of thing which can meaningfully be called *heilsbedeutsam*. The notion of an 'absolute saviour' or an 'eschatological bringer of salvation' serves just this function in Rahner's Christology. In a rich definition of this middle term, Rahner writes,

> We give the title of Saviour simply to that historical person (*geschichtliche Persönlichkeit*) who, coming in space and time, signifies that beginning of God's absolute communication of himself which inaugurates this self-communication for all men as something happening irrevocably and which shows this to be happening.[37]

The concept 'absolute saviour' in this sense clearly is capable of counting as a characterization of Jesus' redeeming significance, and so of being informatively predicated of him. But the ascription of the concept 'absolute saviour' to Jesus Christ does not qualify it as *heilsbedeutsam* and consequently does nothing to advance the argument that its subject, Jesus Christ, can be *heilsbedeutsam*. Rather, given both Rahner's basic methodological decision on this matter (the second way) and his transcendental implementation of that decision, the notion of an absolute saviour will be *heilsbedeutsam* only if it meets the general criteria of what can be significant for salvation. That is, it will have to be shown to be something towards which we can intelligibly be said to be oriented in our concrete existence. If this middle term is to carry out its appointed task, Rahner will have to show how one can say,

to use his own terms, that 'whether reflexively or not, man seeks in
his history after such an absolute bringer of salvation'.[38] The
specific burden of a transcendental Christology is thus to elucidate the human orientation to a saving reality as an orientation
precisely to an absolute saviour.[39] If the *goal* of a transcendental
Christology is to show how Jesus Christ can be *heilsbedeutsam* by
establishing what it is that makes any reality *heilsbedeutsam*, the
method of a transcendental Christology is to show that an 'absolute
saviour' can be *heilsbedeutsam*, in other words, can be that kind of
reality. Should this be established, it would remain to indicate a
way in which 'absolute saviour' can be asserted of Jesus Christ
and the goal would then be achieved, the second way would be
successful.

It is essential to see that this last assertion, namely 'Jesus
Christ is the absolute saviour', is the explicit *assumption* on the
basis of which alone the overall argument can proceed. The aim of
the argument is to show how Jesus Christ can be *heilsbedeutsam*, by
showing how the significance we ascribe to him ('absolute
saviour', and therein 'God–man', 'incarnate Word', and so forth)
can plausibly be said to make a difference to us. But the argument
can never *prove* that Jesus actually has this significance and it is
not designed to do so; the validity of ascribing that significance to
him must be presupposed. Conversely, a demonstration that
ideas like 'absolute saviour', 'God–man', and 'incarnate Word'
are experientially accessible to human beings in a deeply meaningful way does not and cannot show that there actually is an
absolute saviour, or that Jesus Christ is this person. Rahner is
emphatic about this and it lends his version of the second way a
distinctive cast: it is a deliberately more modest project than
christologies fashioned in the second way sometimes are. But it is
necessary to see more precisely how the truth of the belief that
Jesus Christ is the absolute saviour is presupposed in Rahner's
transcendental Christology.

In the first place, belief in Jesus Christ as the absolute saviour is
historically prior to an explicit awareness of our orientation to a
saving reality. 'Man's "transcendental" orientation towards such
a historical redemptive event is only explicitly reflected on when
man meets this event in history.'[40] But temporal priority alone is
not an adequate basis upon which to assert that Jesus Christ as a
particular person can only be presupposed here and not derived

from the transcendentally elucidated idea of an absolute saviour. The asserted temporal dependence of this idea is only a matter of psychological genesis and need not preclude that, once given the idea, the reality of the saviour necessarily follows from it. So Rahner is pressed to articulate a different sort of priority for belief in Jesus Christ as the absolute saviour, with regard to any demonstration that an absolute saviour can have ultimate significance for us. He argues in effect (without explicitly distinguishing this new position from a simply temporal priority) that the basic conviction – 'Jesus Christ is the absolute saviour' – is logically independent of a transcendental justification of the idea of an absolute saviour, and of all that necessarily follows from or is included in the latter. It is logically independent in two distinguishable ways.

First, the argument that an absolute saviour can be *heilsbedeut-sam*, in virtue of a deep structure which orients us towards this kind of object, cannot establish the *actuality* of a saviour. It can only outline the distinctive features of a possible saviour, the actuality of whom (if this saviour *is* actual) must be established in some other way. Or, as Rahner says, an account of the significance of a possibly actual saviour, which is a kind of 'transcendental deduction of Christ's knowability by man', would not 'imply the *necessity* of the fact of Christ, for this was something freely established by God'.[41]

Second, the transcendentally warranted idea of an absolute saviour is also unable to establish the particular identity of the saviour. On the contrary, there is a distinction in principle between the proper grasp of this idea and the knowledge of the saviour as a particular person. 'The *idea* of the God–man and the acknowledgement of Jesus and no one else as the one, unique and real God–man are two quite different perceptions (*zwei verschiedene Erkenntnisse*).'[42] The actuality of the absolute saviour or God–man (as expressed in a proposition such as 'there is an absolute saviour') and more concretely the particularity of the saviour (expressed in a proposition such as 'Jesus Christ is the absolute saviour') are alike incapable of being derived from the idea of an absolute saviour, no matter how thoroughly the credibility of that idea may be established. Consequently, the *truth* of these propositions can certainly never be derived from the warranted assertion that 'an absolute saviour is *heilsbedeutsam*'.[43] It is in this sense that belief in Jesus Christ as the unique redeemer is a logically independent element in the argument which aims to establish that Jesus Christ is *heilsbedeutsam* on the basis of a credible idea of a unique redeemer or absolute saviour. The truth of the belief can enter the overall argument only as a presupposition.[44]

There are technical reasons in Rahner's transcendental argument for belief in Jesus Christ having the status of a presupposition which will come under consideration when that argument is analysed in more detail. But these technical considerations are rooted in a pre-theoretical conviction about the basic character of Christian belief. Christian faith involves an encounter with a particular, historical person which is decisive for the entire life of the believer; the properly developed idea of an absolute saviour alone, no matter how necessary for justifiable belief, 'can of course never be a substitute for the historical experience of Jesus of Nazareth – in other words that reality in which this "idea" has been made real.'[45] And so when Rahner distinguishes between the 'perceptions' of 'the idea of the God–man' and 'the acknowledgement of Jesus', he goes on to say that 'only this second perception, which is one of faith, makes one a Christian'.[46]

While belief in Jesus Christ as the absolute saviour is prior to the transcendental argument that an absolute saviour is *heilsbedeutsam* with respect to the truth of that belief, in a different respect the transcendental argument is logically prior to the belief itself. Showing that an 'absolute saviour' can legitimately be called *heilsbedeutsam* is the *a priori* condition upon which alone belief in Jesus Christ can be meaningful, intelligible and existentially accessible. With respect to its meaningfulness, as opposed to its truth, belief in Jesus Christ presupposes this transcendental argument, rather than being presupposed by it. It is precisely in this respect, as our outline of Rahner's argument has already indicated, that 'a transcendental Christology *per se* is *a priori* to a concrete, historical relationship to Jesus Christ'.[47] The truth of the proposition 'Jesus Christ is the absolute saviour' is presupposed in the attempt to show that he is *heilsbedeutsam*, but it is the transcendental argument which, so Rahner hopes, keeps this from being the sort of assertion before which modern people can simply 'shrug their shoulders'.[48]

The different respects in which belief in Jesus Christ and the warranted idea of an absolute saviour presuppose each other in turn are neatly expressed in a passage from the *Foundations*:

A transcendental Christology as such cannot presume for itself the task and the possibility of saying that the absolute saviour . . . is to be found [in history], and that he has been found precisely in *Jesus* of Nazareth. Both of these statements belong to the experience of history itself which cannot be deduced. *Today,* however, a person would be blind with regard to this actual history if he did not approach it with that reflexive and articulated hope for salvation which is reflected upon in a transcendental Christology. Transcendental Christology allows one to search for, and in his search to understand, what he has already found in Jesus of Nazareth.[49]

A conspectus of the entire argument of Rahner's transcendental Christology is now before us. The argument can be summarily stated in syllogistic form. This may be especially valuable for heuristic purposes, provided that the syllogism is interpreted in light of the various qualifications of the terms, propositions and overall inference that have already been introduced.

1 The absolute saviour is *heilsbedeutsam* (method).
2 Jesus Christ is the absolute saviour (presupposition).
3 Jesus Christ is *heilsbedeutsam* (goal).

While the whole argument can be called that of a 'transcendental Christology', since it is set in motion by the distinctively transcendental procedure involved in warranting the major premise, the argument obviously includes categorial elements as well (principally the particular person introduced as the subject of the minor premise). In fact, the previous discussion allows me to distinguish four different aspects of this argument which bear upon the central problem: (1) Jesus Christ as a particular person; (2) a unique redeeming significance asserted of him; (3) a transcendental argument which attempts to display the meaningfulness of that asserted significance; and (4) the concluding, putatively justified ascription of that meaningfulness to Jesus Christ as a particular person. It is necessary at this point to examine the interaction of these elements in more detail, and thereby understand the argument as a whole more precisely.

THE IDEA OF AN ABSOLUTE SAVIOUR

Turning to the particulars of Rahner's argument, it must be borne in mind that my interest here is in the status of the particularity of Jesus Christ in a modest and self-critical version of what I have called the second way of answering the question, 'how can Jesus Christ be *heilsbedeutsam*? To recapitulate briefly, I have initially defined the second way in terms of the logically and procedurally irreducible distinctness of the question, 'how can there be something which is *heilsbedeutsam*?' from the question, 'how can whatever is *heilsbedeutsam* be ascribed to Jesus Christ?' The answer to the first question supplies the criteria and bases for a definite, predicable (of something particular) characterization of a poss-ible saving reality. This means that on an account like Rahner's, in the last analysis, belief in Jesus Christ as the unique redeemer can be meaningful and accessible because the significance ascribed to him (or, more broadly, what is said of him) thoroughly conforms to the general criteria which establish the character of a saving reality: it is anticipated in the deepest, most inalienable, universal expectations of human beings.

In light of our guiding interest, a more detailed discussion of Rahner's transcendental Christology will have to be limited to two foci. (1) I will consider the way Rahner develops the idea of an absolute saviour under the influence of general criteria for a saving reality; and (2) I will see how, in Rahner's own eyes, Jesus Christ as a particular person, or what he calls the categorial history of Jesus Christ, enters the overall argument of his Christo-logy. That is, I will see how Rahner answers the question, 'how can Jesus Christ be *heilsbedeutsam*?', in a Christology which finds it necessary to justify the possibility of belief in Jesus Christ on grounds independent of his particular identity. In the course of this focused analysis of Rahner's argument, questions and prob-lems will no doubt suggest themselves, but these will have to be passed over in silence. But that is the nature of the case. I am not concerned with the fate of the particularity of Jesus if the second way fails on its own terms, but precisely if it succeeds.

To the question, 'how can any reality be significant for salv-ation?' we have seen Rahner reply: by being the object of a radical orientation of our whole being, on account of which such a reality is capable of affecting us as a whole. This is the ineluctable transcendental condition of the possibility of there being any *saving* reality. Rahner must therefore unfold the idea of an absolute saviour in such a way that we can intelligibly be said to be oriented to such a saviour; working out the idea of an absolute saviour is and must be equivalent to working out the content which is anticipated in the deepest and most comprehensive human orientation. Should there actually be an absolute saviour (or, in the assertoric mood, when we say that Jesus Christ is the absolute saviour), belief in this person will be credible and assimilable precisely in virtue of that orientation, on the strength of which we are able to distinguish belief in a saviour from an untenable mythology. Consequently it is absolutely essential for Rahner to articulate the idea of an absolute, possibly actual saviour in such a way that nothing indispensable to such a saviour falls outside the scope of our fundamental orientation. For anything pertaining to the saviour that is not anticipated in that orientation would thereby lose the basis on which alone it can be credible and meaningful – on which alone, in other words, it can be *heilsbedeutsam*.

Rahner's argument regarding the human orientation toward, or *a priori* openness for, an absolute saviour has three phases in its simplest form.[50] I cannot in this context give an adequate indication of the inner complexity of these phases, but can only attempt to outline the most basic steps of the argument.

1   All human beings in their very essence anticipate the unsurpassable self-communication of God. This first point is reached by taking three distinct assertions cumulatively. (a) It is of the essence of the human person to have (indeed, in a sense, to be) an unlimited openness or 'transcendentality', whose possibilities cannot be limited by any determinate (that is, categorially describable) object or content. The human subject is 'fundamentally and by its very nature (*von sich aus*) pure openness for absolutely everything, for being as such'.[51] (b) The goal and term of this unlimited openness can only be God, as the fullness of being and the intrinsically infinite and incomprehensible mystery. 'When we have said everything about ourselves which can be described and defined, we have still said nothing about ourselves, unless we have included or implied the fact that we are beings who are

referred (*verwiesenen*) to the incomprehensible God.[52] (c) We seek
the goal of this reference or orientation not only as the ever distant
'holy mystery', but as the absolute, insuperable nearness of self-
giving love. Human beings seek this wholly fulfilling immediacy
to God not simply because, as a bare possibility, it supersedes
what would be available to them through a relation to God only as
remote mystery, but because they are already urged and oriented
towards that goal by God's offer of himself.

> We presuppose, therefore, that the goal of the world consists
> in God's communicating himself to it. We presuppose that
> the whole dynamism which God has instituted in the very
> heart of the world's becoming by self-transcendence (and yet
> not as that which constitutes its nature [*Wesen*]) is really
> always meant already as the beginning and first step towards
> this self-communication and its acceptance by the world.[53]

This unlimited 'self-transcendence', which is nothing other than
an orientation towards and striving after the closest possible
union with God, lies at the heart of the transcendental constitution of all persons.[54] Being subjects of the freely offered self-
communication of God, we seek in effect the definitive confirmation and consummation of that offer, which, as long as it remains
only an offer, is ambiguous and not yet definitively present for us.

2 God's self-communication, towards the consummation of
which we are transcendentally oriented, must come to us historically and categorially. There are several distinct features to this
phase of the argument. (a) All transcendental experience must be
'mediated' historically and categorially. 'Man's subjectivity and
his free, personal self-interpretation take place precisely in and
through his being in the world, in time, and in history, or better, in
and through world, time and history.'[55] Consequently, despite its
transcendental dimension, 'the question of salvation cannot be
answered by bypassing man's historicity and his social nature'.[56]
(b) Human freedom, which is rooted in our transcendental make-
up and which extends to the ultimate acceptance or rejection of
God's self-offer, must likewise be mediated categorially. God's
self-communication must therefore take the form of a historical
address to the freedom of human persons. (c) Transcendentally
self-conscious and free beings who live in history are necessarily

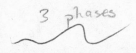

3 phases

social beings, unified in interdependence and intercommunication. 'Hence God's self-communication necessarily turns in the direction of a free history of the human race, and can only happen in *free* acceptance by the free subjects in a *common* history'.[57] (d) The categorial aspect of God's self-offer, should that self-offer be granted its absolute consummation, can be specified more exactly with respect to the 'common history' in which it takes place. God's unsurpassable self-communication must be relatively definite by comparison to that common history as a whole. This is called for not only by the intrinsically unambiguous character of an absolute divine self-communication, but especially by the freedom of the human subject, which would need a categorial reality definite enough to be the basis of an ultimate decision. 'The event of self-communication must therefore be thought of as an event which takes place historically in a specifically spatio-temporal manner and which then turns to everyone and calls upon their freedom.'[58] If 'the divinizing sanctification [*Begnadigung*] of humanity attains its consummation, it must be a concrete, tangible phenomenon (*Greifbarkeit*) in history ... and hence must be an event in such a way as to spread out spatio-temporally from one point.'[59]

3   The combination of these first two phases yields the notion of an absolute saviour as the goal of a fundamental and universal human orientation. We have already adduced a general characterization of an 'absolute saviour' (above, p. 28). The idea, while complex, has two basic and irreducibly distinct aspects. (a) The absolute saviour must be an individual historical person who freely and unreservedly accepts God's loving self-offer. That the saviour must be an individual is already evident from the requirement of relative definiteness (2(d)). The need for the saviour freely to give him or herself wholly over to God's loving will follows from the requirement of irrevocability (1(c)). Unless the saviour freely and manifestly accepts God's self-offer, that offer cannot be definitively present for us as an 'address' to our freedom but must remain ambiguous. (b) The saviour must not simply point to, but must *be* the reality of God's unsurpassable self-communication and commitment to the world. The presence of God's absolute self-communication must, in other words, be irrevocable not only from the side of the human reality in which it

occurs but from God's side as well. In his or her human reality, the saviour is able freely to exist in that state of absolute nearness to God for which we all strive only because God's prior offer of himself enables the saviour to do so (compare 1(c)). Consequently, Rahner argues, the fact that the saviour wholly accepts God's self-communication shows that the latter is not an offer only, but that God has there freely extended himself *ad extra* in an irreversible and unsurpassable way. So the absolute saviour is a single person who is at once a human being and God's definitive pledge of himself to the world. Such a one would constitute that point 'at which a human being means (*bedeutet*) both God's definitive promise of himself, from the deepest ground of his being, *and* the Yes of the world to this God.'[60]

This brief sketch of the way Rahner arrives at the idea of a possible absolute saviour brings into relief one cardinal point: an absolute saviour is, on Rahner's account, the uniquely fit term and object for the orientation towards and desire for salvation in God which characterizes our nature. A possibly actual absolute saviour does not, so Rahner's argument goes, exceed what can intelligibly be said to be anticipated in this basic human striving, nor does it lack anything which this quest necessarily implies. What occurs in the saviour is precisely what all persons look for in virtue of their essence as the fulfilment of their concrete reality. Yet the fulfilment of our existence comes to us through a person distinct from ourselves, and thus through the external object of an orientation (even when that orientation has reached its goal), at least because the consummation of our nature can only be realized through the tangible material of our historical lives.

At this point, it is important to realize, Rahner has completed the properly transcendental portion of his central christological argument. He has justified, and in that (properly Kantian) sense 'transcendentally deduced' the *Heilsbedeutsamkeit* of an absolute saviour, by reference to the constitutive orientation to unsurpassable fulfilment of the concrete human *Wesen*. In essence, if not in detail, the significance which will eventually be ascribed to Jesus Christ can now, Rahner is convinced, be said to be meaningful, intelligible and assimilable.

One of Rahner's primary interests in working out a justified idea of an absolute saviour is to provide a set of concepts which will complement the more familiar but (he argues) less assimilable christological language of incarnation and hypostatic union. He does not suppose that the language of 'absolute saviour' can or should supplant that of 'incarnation'; he takes the latter to be doctrinally necessary.[61] Rather, the concept of an absolute saviour furnishes a basis upon which one can undertake a vigorous clarification and defence of that aspect of the Christian belief in incarnation which, he supposes, is at best obscure in traditional presentations, and is so readily dismissed by modern people – that is, its meaningfulness or significance for salvation.[62] In light of the idea of an absolute saviour, 'it now becomes possible to understand what is really meant by the doctrine of the Hypostatic Union and of the Incarnation of the divine Logos'.[63] Suggestive as it is in its own right, Rahner's attempt to show that these two sets of concepts are substantially translatable has relatively little material bearing on the problems in hand. But his discussions of the theology of incarnation display with particular clarity the basic procedure which governs this first step of his christological argument. Nothing in the idea of a unique redeemer and thus nothing which will eventually be attributed to Jesus, must exceed the reach of, or fail to conform to, those general criteria which establish what kind of reality is *heilsbedeutsam*. Two characteristic examples of the application of this procedural assumption to the theology of incarnation can be briefly considered.

1 Justifying grace and hypostatic union are strictly complementary; not only in reality, but even in our way of conceiving them, they must be regarded as mutually necessary.[64] The proximate, more technical reason for this assumption is that the consummation of human reality at the hands of God, towards which all persons are oriented in grace, is precisely that which occurs in the hypostatic union. 'This very communication [of 'God's reality'] which is aimed at by this "assumption" [in the incarnation] is *the* communication by what we call grace and glory – and the latter are intended for all.'[65]

But why, in turn, must incarnation and hypostatic union be regarded as the same kind of human fulfilment, and correlatively the same kind of divine self-communication, as the fullness of grace and glory which all persons seek? The procedure Rahner uses to warrant the religious meaningfulness of christological assertions demands it, otherwise, a possible (and hence also an actual) incarnation would fall outside the sphere of credibility which our basic human aims define. Therefore Rahner is ultimately compelled to insist upon the mutually complementary character of grace and incarnation, whatever the distinctiveness of the latter may be, by his need to find an answer to the question, 'how can any reality be *heilsbedeutsam*?' 'The advantage of this would be that the incarnation of the Logos would not longer appear merely as something subsequent, a particular event *in* a world already *finished* (and hence in danger of seeming to be something mythological).'[66]

2   The concrete human essence (*Wesen*) is nothing other than a *potentia oboedientialis* for hypostatic union.[67] This fits nicely with Rahner's argument that the fulfilment 'intended for all' in grace is the same as that which is realized in the incarnation, now with an emphasis on what has usually been called the 'mode of union' in the incarnation. God decisively expresses himself *ad extra* in that he 'posits (*setzt*) as his own reality' a *Wesen* which longs to surrender itself so radically to God that it would become precisely God's own reality.[68] It is from this vantage point that Rahner can say 'The incarnation is therefore the unique, *supreme* case of the fulfilment of the essence (*Wesensvollzugs*) of human reality, which consists in the fact that man *is*, in so far as he gives himself up.'[69] Again, the essential point for our purposes is that what Rahner will subsequently say actually occurs in Jesus Christ is itself *heilsbedeutsam* because and in so far as it constitutes the *Wesensvollzug* of human reality. But this only stands to reason. Through a series of intermediate steps, Rahner has simply applied the initial criterion of a saving reality ('that, the lack of which violates the "essence" of man'; compare above, p. 26) to the idea of incarnation, in order to show that the latter can really signal something significant for salvation.

Using both current and more traditional terminology, Rahner has now justified the idea of an absolute saviour, in the limited sense that he has shown how it not only fulfills, but is implied in the basic criterion of a saving reality. As I have already mentioned, since Rahner never requires that one must grasp the orientation to an absolute saviour or God–man, as constitutive of one's own humanity, independently of explicit knowledge of the particular, spatio-temporally and categorially located person

Jesus Christ, this justification does not amount to a proof that there actually is such a universal, essential orientation.[70] However, the negative limit Rahner cautiously imposes upon our access to the orientation which in fact constitutes our concrete nature (namely, his exclusion of the *necessity* of our grasping it apart from explicit reference to Jesus Christ) leaves the epistemic status of this orientation far from clear. In some contexts, for example, when he is explaining the need for a transcendental Christology, Rahner seems to say that we not only need not but indeed cannot know ourselves to be oriented towards an absolute saviour except in connection with explicit faith in Jesus Christ. In other contexts, for example when he is arguing for an 'anonymous Christianity' and a universal 'questing Christology', he seems to say that while we need not, we can grasp and affirm ('pre-thematically', but consciously) this orientation apart from any explicit knowledge of Jesus Christ. Resolving this apparent epistemological antinomy is not essential for the present purposes here.[71]

My concern is rather to assess the status of the particularity of Jesus in Rahner's most modest claims, which need deal only with explicit believers, those whose grasp of their own orientation to an absolute saviour is inseparable from their engagement with Jesus Christ as a particular person. If there is an unavoidable loss of particularity in even this most modest version of the second way, that is, if a Christology which proceeds as Rahner's does turns out to be inconsistent with its own assumption that only Jesus Christ as a particular person can be the 'absolute saviour', the apparently less modest claims involved in a theory of 'anonymous Christianity' will only exacerbate the problem. Conversely, if there is no such problem, objections to a putative loss of particularity when less modest claims are invoked will be indecisive. So I will take Rahner at his most cautious and modest – where the 'orientation to an absolute saviour', as the full answer to the question, 'how can any reality be *heilsbedeutsam*?' can only be grasped and asserted as real in us in connection with knowledge of and reference to Jesus Christ.

Excursus on Rahner's Idea of Incarnation

Before moving on to consider explicitly the place of Jesus Christ as a particular person in Rahner's Christology, it may be useful to make a comment on Rahner's deployment of the ideas of grace in us and the 'unique miracle' of the incarnation.[72] Guided as it is by the need to show that the incarnation is *heilsbedeutsam*, Rahner's conception of the mutually implicative character of grace and incarnation raises an obvious problem for which he provides no clear-cut answer. If the human *Wesen* is really a *potentia oboedientialis* for hypostatic union, how can any person be satisfied with anything less than a hypostatic union, which on Rahner's own account is supposed to be a 'unique', 'supreme' event which happens only once? Or, from a different perspective, what is the ontological difference between uncreated grace in us and the hypostatic union, given Rahner's insistence upon their intrinsic, co-implicative relation? Sometimes more implicitly than explicitly, one can find him offering four distinguishable answers to this kind of question. (a) As historical beings even in our 'transcendentality', we must seek our *Wesensvollzug* in some external, historical person. This might explain how there can be only one hypostatic union but it could not, of course, apply at all to the human being in whom the hypostatic union takes place, who would thus not at all be the supreme *case* of our own *Wesensvollzug*. (b) Each of us finds ourselves in a state of 'sinfulness' and 'radical peril', which 'shows us . . . that the possibility [of hypostatic union] has not in fact been actualized in us'.[73] But this does not really answer the question. One can grant the premise and still ask how, on Rahner's terms, we can permanently and ultimately do without a hypostatic union in our own case, while still holding that this union is *heilsbedeutsam* for us. (c) Our *Wesen* is the same as that of the person in whom the incarnation takes place, 'but the unbridgeable difference is that in his case the "what" (*Wesen*) is uttered as [God's] self-expression, which it is not in our case'.[74] Yet how can this be, if our *Wesen* is precisely the longing for what occurs, for what is uttered, in '*his* case'? (d) In a genuinely evolutionary view of the world, temporal primacy is as good as ontological difference. In other words, in a world which continually surpasses itself by grace toward the life of God, the spiritual creature in whom this movement is first consummated inaugurates a new and final phase of the world's development, so that all who subsequently achieve the same fulfilment do so in dependence upon the one who first crossed the threshold.

This last seems to be the most promising of the four proposals. But aside from making an evolutionary view of the world virtually *de fide*, as the only way of saving the *de fide* ontological supremacy of the hypostatic union (a step Rahner never seems willing to take), the 'ontological difference' in this proposal depends upon a temporal distinction which will (again, by Rahner's own lights) be done away with when the *Wesensvollzug* is consummated in the *visio Dei*.

In sum, it is difficult to see, given Rahner's way of showing that the incarnation is *heilsbedeutsam*, how the humanity of the God–man 'is essentially and always the mediating object of the one act of *latria* which has God as its goal'.[75] None of this is to deny that there could be a consistent Rahnerian way of saying that the incarnation is truly the *principium et ratio essendi* of our own *Wesensvollzug*, but one does not emerge clearly from the texts.

THE CONCEPT OF PARTICULARITY

I have now reached the point where it is possible to begin to clarify the central question. Rahner has developed the idea of a transcendental orientation to an absolute saviour as the necessary condition for the credibility and meaningfulness of belief in Jesus Christ as the absolute saviour. Or, as Rahner sometimes likes to put it, we are all (whether we know it or not is another question) 'on the lookout' for an absolute saviour or God–man; we have an '*Ausschau* within concrete history' for such a person.[76] So the question here is: in what way do we anticipate the individuality of the saviour in our orientation or *Ausschau*? Or, to put it as a question of degree, for precisely how much of the saviour's individuality are we 'on the lookout'?

What we *can* anticipate of the saviour's individuality in our basic orientation is already largely manifest from the analysis of Rahner's justification of the idea of an absolute saviour. The saviour will be a single historical person with a definite significance. That is, the absolute saviour will be some one person in whom certain events, divine and human, come to pass which are decisive for the *Wesensvollzug* of all people. Both Rahner's pre-theoretical and his technical (mainly anthropological) grounds for insisting that the saviour must be found in history

have already been noted.[77] He remarks, in typical fashion, 'The
fact that the salvation of man does not depend merely on the idea
but also on the contingent concrete facts of real history – that
belongs to Christianity.'[78] The need for the saviour to be a single
person he takes to be fairly obvious, given the requirement of
historicity, but he is occasionally explicit about that as well.[79] As
a single historical person, the absolute saviour or God–man will
have some spatio-temporal location and some set of identifying
characteristics. But, as will become more clear momentarily,
these features cannot be further specified within the purview of
our orientation toward an absolute saviour. I will call this indeterminate historical singularity the 'positivity' of the saviour, bearing in mind that I am here using the term in a narrower sense than
has usually been the case. Positivity, taken here to imply a single
historical person with an indefinite spatio-temporal location and
unspecified identifying characterstics, is the 'degree' of
individuality necessarily contained in the idea of an absolute
saviour. And so Rahner says that each person, since our *Wesen* is a
transcendental openness for the absolute self-communication of
God, 'attains his supreme fulfilment . . . only when he believes
that somewhere (*irgendwo*)' there is an absolute saviour.[80]

The precise character and extent of the positivity which we
actually seek comes more clearly to light by contrast with what
Rahner insists we *cannot* anticipate of the saviour's individuality:
our transcendentally oriented *Wesen* cannot anticipate that Jesus
Christ is the absolute saviour. Rahner's usual way of putting this
is to say that we are unable to 'deduce' (*ableiten*) Jesus Christ from
the transcendentally justified idea of an absolute saviour. 'It is, of
course, impossible to deduce *a priori* . . . that the "idea of the
God–man" . . . became fact precisely in Jesus of Nazareth under
the Emperor Augustus and Pontius Pilate, in this particular place
and not somewhere else (*da und nicht dort*), at this particular
moment in time and not at any other (*damals und nicht zu anderer
Zeit*).'[81] From the perspective of our basic transcendental orientation and its content, Jesus Christ is in principle unreachable.
The knowledge of Jesus Christ must come from a different quarter
than our mere *Ausschau* in history. 'That this event of the final
self-transcendence of man into God in the most radical self-
communication of God to man has occurred precisely in Jesus of
Nazareth . . . is accessible only to the historical experience of the

crucified and risen Jesus, to an experience which as such cannot be mediated further.'[82]

The respect in which the individuality of the saviour is beyond the reach of our orientation to an absolute saviour, which Rahner readily acknowledges when he says we cannot 'deduce' Jesus Christ, can be stated with some conceptual precision. It is the *particularity* of the absolute saviour that we cannot anticipate. There are in fact two related respects in which Jesus Christ falls outside the sphere of our transcendental orientation to an absolute saviour; together, these constitute his particularity. In the first place, the concept of an absolute saviour does not and cannot give us any way of making ostensive reference to the saviour. To use Rahner's language, the fact that the saviour actually lived at 'this particular place' and 'this particular moment in time', namely, 'under the Emperor Augustus' and 'under Pontius Pilate', is not included in the idea of an absolute saviour. In the second place, this concept does not enable us to describe definite features of the saviour, for example, that 'under Pontius Pilate', he died by crucifixion. Ostensibility and describability, it seems, mark a particular person and correlatively the concept of particularity. Or, more broadly, having determinate, specifiable features signals particularity.[83] A particular person is therefore one who can bear a proper name, because that person's spatio-temporal location and determinate features support an identifying description which allows us to locate or pick out that person by the use of the name connected with that description.[84]

A clear conceptual distinction and contrast can now be made between positivity and particularity. Looked at with respect to positivity, a person is understood as a single, independently existing, historical individual but without determinate features and a proper name.[85] In this respect, the individual person is conceived as genuinely irreducible, that is, as neither a part or an aspect of a larger whole, nor as divisible into parts which are individuals of the same kind. However, the individual person is here understood and grasped only in so far as he or she is a single, indeterminate human reality, without regard to the definite features in virtue of which the individual can be described and named. A positive individual is not, of course, presumed to exist without some specific features but what these features are is completely indeterminable. Just because a positive individual is only understood to have 'some (indeterminate) features', it can have *any* features compatible with the kind of individual it is. Postivity, in the expressive phrase of Thomas Aquinas, is 'vague individuality'.[86] Looked at with respect to particularity, a person is understood as a fully determinate individual, with a unique spatio-temporal location and specific features, which allow that person to be distinguished from every other individual. Regarded in this way, the individual person is grasped as the possessor of distinctive identifying characteristics and not only as an independent but indeterminate human subject. Particularity, in another phrase of Thomas's, is individuality *determinatum distinguens*, individuality distinguished by its various specific determinations.[87] Positivity and particularity thus signal two different aspects under which an individual may be conceived, and also under which that individual may be grasped or known: abstractly, without respect to its determinate features; and concretely, with respect to its determinate features.

This explanation of a distinction between positive individuality and particular individuality may usefully be complemented by some logico-grammatical considerations. I will assume for these purposes that an individual (that is, something irreducible and capable of independent existence) can only enter discourse as a subject, never as a predicate. Suppose we are dealing with some single individual, for example, 'the chair of the Religious Studies Department'.[88] This individual can enter discourse as the subject of propositions in two different ways, which employ two different kinds of expression.

1 As the subject of a proposition, 'the chair of the Religious Studies Department' can be spoken of using (a) indefinite pronouns (for example, '*someone* works in the office on the second floor'); (b) concrete nouns with indefinite qualifiers ('*some fellow* answers the phone when the secretary buzzes'); or (c) quantifying expressions ('*there is a person who* makes important decisions around here'). The sorts of indefinite expressions which serve as subjects in these propositions do not introduce, nor do they include, the determinate identifying features of 'the chair of the Religious Studies Department'. They simply introduce and (ordinarily) assert the positivity of an individual, without specifying who that individual actually is.[89]

2   This same individual can be spoken of using (a) demonstratives (for example, '*this* is the person working in the office on the second floor'); (b) proper names ('*Hans Frei* answers the phone when the secretary buzzes'); or (c) descriptions ('*the teacher of modern Christian thought* makes important decisions around here'). These sorts of expressions in some way introduce the determinate features of the 'chair of the Religious Studies Department' and so introduce this individual as a particular person, who can be identified as such.[90]

From a logico-grammatical perspective, then, the distinction between positivity and particularity can be understood in terms of the distinction between indefinite and definite subject expressions. This can be applied to the problem at hand. If one asserts, on whatever grounds, the positive reality of an absolute saviour, then one is entitled to remarks like 'there is an absolute saviour' (or, more fully, 'there is someone who is the absolute saviour'), or 'somewhere there is an absolute saviour'. On the other hand, if one can assert the particular reality of the saviour, then one is entitled to statements like, 'this person is the absolute saviour', 'Jesus Christ is the absolute saviour', and 'the man from Nazareth who was crucified under Pontius Pilate is the absolute saviour'. Rahner, as has been seen, uses both kinds of phrases; my aim has been to highlight the difference between them.

Several supplementary remarks are in order, pertinent to the application of this distinction between positive individuality and particular individuality to Rahner's Christology. First of all, I have observed in several contexts Rahner's pre-theoretical conviction that the whole panoply of Christian belief hangs upon 'the contingent, concrete facts of real history'.[91] In order to work this conviction about the character of Christian belief into a theoretical context which accommodates the demands of the second way, Rahner must, as can now be seen, take the notion of 'the contingent facts of real history' in two different senses, serving two different purposes. On the one hand, if the Christian belief in redemption and redeemer necessarily involves a reference to 'real history', and if that belief must, on the second way, uniquely fulfil general criteria of meaningfulness and existential assimilability, then in at least some sense the historical component of that belief also must fit those general criteria. So the idea of an absolute saviour ordinarily includes what I am calling the 'positive individuality' of the saviour. On the other hand, precisely because the Christian belief in a unique redeemer involves a personal appropriation of 'real history', it must, in some sense, be impossible to reach that belief simply by reflection upon an idea. So, Rahner maintains, the idea of an absolute saviour does not include the 'particular individuality' of the saviour, nor does it provide the raw material for a 'deduction' of the saviour's particularity.

This brings me, secondly, to the matter of whether Rahner is aware of the distinction I am using to understand him. If explicit awareness of a distinction means using concepts consistently in a way which honours the distinction, then Rahner is not explicitly aware of a difference between positivity and particularity. Sometimes he uses phrases such as 'concrete facts' and 'real history' in a way which conforms to the notion of positive individuality; at other times, the same phrases seem to imply what I have called particular individuality. It is usually evident from the context which sense such terms and phrases have at any given point, but Rahner never recognizes this distinction of use in an explicit distinction of terms. At the same time, the distinction I have outlined is functionally inescapable for Rahner, since he needs (as he is well aware) to differentiate what we cannot grasp of the absolute saviour's individuality or historicity on the basis of our transcendental orientation alone from what we must grasp of the saviour's individuality on that basis alone. So Rahner in the same breath can speak of the saviour as 'historical' in two different senses, as the structure of his Christology requires. A transcendental Christology sees the 'God–man' as 'the point of intersection between the ultimate self-transcendence of the world reaching out to God and the self-bestowal of God upon the world in its most radical form (both taking place in history),' that is, it sees the 'God–man' as a positive individual. By contrast, 'the fact that this event has taken place in Jesus of Nazareth is ascertainable only through the historical experience of the crucified and risen Jesus' – that is, through the experience of a particular individual, namely Jesus Christ.[92]

JESUS CHRIST

I am now in a position to say more precisely than before what Rahner has actually justified in the properly transcendental portion of his Christology, assuming for the present purposes that his basic argument is sound. By appeal to a universal orientation or *Ausschau*, he has established that a *positive* saviour is, or would be, *heilsbedeutsam*. It has, of course, been assumed throughout that Jesus Christ as a *particular* person is in fact the saviour in question. This assumption brings a question to the fore which I have naturally been unable to treat in this endeavour to locate precisely the boundaries of 'the idea of an absolute saviour'. How do we actually know Jesus Christ, to whom this unique significance is ascribed? How do we identify and describe him as a particular person, given that the determinate features which enable us to do so are in no way included in the idea of an absolute saviour, or in our orientation to such a saviour? It will be useful to discuss this matter briefly before assessing the actual status of Jesus Christ as a particular person in Rahner's Christology.

Jesus Christ is identified and known, on Rahner's account, through a self-involving engagement with him in the historical dimension of one's life, a 'concrete encounter' which alone discloses him to us as a particular person.[93] Here the realm of the categorial enters Rahner's Christology in the full sense, although in one respect (namely, the positivity which pertains to all categorial realities) it has been anticipated in the transcendental justification of the notion of an absolute saviour. That is, in the encounter with Jesus Christ we are concerned with a spatio-temporally limited human reality who is the subject of certain definite describable features and not of any others. Precisely this concrete, categorially explicit relationship, and thus the one who is encountered in it, cannot be derived from or absorbed into the idea of an absolute saviour.[94] This is the christologically signifi-cant sense of Rahner's axiom that the categorial is 'irreducible' to the transcendental.[95] Of course, it is the particular person whom we identify as such in this irreducible encounter that we believe to be the transcendentally anticipated absolute saviour, and to whom we ascribe this (independently justified) dignity and significance. This belief and ascription constitute the funda-mental assumption, what has been called the 'minor premise', of Rahner's overall christological argument:

> The common Christian relationship to Jesus Christ . . . is present (*gegeben*) in and through the 'faith' that in the

encounter with him in the unity and totality of his word, his life and his victorious death the all-encompassing and all-pervasive mystery of reality as a whole and of each individual life, the mystery which we call God, 'is present' for our salvation . . . Therefore this relationship can also be characterized as a relationship to the absolute and eschatological saviour.[96]

Remarks like this ('in the unity and totality of his . . . life') might lead one to suppose that any number of actions and events in the specific cumulative pattern which constitutes Jesus' particularity might be minimally sufficient for us to identify him as a particular person. Rahner is willing to say this, in so far as the whole life of Jesus is part of the 'content' or 'object' of faith.[97] However, the issue at hand is not simply what features of Jesus enable us to identify him, but which features minimally enable us to identify him as the one whom we believe to be the absolute saviour. Here, Rahner insists, only two determinate features are at once necessary and sufficient to identify Jesus as a particular person in such a way that we can take him to be the absolute saviour, that is, to identify the subject of the assumption, 'Jesus Christ is the absolute saviour'. As he puts it, 'in fundamental theology we really only have to prove that two theses are historically credible in order to establish in fundamental theology the grounds of faith for orthodox Christianity's whole Christology.'[98] These features are: (1) that 'Jesus understood himself . . . as the *eschatological* prophet, as the absolute and definite saviour', and not only as one in a continuing series of divine messengers; and (2) 'the resurrection of Jesus'.[99] By contrast, 'all other assertions about Jesus as the Christ can be left to faith itself as the content of faith'.[100]

Jesus' self-understanding and his resurrection, taken as historically accessible particularizing features, are an adequate basis upon which we can find in him what we are always already on the lookout for in virtue of our concrete nature (even if we may be aware of this *Ausschau* only after its fulfilment), namely the absolute saviour. 'Jesus, then, is the historical presence of this final and unsurpassable word of God's self-disclosure: this is his claim and he is vindicated in this claim by the resurrection . . . In this sense in any case he is the "absolute saviour"'.[101]

There is, so Rahner argues, a suggestive fitness here: Jesus Christ as identified in his 'messianic' self-understanding and his resurrection from the dead seems a materially appropriate subject for the ascription of that ultimate redeeming significance which we all seek in our basic transcendental orientation. 'A God–man as radical question in death and as radical answer in what we call "resurrection", [is] what we seek. We find this in Jesus, simply because *he* exists *in this way* and no one else in history has laid such a claim to this, and because this claim of his has been believed.'[102] By drawing attention to this apparent fitness Rahner is not arguing that belief in Jesus Christ as the absolute saviour is historically demonstrable; faith in Jesus Christ is a self-involving commitment of the whole person which is beyond demonstration.[103] Rather, Rahner is indicating a kind of coherence between the idea of an absolute saviour, which is meaningful and credible for us on *a priori* grounds (namely, its congruity with certain general criteria), and the particular life of Jesus. This congruity, he argues, makes it at least 'not absurd' for Christians to believe in him as the absolute saviour.[104]

Recollection of the overall structure of Rahner's basic christological argument, which was summarized in the form of a syllogism, shows that the entire argument is now in place. By developing the idea of an absolute saviour, he has given a clear answer to the distinguishing question of the second way, and with the same stroke has warranted the proposition which epitomizes the specifically transcendental aspect of the argument (which has been called his 'major premise'). He has shown that 'an absolute saviour is *heilsbedeutsam*', in answer to the question, 'how can there be something which is *heilsbedeutsam*?', by deploying a general criterion for a saving reality (namely, that such a reality be the object of an *a priori* orientation to ultimate fulfilment which is constitutive of our concrete nature), and by demonstrating that an absolute saviour would be a uniquely and unsurpassably suitable object for such an orientation. In a second and separate step, Rahner has now introduced a particular person, Jesus Christ, into the argument and shown how he can be accepted as the absolute saviour. This was accomplished by isolating identifying features of Jesus on the basis of which he can intelligibly be said to be the saviour whom we all seek, although the knowledge that he actually is this saviour remains accessible only to faith. So grounds of credibility have been established, of a quite different sort in each case, both for the meaningfulness of any belief in an absolute saviour, and for the feasibility of belief specifically in Jesus Christ as the absolute saviour.

By the procedure of combining these two kinds of credibility, by combining, that is, general criteria of a saving reality with identifying reference to Jesus Christ as a particular person, Rahner asserts the conclusion at which his entire argument has aimed: Jesus Christ is *heilsbedeutsam*. This conclusion, of course, is taken for granted by both ways of trying to show how Jesus Christ can be *heilsbedeutsam*. My interest lies in the distinctive manner in which Rahner reaches this shared conclusion.

It seems that for Rahner, one must in principle make a radical distinction between the criteria which establish that an absolute saviour is *heilsbedeutsam* and the criteria which indicate that Jesus Christ is the absolute saviour. The criteria which establish the character of a possible saving reality are those constituted by a universal human orientation to ultimate fulfilment. These criteria, and therefore the idea of an absolute saviour which conforms to them, are by nature logically general; they mark off the 'kind of thing' which is significant for salvation. Such criteria include no reference to Jesus Christ as a particular person – that is, no ostention and description of him. By contrast, it is specific features of Jesus's own life which provide the grounds or criteria for saying that he is in fact the absolute saviour. Hence the distinctiveness of Rahner's procedure and of the second way which he exemplifies. While Jesus Christ is in fact the absolute saviour on account of specific features of his own life, we can say that Jesus Christ is actually significant for us because we can ascribe to him a status and function the credibility, meaningfulness and intelligibility of which can and must be justified independently of, and without reference to, him as a particular person. The remainder of this discussion of Rahner will be devoted primarily to charting the implications of this procedure.

Excursus on Rahner's conception of our knowledge of Jesus

A problem arises in connection with the way Rahner thinks we *identify* (that is, locate or pick out) Jesus as a particular person, one which I can only mention briefly here but which would be worth a more detailed examination. Without explicitly taking up the matter, Rahner assumes that we can identify Jesus Christ on the basis of his self-understanding and the resurrection alone. He must assume this, since these are the only particularizing features of Jesus which he allows into the domain of fundamental theology, that is, into an account of the 'grounds of faith', the bases upon which we call Jesus the absolute saviour. But it is not clear that we can identify Jesus on the strength of either of these features, at least as Rahner understands them.

1 Jesus' self-understanding (confining ourselves here to the less problematic 'objectified', 'thematic' aspect) is, strictly speaking, part of his own conscious experience. It is widely argued, in Strawson's words, that 'the principles of individuation of such experiences essentially turn on the identities of the persons to whose histories they belong'.[105] This would mean that we can only ascribe this self-understanding to Jesus, as distinguished from anyone else, if we can first locate Jesus on the basis of overt words and deeds which allow us to attribute to him the self-understanding in question. Rahner never explicitly denies this but taking it seriously would mean introducing the ostensible and describable 'history' of Jesus into fundamental theology and explaining how the history which actually identifies Jesus, and not only the consciousness which is presumed to underlie that history, can serve as a fit basis for calling him the absolute saviour.

2 The resurrection does not seem to be the sort of event which admits of a definite description, a point Rahner stresses.[106] But this indicates that the resurrection, taken by itself, does not enable us to identify its subject. Rather, the resurrection is only accessible to us in its distinctive place as the climax of the coherent, particularizing pattern of Jesus' life. This would lead to the same practical conclusion as point 1 above.

Valuable though it would be to pursue these considerations for their own sake, they are secondary for my purposes. I am concerned about the fate of Jesus as a particular person in a Christology like Rahner's if he *can* successfully identify Jesus and similarly, as has already been mentioned, if he *can* show that we all have a transcendental orientation to an absolute saviour. So I will assume that identifying reference to Jesus is possible on Rahner's terms.

THE LOSS OF PARTICULARITY

I have now laboured at some length to give an account of the structure of Rahner's Christology. While this has entailed a, perhaps wearisome, delay in getting at the issue, it was unavoidable on two counts. First, I am inquiring into the consistency of Rahner's christological procedure or method with the conviction that Jesus Christ is the 'absolute saviour' precisely as a particular person. Rahner does not really consider this issue explicitly, and, like most followers of the second way, seems not to see that there might be a problem here. Consequently, it was necessary to outline in some detail the context in which the consistency of method and conviction does become a problem for Rahner, so that the plausibility of the ensuing argument, which aims to specify the nature and import of that problem, might be clear. Second, Rahner's difficulty is precisely a structural one; it is a function of the way he uses a number of complex terms (a name and several concepts) in a large-scale argument. Because the difficulty lies embedded in Rahner's most basic decisions about how to proceed in Christology and not simply in some missing concept, distinction or refinement, which could easily be supplied, I have focused my attention upon the overall argumentative structure in which those decisions are worked out. For it seems as though Rahner's method will not, in fact, allow him to say that Jesus Christ is *heilsbedeutsam*, in the sense in which, he insists, this belief is to be held in the Christian church, and as such is to be the presupposition and norm of any Christology, specifically, of any attempt to explain how it is that Jesus Christ can be *heilsbedeutsam*.

In order to see how this is so, what Rahner takes to be an essential feature of the Christian conviction that Jesus Christ is the absolute saviour should be borne in mind. The truth of this belief or its obvious equivalent is acknowledged not only by Rahner, but by theologians of both the first and second ways generally, that is, by all theologians who hold that Jesus Christ actually is ultimately significant for salvation and try to give an account of how this can be so. However, 'Jesus Christ is the absolute saviour' is not simply taken to be true on both sides; it is taken to be true in a specific *sense*. The Christian conviction taken for granted in both types of Christology is that Jesus Christ is the absolute saviour precisely as a particular person. This very person Jesus of Nazareth, and thus the actions and events which constitute his life and correlatively enable us to identify him as distinct from all other persons, is *heilsbedeutsam*. Or, to put the point more generally, the Christian belief in an absolute saviour and in salvation is essentially and necessarily tied to Jesus Christ. Because the Christian belief in redemption is necessarily tied to Jesus Christ, it cannot be regarded as a paraphrase of some more basic belief, from which Jesus Christ is absent, that the world is redeemed. Jesus Christ, and hence the actions and events that make up his life, is not, for theologians of either way, an optional enrichment of the Christian belief in redemption.

Rahner himself is quite clear about this: 'Catholic faith and its dogmatics as they have been understood up to now, and also as they will have to be understood in the future, remain indissolubly bound up (*unablösbar gebunden*) not only with the historical existence of Jesus of Nazareth, but also with the historical events of a specific kind which took place during his life.'[107] What Christian faith and theology have to say about salvation and a saviour are 'indissolubly bound' to Jesus Christ as a particular person, so that, it would seem, an admissible account of 'that which is significant for salvation' cannot fail to include and be governed by reference to Jesus Christ. Rahner can also cast this assumption about the basic sense of the belief that 'Jesus Christ is the absolute saviour' in more negative terms. Thus, he insists, where 'Jesus is nothing more than one of the relatively numerous exemplary persons (*vorbildlichen Menschen*), one would no longer be dealing with Christianity'.[108] In other words, only Jesus Christ can be the absolute saviour. Any conception of that which is ultimately significant or significant for salvation which could apply to other individuals, either instead of Jesus or in addition to Jesus, does not seem to be for Rahner an account of salvation and a saviour which is admissible in Christian faith and theology. In these positive and negative senses 'Jesus Christ is the absolute saviour' functions as a norm even for those numerous Christologies of the second way which, in contrast to Rahner's, are not

nearly so clear that this belief must have the status of a presupposition in the attempt to show how Jesus Christ can be
heilsbedeutsam.

This characterization of the specific sense of the Christian
belief in Jesus Christ as the absolute saviour can usefully be
amplified in a logico-grammatical vein. From this point of view,
the sense the belief is assumed to have by theologians of both the
first and the second ways amounts to insisting that the subject of
'Jesus Christ is *heilsbedeutsam*' has a clear priority over the predicate. That is, on analogy with the broadly Aristotelian analysis of
the general priority of subjects over predicates, this specific
predicate ('is *heilsbedeutsam*') is always consequent upon this particular subject ('Jesus Christ'); it can properly enter discourse
only as the explicit or implied predicate of this subject. This is so
in two different respects. First, right speech about salvation and a
saviour *requires*, as has already been noted, some identifying
reference to Jesus Christ. Rahner calls this requirement the
indissoluble bond of the Catholic faith to 'the historical existence
of Jesus of Nazareth'. I shall call it the 'logical indispensability' of
Jesus Christ to the Christian belief in redemption. Second, language about salvation (precisely in Rahner's sense of the
Wesensvollzug of human reality) and a saviour *depends* upon Jesus
and the actions and events of his life; 'salvation' and 'an absolute
saviour' must be understood and conceived in a way which
evinces this dependence and perhaps, in some circumstances,
maximizes it. This dependence is what Rahner calls the bond of
Catholic faith to 'the historical events of a specific kind which
took place during his life'. I shall call it the 'material decisiveness'
of Jesus Christ for the Christian belief in redemption.[109]

All of this may seem rather obvious and Rahner certainly takes
it for granted. But the question is not whether Christian belief in
Jesus Christ typically has that specific sense on which I have just
focused, but whether it functions in this sense in actual
theological practice, among theologians who insist that it should
and must do so. Therefore, in the present case, the issue is
whether Rahner's attempt to conceptualize, explain and defend
this belief in a christological theory ends up honouring that belief
in the sense in which, by his own lights, it must.

We know what sense Rahner thinks 'Jesus Christ is the absolute
saviour' should have in Christology but it seems impossible for it

to have this sense in his Christology. The reason is clear from the way Rahner proceeds. Any reality, object, or person can be significant for our salvation (*heilsbedeutsam*) only because and in so far as we are oriented toward it by our very nature; only by falling within the scope of this transcendental orientation can any reality affect us as a whole and so be genuinely saving. But we are not, and cannot be, oriented in this way toward Jesus Christ; he himself can in no way be derived or deduced from our transcendental orientation and its content. Therefore, Jesus Christ is not, and cannot be, *heilsbedeutsam*, significant for salvation.

The same kind of argument applies when Rahner ascribes a specific characterization of that which is *heilsbedeutsam*, namely the status of the 'absolute saviour' (or whatever cognates he might want to employ), to Jesus Christ. An absolute saviour is *heilsbedeutsam* in that he or she is the object of an *a priori* orientation towards, or *Ausschau* for, supreme fulfilment. But Jesus Christ himself, and thus the actions and events which make up his life, is not a part of, or included in, the universal orientation in virtue of which alone an absolute saviour is *heilsbedeutsam*. Therefore, as Jesus Christ in his particularity is not, and cannot be, *heilsbedeutsam*, so also he is not, and cannot be, the absolute saviour.

In this way, Rahner's use of general criteria to define the arena of 'significance for salvation' seems inconsistent with his basic assumption about the way in which Jesus Christ is the absolute saviour. According to that assumption, any account of 'that which is significant for salvation' must include some reference to Jesus Christ as a particular person. But, as my argument indicates, Rahner's account of the meaningfulness, credibility and existential assimilability of 'an absolute saviour' fails to include any reference to Jesus Christ as a particular person. Indeed, that omission is not accidental, as though it were simply an oversight but is, rather, the inevitable result of the way Rahner structures his Christology. For on Rahner's account, it is conformity to a general criterion – namely, a universal pre-thematic human orientation to absolute fulfilment – which alone ultimately secures the *Heilsbedeutsamkeit* of 'an absolute saviour'. Since Jesus Christ as a particular person cannot be included in that orientation, but rather must be the object of a personal historical encounter, it appears that the significance for salvation of an absolute saviour will inevitably be secured in a way which involves no reference to Jesus Christ.

Seen in this light, Rahner's most basic procedural decision (the second way), and the method he develops in conformity with that decision (transcendental Christology), lead his Christology to face two alternatives which are equally unacceptable to him. On the one hand, he can hold that 'Jesus Christ is the absolute saviour' in the sense that his procedure requires, whereby 'the absolute saviour' is indeed *heilsbedeutsam*, because such a saviour uniquely and unsurpassably fulfills general criteria which define the character of a saving reality. But this procedure will not allow him to hold the belief in the sense in which he insists it is rightly held in the Christian church and necessarily honoured in theology. For if an absolute saviour is truly *heilsbedeutsam* in this way, then belief in an absolute saviour not only does not require or depend upon identifying reference to Jesus Christ, it *cannot* do so, since the ultimate significance of such a saviour must depend upon criteria which are logically general and, at least implicitly, known and accepted by all. On the other hand, Rahner can assert that 'Jesus Christ is the absolute saviour' in the sense in which he insists this belief must be held in the Christian church, where identifying reference to Jesus Christ is logically indispensable and materially decisive for any belief in an absolute saviour. But this would mean that the Christian belief in an absolute saviour does not actually reach a saving reality, since it is necessarily tied to Jesus Christ who, in his particularity, falls short of the domain of ultimate significance defined by general criteria for a saving reality and indeed is excluded from it. In brief, it looks as though Rahner's basic procedure in Christology will let him have *either* Jesus Christ *or* his saving significance, but will always stop him from having both. It appears that in Rahner's theology, the sense which 'Jesus Christ is the absolute saviour' must have, it cannot have.

This argument can perhaps usefully be amplified by applying the distinction I have introduced between particular individuality and positive individuality. Like any individual, Jesus can be looked at and understood concretely as a particular person, or abstractly as a positive person. As a particular person, and thus in his complete and proper individuality, Jesus Christ is the bearer of a proper name, who has determinate, describable features and who is located in a unique stretch of space and time (he was 'born under the Emperor Augustus', and 'suffered under Pontius Pilate'), all of which allows us to distinguish him from every other individual. Precisely as a particular person (as, in Rahner's terms, a 'concrete fact' of 'real history', accessible only through an irreducible 'historical experience', and not on the basis of the idea of an absolute saviour), Jesus Christ would seem not to be the absolute saviour, since as a particular person he necessarily lies outside the sphere of the inner orientation which alone renders an absolute saviour, whether possible or actual (that is, whether the 'idea of an absolute saviour' is simply entertained, or asserted to obtain in reality), meaningful, intelligible and existentially accessible for us. Because Jesus Christ cannot be the absolute saviour as a particular person, when Rahner asserts in the context of his Christology and the second way that 'Jesus Christ is the absolute saviour', this status and significance can apply to Jesus only as a positive person or 'vague individual'. That is, on Rahner's procedure, Jesus Christ can be the absolute saviour only in abstraction from and without regard for, his proper name, determinate features and unique spatio-temporal location, without, in other words, everything which makes him *Jesus* and so distinguishes him from any other individual. He is the absolute saviour only with respect to the bare form of individuality in him, that is, only in so far as he is an indeterminate, independently existing human subject. For in this respect alone do we anticipate him in our transcendental orientation and so in this respect alone can we, on Rahner's account, rightly consider him significant for salvation.

Rahner's more negative formulation of the assumption that 'Jesus Christ is the absolute saviour' may further help us to see the difficulty into which he is led by his christological method. According to this assumption, it is not simply the case that Jesus Christ is in fact the absolute saviour, that is, that the predicate 'absolute saviour' in fact applies to him. Jesus Christ is not one of many possible or actual 'exemplary (*vorbildlichen*) persons'; rather, only he can possibly be the 'absolute saviour' or *vorbildlicher Mensch*. Therefore, if this conviction is to be maintained in its theological explication and defence, the notion of an absolute saviour, as that which is ultimately significant for us, cannot be conceived in such a way that it could apply to someone else as readily as to Jesus. Yet this seems to be just the way in which 'an absolute saviour' is conceived in Rahner's transcendental Christology. The notion of an absolute saviour is of ultimate significance for us in virtue of its congruity with a general, anthropologically rooted criterion of significance for salvation. But it seems thoroughly conceivable that 'Socrates' or 'Martin Luther King' could be 'the absolute saviour' in just this sense and on just this basis. That is, another subject could conceivably be *heilsbedeutsam* in the very way in which, Rahner assumes, Jesus is in fact so, namely, by being the actualization of that for which all persons are necessarily on the lookout.

It may be useful here to recall the logico-grammatical distinction between positivity introducing expressions and particularity introducing expressions. Given the way Rahner justifies the meaningfulness and credibility of 'an absolute saviour', it seems, I have just argued, that the idea of an absolute saviour remains *heilsbedeutsam* in the same sense, and for the same reason, regardless of the particular subject ('Jesus', 'Socrates', etc.) to which it might be applied. Indeed, this appears to be the case even if there is no particular subject at all, but only a 'positivity introducer' like 'someone' or, to use one of Rahner's own phrases, 'somewhere there is' (an absolute saviour).[110] 'Absolute saviour', in other words, functions as an adequate (if not complete) characterization of that which is ultimately meaningful, intelligible and existentially assimilable quite apart from its ascription to Jesus Christ. Consequently, 'Jesus Christ' seems neither logically nor materially necessary to the judgment that he is the absolute saviour; any proper name, or no proper name at all, could serve the purpose which his does when it is introduced here – that of some subject which completes the assertion that the transcendentally justified saviour is actual.

It is important to note that I am not faulting Rahner for maintaining that the bare idea of 'an absolute saviour' is not necessarily an identifying description of Jesus Christ and in that sense could apply to someone else. The difficulty, rather, is that on his account 'an absolute saviour' signals something *significant for salvation* whether it is applied to Jesus, some other person, or no particular subject at all. It is this which seems deeply inconsistent with Rahner's assumption that Jesus Christ as a particular person, and only he, can be the absolute saviour.[111] Rahner, of course, always insists that the name of Jesus is the only one which belongs as the subject of 'absolute saviour', but this seems to be, in his own sense of the terms, a relatively meaningless, incredible dogmatic posit.

It seems, then, that Rahner's actual Christology is inconsistent with some of his most basic christological assumptions and commitments; Jesus Christ appears to be the absolute saviour for Rahner not in so far as he is Jesus, but only in so far as he is 'someone'. Indeed, the question reasonably can be raised whether in Rahner's Christology it must finally be *false* to say that 'Jesus Christ is the absolute saviour', although this proposition can be saved by giving it a forced sense which fits with the overall argument (forced, that is, because 'Jesus Christ', an expression which introduces a particular person, must be treated as though it does not). This suggests that there is a serious, perhaps fatal, equivocation in Rahner's central and most characteristic christological argument. Belief in Jesus Christ as the absolute saviour, which it has been shown functions like a 'minor premise' in Rahner's Christology, ends up meaning one thing as the Christian conviction which is the presupposition and norm of christological argument, and quite another thing in the context of the argument itself. Rahner, to be sure, intends otherwise. It will be necessary, therefore, to examine in the next chapter the ways he might respond to the argument that the formal structure of his Christology yields results which are inconsistent with some of his most basic christological convictions. It will also be necessary to turn in some detail from the formal structure of Rahner's Christology to his treatment of the life of Jesus, especially to those actions and events in which he takes Jesus' redemptive significance to be focused. If the argument about the formal structure of Rahner's Christology is correct, and he applies that position consistently, then one would expect the central redemptive events of Jesus' life to become so attenuated in his Christology that they no longer include any definite, unambiguous reference to Jesus himself. Only by examining in detail his treatments of these events, however, will it be possible to see whether this actually is the case.

NOTES

1   Karl Rahner, 'Jesus Christ, IV: History of Dogma and Theology', in *Sacramentum Mundi: An Encyclopedia of Theology*, ed. Karl Rahner et al. (6 vols, New York: 1969), vol. 3, p. 197, col. 1 (hereafter 'Jesus Christ').

2   Karl Rahner, *Schriften zur Theologie* (hereafter *SzT*) (16 vols, Einsiedeln: 1954–84), vol. 9, p. 98. The English translation is Karl Rahner, *Theological Investigations* (hereafter *TI*), tr. Cornelius Ernst et al. (20 vols, New York: 1961–83), vol. 11, p. 87. On the practice I will follow in citing Rahner, and the use of the standard English translations, see the Preface. On transcendental theology as the way to answer questions of possibility, cf. also *SzT*, vol. 8, p. 44; *TI*, vol. 9, p. 29. 'A transcendental question (*Fragestellung*) asks about the necessary conditions of the possibility of knowledge or action in the subject itself'.

3   *SzT*, vol. 8, p. 44; *TI*, vol. 9, p. 29. The fact that the 'human subject' is the *terminus* of the transcendental inquiry in theology does not, of course, limit the conditions of Christian faith and action to the 'merely human'. On the contrary, as Rahner frequently points out, the 'human subject' is radically (although not, strictly speaking, by 'nature') affected by the grace of justification, which as a universal divine action *ad extra* enters into the transcendental constitution of the human subject: 'God's offer of himself belongs to all men, and is a characteristic of man's transcendence and his transcendentality.' Karl Rahner, *Foundations of Christian Faith: An Introduction to the Idea of Christianity* (hereafter *Foundations*), tr. Willian V. Dych (New York: 1978), p. 129. Karl Rahner, *Grundkurs des Glaubens: Einführung in der Begriff des Christentums* (hereafter *Grundkurs*), (Freiburg: 1976), p. 135.

4   *Foundations*, p. 20; *Grundkurs*, p. 31. Cf. also *TI*, vol. 11, p. 89; *SzT*, vol. 9, p. 101.

5   *Foundations*, p. 85; *Grundkurs*, p. 93.

6   See, e.g., the contrast between 'transcendental, *a priori* theology' and 'descriptive (*kategorial*), historical, *a posteriori* theology' in *TI*, vol. 9, p. 30; *SzT*, vol. 8, p. 45.

7   *Foundations*, p. 140; *Grundkurs*, p. 145.

8   Thus Rahner can say that this 'relationship of mutual conditioning' (*gegenseitigen Bedingungsverhältnis*) is one in which 'knowledge of the *a priori* conditions which make knowledge possible in the subject necessarily constitutes also an element in the actual knowledge of the object itself, both with regard to the question of what the nature of the object known is as a matter of metaphysical necessity, and also with regard to the question of what the concrete historical

conditions of this object are' (*TI*, vol. 11, p. 87; *SzT*, vol. 9, p. 98). However, the very constitution of the human subject is such that 'he experiences the act of self-realization of his own transcendentality as communicated (*vermittelt*, 'mediated') to him through the *a posteriori* experience of the object which of itself manifests itself to him or refuses to manifest itself to him' (*TI*, vol. 11, p. 88; *SzT*, vol. 9, p. 99). The background of this notion of a mutual conditioning between the transcendental and categorial aspects of experience, and by extension of theology, lies in Rahner's early metaphysics of knowledge. Even on the supposition of the ultimate identity of being and self-present knowing, 'the return (*Rückkunft*) into oneself, the being reflected into oneself, which constitutes the essence of knowledge, is only possible for man by reaching out (*durch eine Auskehr*) to an other, different from him', Karl Rahner, *Hörer des Wortes: Zur Grundlegung einer Religionsphilosophie*, ed. J. B. Metz (Munich: 1963), pp. 147–8. Correlative with this mutual conditioning in human knowledge, 'Historicity results from the specifically human spiritual constitution (*Geistigkeit*), so that it is the historicity of the human spirit as such' (*Hörer des Wortes*, p. 173).

9   *Foundations*, p. 269; *Grundkurs*, p. 264.

10 Karl Rahner, *Spirit in the World* (no tr. given) (London: 1979).

11 Cf. above, n. 8. For a detailed exposition of these two books and the approach to theology which they suggest, with references to the extensive secondary literature, cf. Anne Carr, *The Theological Method of Karl Rahner* (Missoula, Mont: 1977).

12 *TI*, vol. 6, p. 131; *SzT*, vol. 6, p. 160. On the credibility of the specific contents of Christian faith as the proper concern of fundamental theology, cf. 'Jesus Christ', p. 193, col. 1: 'The fact that a divine revelation has taken place (and in Jesus Christ in particular) can probably only be shown to be credible today by continual reference to what has been revealed and as such appears credible.' Rahner here clearly distinguishes formally between credibility and content, while at the same time insisting that it must be features of the content of Christian belief that render Christian belief credible. On the strictly formal character of this distinction, cf. *Foundations*, p. 238; *Grundkurs*, p. 236. Rahner's insistence that the material of fundamental theology must be the same as that of dogmatic theology (even if the extension of the latter is, in practice, much wider), but viewed under a certain aspect, is a response to what he calls 'old' or 'traditional' fundamental theology. The latter, as he sees it, sought to ground the credibility of Christian faith without reference to its content but rather by appeal to the authority intrinsic to its source. *Locutio Dei attestans*, for example, is taken in this 'old' fundamental theology to be a general feature of all reve-

lation and, as such, a ground of its credibility (cf. *TI*, vol. 6, p. 127; *SzT*, vol. 6, p. 154).

13 *TI*, vol. 6, p. 129; *SzT*, vol. 6, p. 157.

14 *Foundations*, p. 207; *Grundkurs*, p. 207. The necessity of fundamental theology, especially its transcendental aspect, will be considered in more detail when its christological application is examined. Cf. below, nn. 23, 31, 36.

15 Karl Rahner, *Ich Glaube an Jesus Christus* (hereafter *Ich Glaube*) (Einsiedeln: 1968), p. 14.

16 *TI*, vol. 1, p. 185; *SzT*, vol. 1, p. 206. The same basic question can be put in a variety of ways. So Rahner will stress the need for a 'picture of the world' in which Jesus Christ is 'meaningful' (*sinnvoll*) (*TI*, vol. 1, p. 198; *SzT*, vol. 1, p. 219). Theology, he says, has to 'render intelligible' (*verständlich machen muß*) faith in a historical redeemer (*TI*, vol. 11, p. 100; *SzT*, vol. 9, p. 112). It must ask the question, 'whether and how *Jesus Christ* is the Christian answer to the human question of meaning (*Sinnfrage*)' (*SzT*, vol. 15, p. 209; this volume of the *Schriften* has not yet been translated into English).

17 The development of the position just outlined will be discussed at length in chap. 4. It has been briefly introduced here simply for the purpose of a clarifying contrast with Rahner's own view.

18 *Foundations*, p. 230; *Grundkurs*, p. 227.

19 Karl Rahner, 'Transcendental Theology', *Sacramentum Mundi*, vol. 6, p. 288, col. 1.

20 *SzT*, vol. 15, p. 234.

21 This posture, which takes 'how can Jesus Christ be *heilsbedeutsam*?' to be in fact two distinct questions, is nicely captured in a passage from *Ich Glaube*, p. 14 (part of which has already been cited; cf. n. 15): 'For if the "act" which seeks or explicitly finds Jesus Christ is supposed to be significant for salvation, then it must bear on (*betreffen*) the fulfilment of one's *whole* existence with all its necessary structures and relations, and it can therefore be specified (*bestimmt*) by means of all the characteristics which such an existence has and realizes. All these characteristics must agree on the one hand in signifying *necessary structures of existence*, because otherwise they could have nothing to do with a religious question of salvation, and on the other hand in being related precisely to *concrete history*, [i.e., that of Jesus].'

22 *TI*, vol. 9, p. 41; *SzT*, vol. 8, p. 60.

23 *Foundations*, pp. 207–8; *Grundkurs*, p. 207. Cautions of this kind against 'mythology' abound in Rahner's writings ('I have used this word often', *SzT*, vol. 15, p. 226), but they are usually quite brief and serve simply to highlight Rahner's conviction that whatever is *heilsbedeutsam* must be presented in such a way that it is credible in

its own right. One example, typical in substance but noteworthy for its uncharacteristic rhetorical pungency, is *TI*, vol. 9, p. 40; *SzT*, vol. 8, p. 59. 'Let us look dispassionately at today's real cultural situation: if a modern man who has not been brought up as a Christian hears the words 'Jesus is God made man', he will straight away reject this explanation as mythology which he cannot begin to take seriously nor to discuss, just as we do when we hear that the Dalai Lama regards himself as a reincarnation of Buddha.' This example recurs in *SzT*, vol. 15, p. 232.

24   *TI*, vol. 16, p. 202; *SzT*, vol. 12, p. 254. Cf. also *TI*, vol. 12, p. 165; *SzT*, vol. 9, p. 502: 'According to the doctrine of the Church herself an individual can already be in possession of sanctifying grace . . . positively oriented by grace towards his supernatural and eternal salvation even before he has explicitly embraced a credal statement of the Christian faith and been baptized.'

25   *Foundations*, p. 147; *Grundkurs*, p. 152. Cf. *SzT*, vol. 9, p. 507; *TI*, vol. 12, p. 170. Grace 'implies a real alteration of consciousness . . . It would be a miraculous, almost mythological notion (*Vorstellung*), if one supposed that this grace of faith were given only in the instant in which the preaching of the gospel strikes the hearer.'

26   *TI*, vol. 16, p. 200; *SzT*, vol. 12, pp. 251–2.

27   *SzT*, vol. 12, p. 252; *TI*, vol. 16, p. 200.

28   *TI*, vol. 11, p. 237; *SzT*, vol. 9, p. 249.

29   The second way has in fact been undertaken with astonishing inventiveness, as two clearly non-transcendental examples indicate. John Locke, who was perhaps the first writer expressly to distinguish the question of our need for salvation from that of our need for Jesus Christ (cf. *The Reasonableness of Christianity*, nos 234ff., ed. I. T. Ramsey, (Stanford, Calif: 1958), pp. 56–77), explains the need for salvation without invoking any technical anthropology but simply by appealing to common morality (common, that is, to the emerging English middle class). In our own day, Wolfhart Pannenberg avoids any explicit transcendental procedure in Christology and invokes a broadly transcendental anthropology only in passing, yet he follows the second way in his insistence that the saving significance attributed to Jesus Christ can only be maintained if 'that kind of thing' can independently be shown to be feasible. With regard, for example, to Jesus' death in the place and stead of sinners, 'if substitution is not a universal phenomenon in human social relationships . . . then it is not possible to speak meaningfully of a vicarious character of the fate of Jesus Christ' (*Jesus – God and Man*, 2nd edn, tr. Lewis S. Wilkins and Duane A. Priebe (Philadelphia: 1977), p. 268). In light of this kind of remark, statements like, 'The task of Christology is to establish the true

understanding of Jesus' significance from his history', apply for Pannenberg only to the *genesis* of an account of Jesus' significance, not to the justification of its religious meaningfulness (*Jesus – God and Man*, p. 30).

30 *TI*, vol. 9, p. 35; *SzT*, vol. 8, pp. 51–2.

31 *TI*, vol. 11, p. 100; *SzT*, vol. 9, p. 112. It is just this transcendental theology which, as transcendental Christology, 'asks about the *a priori* possibilities in man which make the coming of the messsage of Christ possible', and thus keeps the ascription of saving significance to Jesus Christ from being, 'a mythological overlay on historical events' (*Foundations*, p. 207; *Grundkurs*, p. 207).

32 Cf. above, n. 18.

33 *SzT*, vol. 8, p. 51; *TI*, vol. 9, p. 35. The same point can be put with an emphasis on the categorial aspect of human life. 'Faith has to do with the comprehensive interpretation (*Deutung*) of all existence, and the Christian faith (as proclamation of historical events of salvation) makes assertions about *all* dimensions of human exist- ence' (*SzT*, vol. 7, p. 61; *TI*, vol. 7, p. 55).

34 *TI*, vol. 11, p. 100; *SzT*, vol. 9, p. 112. Or, as Rahner puts the same point in a parallel passage, 'If they [saving realities] are to address man as man, he must address himself to them with his whole being, that is, he must discover that he is by his very nature forced to turn to them. But if he approaches them with his whole being, his theology is transcendental' ("Transcendental Theology", p. 288, col. 1). 'By nature' here is an ellipsis for 'by nature supernaturally elevated through the offer of beatifying grace'. So Rahner writes, 'We can and must say that this transcendental reference (*Bezogen- heit*) to a reality of supernatural verbal revelation, to a mystery that has been revealed, is thought of throughout as constituted by God's grace itself' (*TI*, vol. 11, p. 93; *SzT*, vol. 9, p. 105). In the more precise terminology of an earlier essay on nature and grace, persons are oriented toward a saving reality in their 'concrete quiddity', but not by 'pure nature'. 'Man's concretely experienced quiddity (*Wesen*) differentiates itself into the supernatural existential as such and the "remainder" – the pure nature' (*TI*, vol. 1, p. 315; *SzT*, vol. 1, p. 342). However, transcendental *Christology* does not have to be concerned about this distinction but only with the orientation to a saving reality itself (cf. *Foundations*, p. 208; *Grundkurs*, p. 208).

35 So Rahner says

> Transcendental Christology appeals to a person who (as we know at least from the universal revelation in grace which has become reflexive in Christianity) already has at least unthematically a finality and dynamism imparted by God

himself towards God's self-communication, and it asks him whether he could not appropriate this orientation (*Ange-richtetheit*) as his own in freedom and from out of his own inner experience, an experience which unthematically at least belongs to his transcendental constitution.

It is in this sense that 'a transcendental Christology takes its starting point in the experiences which man always and inescapably has' (*Foundations*, p. 208; *Grundkurs*, p. 208).

36   *TI*, vol. 11, p. 93; *SzT*, vol. 9, p. 104. The reference in Rahner's text at this point is to transcendental theology as a whole, not only to transcendental Christology. Cf. a similar remark in *SzT*, vol. 8, p. 52; *TI*, vol. 9, p. 35: 'The saving significance (*Heilsbedeutsamkeit*) of a theological object, which is a necessary moment of every theological object, can be ascertained by asking about the *saving receptivity (Heilsempfänglichkeit)* of man *for* this object.' These later formulations are perhaps bolder than Rahner's earlier ones, but this same basic position is maintained as early as the seminal article 'Current Problems in Christology', (in *SzT*, vol. 1; *TI*, vol. 1), viz., that an adequate account or 'thick description' of a theological object is insufficient in principle to explain how that object can be accessible or 'meaningful' (*sinnvoll*) for us, so that the basic meaningfulness of the object must be explained by a subjective *a priori* reference to the object in question. 'It is not only the knowability of the *object* which must be examined, but also the distinctive nature of the *subject* and *his* specific openness with regard to just that object' (*TI*, vol. 1, p. 186; *SzT*, vol. 1, p. 206). Even at this early point, Rahner asserts that 'without such a fundamental deduction, and unless it is brought home to man as something really achieved, the historical message concerning Jesus the Son of God is always in danger of being dismissed as a mere piece of mythology' (*TI*, vol. 1, p. 187; *SzT*, vol. 1, p. 208).

37   *TI*, vol. 5, pp. 174–5; *SzT*, vol. 5, p. 237. Cf. *Foundations*, pp. 193–4; *Grundkurs*, pp. 194 – 5.

38   *SzT*, vol. 10, p. 237; *TI*, vol. 13, p. 222.

39   Cf. *TI*, vol. 11; p. 96, *SzT* vol. 9, p. 108: 'Christology in transcendental theology would have to develop the concept of an absolute mediator of salvation.'

40   'Jesus Christ', p. 197, col. 1. Cf. also *TI*, vol. 5, p. 187; *SzT*, vol. 5, p. 216. 'Naturally, the historical nature of human and also metaphysical knowledge permits us in actual fact to formulate such a formal scheme with such clarity only because we already know about the fact of the Incarnation, all of which is possible only *post Christum natum*.'

41   *TI*, vol. 1, p. 186; *SzT*, vol. 1, pp. 206–7. Similarly, Rahner writes, 'We can deduce (*ableiten*) from the transcendence [of the human *Wesen* towards absolute fulfilment through the free self-communication of divine love] no exigency (*Forderung*) of such fulfilment' (*TI*, vol. 4, p. 110; *SzT*, vol. 4, p. 143). Since the independence of the redeemer's actuality is primarily logical rather than temporal, the whole issue of whether and to what degree the idea of a unique redeemer is accessible apart from the knowledge of the redeemer's actuality is relatively unimportant. The logical distinction Rahner maintains between the two holds precisely when the actuality of the redeemer is known; the fact that the saviour is actual always remains independent of and not derivable from the idea of a redeemer and from the argument which establishes that such a fact can be *heilsbedeutsam*.

42   *TI*, vol. 5, pp. 187–8; *SzT*, vol. 5, p. 217. Cf. also *TI*, vol. 5, p. 11; *SzT*, vol. 5, p. 20. Rahner is at least marginally aware of the distinction I have just made between the actuality and the particularity of the saviour, but he does not devote any explicit attention to it. Thus, in a passage to which I have already made reference (cf. previous note), he distinguishes between 'what is contained in Christ, who can in fact be known only by obediently listening to a messsage which has gone forth in history' (particular identity), and 'the *necessity* of the fact of Christ' (actuality) (*TI*, vol. 1, p. 186; *SzT*, vol. 1, pp. 206–7). Cf. also below, nn. 43, 49.

43   The lineaments of this position are already visible in Rahner's early philosophy of religion, where the christological application of the position has not yet been worked out.

The philosophy of religion, which is the knowledge of man as unlimited spirit before the free God of a possible revelation, can make no decision (*Vorentscheidung*) concerning the possible content of such divine speech, indeed not even concerning the question of whether such speech occurs. The constitution of a hearer of the speech *or* the silence of God allows the religion of the revelation which has actually been issued by the divine speech to be founded (*beruhen*) wholly on itself, with regard both to its existence and its content (*nach Dasein und Sosein*). (*Hörer des Wortes*, p. 213).

44   It might be objected at this point that the stated task of Rahner's transcendental Christology is only to show *how* Jesus Christ *can be heilsbedeutsam*, not *that* he *is heilsbedeutsam*. But the logical structure of Rahner's argument indicates that both expressions are acceptable, as long as their proper sense is understood. What I have called the

primary burden of a transcendental Christology is, in logico-grammatical terms, to warrant predicating *heilsbedeutsam* of 'absolute saviour' or 'God–man.' As I have just stressed, the warranted assertion that 'an absolute saviour is *heilsbedeutsam*' is logically indifferent to the actuality and identity of the saviour; in these respects, the statement 'Jesus Christ is the absolute saviour' can only be presupposed. However, it can be presupposed in two different modes: as a hypothetical proposition (so it would be for the unbeliever), or as a truth assertion (so it ordinarily is for the believer). The modality in which the presupposition is held determines the modality of the proposition towards which the whole argument is directed. If 'Jesus Christ is the absolute saviour' is held hypothetically, then the argument will only show *how* 'Jesus Christ is *heilsbedeutsam*' is possible. If the presupposition is held assertorically, then it will also show *that* 'Jesus Christ is *heilsbedeutsam*.'

  TI, vol. 11, p. 96; *SzT*, vol. 9, p. 107.

46 *TI*, vol. 5, p. 188; *SzT*, vol. 5, p. 217.

47 *Foundations*, p. 207; *Grundkurs*, p. 206.

48 Cf. *SzT*, vol. 15, p. 232. Without the transcendental justification of the idea of an absolute saviour (in this passage, more specifically, the idea of a resurrection from the dead), which shows that this is not 'an absolutely meaningless (*sinnlose*)' sort of thing, or one 'which has absolutely nothing to do with us in our concrete experience of existence', there is no way of preventing the consequence that 'fundamentally we also could only hear the message of the resurrection of Jesus with a shaking of the head or a shrug of the shoulders'.

49 *Foundations*, pp. 211–12; *Grundkurs*, pp. 210–11.

50 This outline of the way Rahner arrives at the essential content of the idea of an absolute saviour is congruent with his own brief summaries in *TI*, vol. 11, pp. 93–4; *SzT*, vol. 9, pp. 105–6 and *Foundations*, pp. 208–12; *Grundkurs*, pp. 208–11. It follows neither of these somewhat different summaries in detail. The currently available surveys of Rahner's theology typically contain some account of 'the idea of an absolute saviour' and cognate issues. Cf. e.g., Karl-Heinz Weger, *Karl Rahner: An Introduction to His Theology*, tr. David Smith (New York: 1980), pp. 152–71. However, as far as I have been able to discover, none of the literature on Rahner's Christology (or indeed his theology as a whole) explicitly takes up the specific issue with which I am concerned. For that reason, my analysis of Rahner will not include an explicit conversation with that literature.

51 *Foundations*, p. 20; *Grundkurs*, p. 31. Cf. a characteristic remark from *Hörer des Wortes*, where a detailed argument regarding the necessity and structure of this 'openness' is developed. 'In so far as judgements and free activities necessarily belong to human existence, the pre-app-

rehension of being belongs absolutely to the fundamental condition of
human existence, in the infinity which belongs to it in itself' (p. 83).

52 *TI*, vol. 4, p. 108; *SzT*, vol. 4, p. 140.

53 *TI*, vol. 5, p. 173; *SzT*, vol. 5, p. 201. Other passages bring out more
    clearly the fact that the quest for this goal is necessarily supported
    by the antecedent offer of grace. 'This infinite term (*Woraufhin*) of
    the transcendental movement opens itself to man in self-
    communication, at least in the form of an offer, as the free wonder of
    ecstatic love, which aims at absolute nearness and immediacy and
    bears in this self-communication the transcendental movement of
    man itself' (*SzT*, vol. 9, p. 106; *TI*, vol. 11, p. 94). Rahner's employ-
    ment of an 'evolutionary view of the world' in some discussions
    enables him to emphasize the striving, seeking character of this
    complex 'reference' to God much more clearly than I can do here.

54 Rahner's terminology here is less precise than one might wish. In
    the passages just quoted (cf. previous note) from *TI*, vol. 5; *SzT*, vol.
    5, he explicitly denies that an orientation to the unsurpassable
    self-communication of God is identical with the human *Wesen*.
    Elsewhere, however, he insists that '[Man] in his own *Wesen*, in his
    original (*ursprünglichen*) ground, in his *nature*, (*Natur*), is the needy,
    striving reference towards this fullness' (*SzT*, vol. 4, p. 140; *TI*, vol.
    4, p. 108, my emphasis). At other times he simply uses the noncom-
    mittal phrase *von sich aus* (cf. above, nn. 51, 34). The terminological
    difficulty, as I have already indicated (cf. n. 34), lies in the ambi-
    guity of the term *Wesen*. It can stand for 'pure nature' (and so it
    should be taken where it is *contrasted* with the transcendental orient-
    ation to immediacy with God), or it can stand for 'the concretely
    experienced *Wesen* of man' (*SzT*, vol. 1, p. 342; *TI*, vol. 1, p. 315), viz.,
    historically existing human nature under the offer of grace, for
    which 'the capacity for the God of personal love, which bestows
    itself, is the central and abiding existential' (*SzT*, vol. 1, p. 339; *TI*,
    vol. 1, p. 312) (and so it should be taken when it or its equivalent is
    in some way *identified* with our orientation to divine immediacy).

55 *Foundations*, p. 40; *Grundkurs*, p. 51.

56 *Foundations*, p. 40; *Grundkurs*, p. 51. Cf. above, n. 8.

57 *TI*, vol. 5, p. 174; *SzT*, vol. 5, p. 201.

58 *TI*, vol. 5, p. 174; *SzT*, vol. 5, p. 202. Cf. the parallel discussion in
    Foundations, p. 193; *Grundkurs*, pp. 193–4.

59 *TI*, vol. 5, p. 181; *SzT*, vol. 5, p. 210.

60 *SzT*, vol. 9, p. 213; *TI*, vol. 11, p. 201. Cf. *TI*, vol. 5, p. 176; *SzT*, vol. 5,
    p. 203. 'This Saviour, who represents the climax of this self-
    communication, must therefore be at the same time (*in einem*) God's
    absolute pledge (*Zusage*) by self-communication to the spiritual
    creature as a whole *and* the acceptance of this self-communication

by the Saviour; only then is there an utterly irrevocable self-communication from both sides, and only thus is it present in the world in a historically communicative manner.'

61 Cf. *TI*, vol. 1, p. 150; *SzT*, vol. 1, p. 170; *TI*, vol. 4, pp. 105–6; *SzT*, vol. 4, pp. 137–8. Much more recently, cf. *SzT*, vol. 15, pp. 217–8, pp. 227–8, and especially p. 225. There Rahner says that if one should come to the realization, with respect to the relation between one's own Christology and 'the' traditional Christology, 'that the two things have nothing to do with one another or contradict one another, then that would be a sign that one's own Christology was wrong, and not the contrary. Allow me to say this here, because in my whole life I have never had another view (*Meinung*) of this matter.'

62 Cf., *inter alia*, *Foundations*, pp. 292 – 3; *Grundkurs*, p. 286.

63 *TI*, vol. 5, p. 176; *SzT*, vol. 5, p. 203. Rahner makes and discusses this kind of assertion frequently. Cf., e.g., *Foundations*, pp. 197 – 8; *Grundkurs*, p. 198; *Ich Glaube*, p. 45; 'Jesus Christ', p. 204, cols. 2–205, col. 1.

64 Cf. *SzT*, vol. 5, p. 211; *TI*, vol. 5, p. 182. 'In any case, nothing stands in the way theologically of the assumption that grace and hypostatic union can only be thought together, and as a *unity* signify the one *free* decision of God for the supernatural order of salvation.' Cf. also, *TI*, vol. 11, p. 108; *SzT*, vol. 9, p. 120; *TI*, vol. 4, pp. 67–9; *SzT*, vol. 4, pp. 92–4.

65 *TI*, vol. 5, p. 182; *SzT*, vol. 5, pp. 210–11.

66 *TI*, vol. 1, p. 164; *SzT*, vol. 1, p. 185. Cf. *TI*, vol. 5, p. 180; *SzT*, vol. 5, pp. 208–9. We can now see that 'mythological' means 'not credible', precisely in the sense of 'not genuinely the object of our orientation to salvation'.

67 'This *potentia* cannot be an individual capacity *next to* other possibilities in the human state of being (*Seinsbestand*), but is materially identical with the human essence' (*SzT*, vol. 4, pp. 142–3; *TI*, vol. 4, p. 110). Cf. also the remark that our 'indefinable nature . . . When assumed by God as *his* reality, has arrived at the point to which it is always on the way in virtue of its own essence (*Wesen*)' (*SzT*, vol. 4, pp. 141–2; *TI*, vol. 4, p. 109). Cf. *TI*, vol. 1, pp. 183–4; *SzT*, vol. 1, pp. 204–5.

68 Cf. on this *TI*, vol. 4, pp. 114–16; *SzT*, vol. 4, pp. 148–50; the cited phrase is from *TI*, vol. 4, p. 114; *SzT*, vol. 4, p. 148.

69 *SzT*, vol. 4, p. 142; *TI*, vol. 4, p. 110. Cf. *TI*, vol. 5, p. 205; *SzT*, vol. 5, p. 234.

70 Cf. above, pp. 27–9. This is quite apart from the fact that Rahner calls upon a variety of theological and anthropological assumptions in working out a justified idea of an absolute saviour; he is willing to

defend most of these assumptions in their own places.

71 For some remarks focused specifically on the christological import of 'anonymous Christianity', cf. chap. 3, pp. 84–8. A sympathetic exposition of Rahner's view of anonymous Christianity and attendant issues may be found in Weger, *Karl Rahner*, pp. 86–141. For a useful account of Rahner's view in relation to a range of recent Catholic and Protestant alternatives, cf. George A. Lindbeck, '*Fides ex auditu* and the Salvation of Non-Christians', in *The Gospel and the Ambiguity of the Church*, ed. Vilmos Vajta (Philadelphia: 1974), pp. 92–123.

72 *TI*, vol. 4, p. 112; *SzT*, vol. 4, p. 145.

73 *TI*, vol. 4, p. 110; *SzT*, vol. 4, p. 143.

74 *TI*, vol. 4, p. 116; *SzT*, vol. 4, p. 150.

75 *TI*, vol. 3, p. 45; *SzT*, vol. 3, p. 59.

76 The phrase is from *Ich Glaube*, p. 33. Cf. *TI*, vol. 1, p. 187; *SzT*, vol. 1, p. 208. 'Accordingly [man] looks out – and looks out in the course of his history – to see whether the supreme fulfilment (however free it may remain) of his being (*Wesens*) and his expectation is not on the way to meet him.' Cf. also *Hörer des Wortes*, p. 197, p. 217.

77 On Rahner's pre-theoretical convictions about the character of Christian belief, cf. above, p. 31. On the theoretical side, cf. pp. 35–6.

78 *TI*, vol. 5, p. 188; *SzT*, vol. 5, p. 217.

79 'If one were to say that the *whole* history of the one humanity is the concrete reality in which the mystery of God is brought to experience and is promised to man . . . then it would still have to be said that this history is a one-way street, and as such must exhibit one point in which, as the history of God's self-communication, it comes to its high point' (*Ich Glaube*, p. 33).

80 *TI*, vol. 4, p. 111, *SzT*, vol. 4, p. 144. My use of 'absolute saviour' is an ellipsis for a much longer construction in the text.

81 *TI*, vol. 5, p. 11; *SzT*, vol. 5, p. 20. Rahner makes this kind of remark often. Cf. *TI*, vol. 1, p. 186; *SzT*, vol. 1, p. 207; *TI*, vol. 9, p. 30; *SzT*, vol. 8, p. 45; *TI*, vol. 11, p. 227; *SzT*, vol. 9, p. 239; *Ich Glaube*, p. 35, p. 61; *Foundations*, pp. 206–7, pp. 211–12; *Grundkurs*, p. 206, pp. 210–11.

82 *SzT*, vol. 9, p. 239; *TI*, vol. 11, p. 227.

83 This last, broadest concept of particularity applies to any created reality and even, in a sense, to the particularity of God (but only when a variety of important distinctions are made regarding the way in which descriptive terms apply to God). In this discussion, however, 'particular' and 'particularity' will normally connote 'human person', as will the concepts 'individual' and 'positivity'.

84 On the distinction and relation between proper names and identifying descriptions in the sense in which I am using the terms

here, cf. P. F. Strawson, *Individuals: An Essay in Descriptive Metaphysics*
(London: 1959), p. 20, pp. 25–6.

85 The fact that a positive reality of some kind is *conceived* as 'independently existing' does not mean, of course, that it is *affirmed* to be
actual. Thus the fact that we are oriented towards an absolute
saviour in a way which includes the positivity of the saviour is not to
be confused with an assertion of the saviour's existence; the concept
of positivity simply specifies the form a saviour will have, should
there be one.

86 *Summa Theologiae*, I, 30, 4, r. For citations from the *Summa Theologiae*, I
have used the Marietti manual edition of the Leonine text: *S. Thomas
Aquinatis Summa Theologiae*, ed. Peter Caramello (4 vols, Turin and
Rome: 1948–52). From here on, Thomas's *Summa Theologiae* will be
cited by part number only (I, I–II, II–II, III), followed by question,
article and location within the article.

87 I, 30, 4, r. Thomas deploys this distinction between positive
('vague') and particular ('determinate') individuality in a complex
variety of ways in his Christological and Trinitarian discussions.
For an analysis of his use of a logico-grammatical form of this
distinction in Christology, cf. chap. 5, pp. 176–89.

88 A descriptive phrase like 'chair of the Religious Studies Department' can, of course, be a predicate as well as a subject. But, so the
argument goes, it only introduces an *individual* into a proposition
when it functions as a grammatical and logical subject, and it is in
this use that I am considering it here. Used in this way, such a
phrase is an example of 2(c) in the brief taxonomy that follows of
subject expressions which introduce individuals.

89 Each of the *propositions* I have used as examples in point 1 could
enable someone successfully to identify the individual in question,
if that person were sufficiently familiar with the context of reference
for the *predicate* to serve as an identifying description. The indefinite
'positivity introducing' subject carries no identifying or particularizing load in such cases. Rather, the descriptive predicate
alone must function as the linguistic basis of identification; it can do
so because it is capable of serving as, or being included in, the
subject of another proposition, which latter would be logically prior
for purposes of identification. Should the predicate in such propositions be unable to bear the burden of identification, either, for
example, because one has insufficient familiarity with the context of
reference, or because the predicate is in some way incapable of
functioning as an identifying description, then no identification –
no reference to a particular individual – will be possible, even
though reference to some indeterminate individual is achieved.

90 In contrast to subject expressions of the first kind, these 'par-

ticularity introducing' expressions are always capable of serving to identify the individual they introduce and will do so given sufficient acquaintance with the context of reference. In this case, the various predicates will not serve to identify but only to characterize, classify, or otherwise qualify a particular already identified. In some cases, it may again be the predicate which enables identification of the individual introduced by the subject (cf. previous note), but this will be the case only when (a) the person doing the identifying is unfamiliar with the determinate features introduced by the class 2 subject expression, and (b) the predicate itself is capable of serving as class 2 subject.

91 Cf. above, nn. 78, 79.

92 *TI*, vol. 11, p. 227; *SzT*, vol. 9, p. 239.

93 The knowledge and identification of Jesus Christ must in fact be mediated by the apostolic witness (cf. *Foundations*, pp. 275–6; *Grundkurs*, p. 271), and hence by the testimony of Scripture and the Church. But this is tangential for our purposes, especially since Rahner says, 'Fundamentally, Jesus convinces us of the Church and Scripture, and not the reverse' (*SzT*, vol. 15, p. 220).

94 Cf. above, no. 82; also *Ich Glaube*, p. 61: 'The encounter with the concrete Jesus of the Gospels discovers (*erfährt*) without abridgement, in the concreteness and underivability of this historical form (*Gestalt*), *the* man who seeks the inconceivable infinity of the absolute God [i.e., who is the absolute saviour].'

95 Cf. above, pp. 17–18.

96 *Foundations*, pp. 204–5; *Grundkurs*, p. 204.

97 Cf. *Foundations*, p. 238; *Grundkurs*, p. 235.

98 *Foundations*, p. 245; *Grundkurs*, p. 243. I have already discussed the convictional and theoretical senses in which Rahner insists that 'Christology's assertion of faith about Jesus refers to a quite definite historical person and to historical events. Hence it implies historical assertions' (*Foundations*, p. 233; *Grundkurs*, p. 230. Cf. the discussion above, pp. 46–7). These historical assertions, he goes on to say, 'may perhaps really be found within an assertion of faith, but there at least they are meant in a really historical sense'; consequently for Rahner, they must be 'historically credible' according to the criteria of historical – critical exegesis (ibid.; cf. *TI*, vol. 11, pp. 191–2; *SzT*, vol. 9, p. 204). Note that 'credible' here is used minimalistically; a historical claim (e.g., about Jesus) is 'credible' if it cannot be shown by responsible critical means to be absolutely and unambiguously false. It is rather unlikely that this would actually occur, given Rahner's conception of the probable, only relatively certain character of historical knowledge (cf. *TI*, vol. 11, p. 206, p. 202; *SzT*, vol. 9, p. 218, p. 214, also *Foundations*, p. 252; *Grundkurs*, p. 249).

99   *Foundations*, p. 246; *Grundkurs*, p. 243.

100   Ibid.

101   *Foundations*, p. 280; *Grundkurs*, p. 275. Cf. *SzT*, vol. 15, pp. 214–15.

102   *Ich Glaube*, p. 38. Rahner sometimes finds the fitness of the particularity of Jesus with the content of our *a priori* anticipation less obvious. 'And so the incarnation of God is the absolute and yet the obvious mystery. One could almost think that what is strange, historically contingent and hard about it is not the thing in itself but the fact that the obviously (*selbstverständliche*) absolute mystery has taken place precisely in Jesus of Nazareth there and now' (*TI*, vol. 4, p. 120; *SzT*, vol. 4, pp. 154–5).

103   'No one can be compelled by discussions to believe precisely in Jesus of Nazareth as the absolute presence of God' (*Ich Glaube*, p. 35). Therefore, just as it would be false to suppose 'that this absolute assent of faith to Jesus Christ has nothing at all to do with the data of history, with which exegetical reflection is concerned', so also 'it would be . . . false to believe that the content and certainty of faith in Jesus Christ are the mere product of historical reflection, as it is pursued in exegesis' (*SzT*, vol. 9, p. 203, p. 204; *TI*, vol. 11, p. 192, p. 193).

104   Cf. *TI*, vol. 5, p. 13; *SzT*, vol. 5, p. 22. Rahner elsewhere puts it more strongly; not only is it not absurd but it is 'not so difficult' to find the absolute saviour in Jesus of Nazareth. Cf. *Ich Glaube*, p. 33; *TI*, vol. 13, p. 200; *SzT*, vol. 10, p. 214.

105   Strawson, *Individuals*, p. 41. The sorts of 'experience' or 'private particulars' (viz., 'sensations, mental events and, in one common acceptance of this term, sense-data') to which Strawson refers here are much less complicated than an individual's whole 'self-understanding'. But in so far as one locates both, however differently, in 'consciousness', precisely in contrast to the outward, ostensible history of an individual (as Rahner does), the logic of the issue remains basically the same.

106   Cf. *TI*, vol. 11, p. 208; *SzT*, vol. 9, p. 220; *Foundations*, p. 266; *Grundkurs*, p. 262.

107   *TI*, vol. 13, p. 201; *SzT*, vol. 10, p. 215.

108   Karl Rahner, *Im Gespräch*, ed. Paul Imhof and Hubert Biallowons (Munich: 1982), vol. 1, p. 163. Cf. also *TI*, vol. 4, p. 120; *SzT*, vol. 4, p. 155. 'When the longing for the absolute nearness of God . . . looks for *where* this nearness came – not in the postulates of the spirit, but in the flesh and in the housings of the earth: then no resting place can be found except in Jesus of Nazareth, over whom the star of God stands.'

109   The precise import of the labels 'logical indispensability' and 'material decisiveness' will be treated later on; they need not detain us here.

110 Cf. above, n. 80.
111 The issue of what constitutes an identifying description, as distinguished from a non-identifying characterization, will be taken up in more detail in the next two chapters.

3

The Loss of Particularity in Light
of Rahner's Responses

One of the primary tasks of Christian theology, it can be argued, is to describe with conceptual precision, as far as it is able, the distinctive, complex and infinitely rich patterns of Christian speech and action, and hence of the one real world rendered in the Bible – the world in which believers seek to live and think. While it differs in some important respects, this characterization is not incompatible with Rahner's insistence that 'fundamental' theology seeks to specify the grounds 'existentially effective today for faith in the real event of Christian revelation and its central contents'.[1] In either case, theology charts the logic of Christian belief, including its 'grounds', under the guidance of rules or parameters appropriate to the issue at hand. While these rules may be only implicit, when the issue is the place of Jesus Christ as a particular person in an account of what he is (that is, in an account of redemption and a redeemer), Christian speech and action, so Rahner would agree, stipulate a definite rule for theology. Any appropriate account of redemption and a redeemer are, in his phrase, 'indissolubly bound' to Jesus Christ as a particular person. As has been seen in a preliminary way, this 'indissoluble bond' is in fact constituted by two distinguishable logical relations. In the first place, Jesus Christ in his particularity is 'logically indispensable' to any acceptable explanation of what he is. This first relation is a necessary but not sufficient condition for the second, namely the 'material decisiveness' of Jesus Christ for the Christian belief in salvation and 'an absolute saviour'.

I have argued that this 'indissoluble bond' does not in fact exist in Rahner's theology and that his theology is, as a result, inconsistent with his own assumptions about the sense in which

Jesus Christ is the 'absolute saviour'. His Christology is radically structured by the aim of finding general criteria of significance for salvation (of that which is *heilsbedeutsam* or ultimately significant), criteria which direct the formulation and evaluation of any theologically usable concept of a 'saviour'. By their very nature, these general criteria are not 'indissolubly bound up' with the identifying description of any particular person. Such criteria, and any more definite characterization of 'that which is signifi-cant for salvation' which is developed in conformity with them, have the logical status of a generality in two distinguishable respects. They do not describe or necessarily include reference to any particular individual; correlatively, they can include, and are fit to be applied to, many particulars. Consequently, so the argument goes, any saving significance attributed to Jesus Christ on the basis of its conformity with these criteria is not, and indeed cannot be, logically and materially bound up with him. The very structure of his Christology prevents Rahner from honouring the two-fold rule he himself enunciates regarding the place of Jesus Christ in any acceptable Christology. The two aspects of that rule (which I have formulated in somewhat more general terms than Rahner himself does) will therefore serve as a useful and fitting standard for the classification and analysis of responses Rahner might make to the charge that he has unwittingly abandoned the rule in his own theology.

THE LOGICAL INDISPENSABILITY OF JESUS CHRIST: RAHNER'S DEFENCE

One line of defence against the charge which has been brought stands out clearly in Rahner's Christology. The defence rests on an appeal to the proper way of understanding the distinction and relation between our inner orientation to an absolute saviour and Jesus Christ as a particular person, or more generally between the transcendental and the categorial. When this relation is grasped correctly, Rahner argues, the contention becomes manifestly groundless that an attempt to give a transcendental account of the meaningful possibility of redemption through a historical person inevitably subverts the requirement that this redemption is in fact 'indissolubly bound up with' Jesus of Nazareth. In other words,

when the relation between transcendental and categorial experience is rightly appreciated, a transcendental Christology (and the
second way of which it is a leading instance) does not, contrary to
the argument in the last section of chapter 2, sacrifice the 'logical
necessity and indispensability' of Jesus Christ as a particular
person for the Christian belief in salvation and a saviour.[2] I will
consider first the specific, then the general form of this argument.

1   Rahner frequently insists that the transcendental justification
of the meaningfulness of an absolute saviour cannot and need not
establish that Jesus Christ as a particular person is the absolute
saviour. The idea of an absolute saviour does not enable us to
'deduce' Jesus Christ in his particularity; rather, Jesus is grasped
and affirmed as the saviour in a concrete historical 'encounter'
with him.[3] Rahner seems clearly to recognize – in fact, to insist
upon – the limitations of a 'transcendental Christology'. Consequently, he maintains, 'the fact that by itself it cannot establish
(*begründen*) a concrete relationship precisely to *Jesus* as the Christ'
constitutes no argument against a transcendental Christology
and the overall procedure it implies.[4] He cannot be faulted, in
other words, for failing to do what he explicitly disavows.

I have not argued, however, that Rahner's christological
procedure excludes the logical indispensability of Jesus Christ
because it fails to *prove* that Jesus Christ is the absolute saviour.
My argument seems consistent with Rahner's assumption that
there is no demonstrative argument (that is, one with the force of
necessity) which could conclude that Jesus Christ in his particularity is the absolute saviour. Correlatively, it seems consistent with his rejection of any attempt to analyse 'Jesus Christ' out
of the concept of an 'absolute saviour'. Indeed, it is in part the
acceptance of these assumptions which might reasonably cause
one to wonder whether the distinctive logic of the faith 'experience' of or 'encounter' with Jesus Christ is adequately maintained
in Rahner's Christology. For, according to the logic of that
encounter, Rahner would agree, Jesus Christ 'is the absolute
saviour' precisely as a particular person. That is, Christians call
Jesus the 'absolute saviour' on the strength of specific events in
his particular life (for example, his crucifixion and resurrection),
as we come to know that life in a personal encounter. This
encounter recognizes, to use Rahner's phrase, an 'indissoluble

bond' of 'that which is significant for salvation' (and thereby of 'the idea of an absolute saviour') to Jesus' particular life, and especially to those climactic events.[5] Thus the particularizing features of Jesus' life are necessarily ingredient in, and ultimately constitutive of, 'that which is significant for salvation'. Consequently, according to the logic of the faith encounter with Jesus Christ, there can be no adequate or appropriate definition of 'that which is *heilsbedeutsam*' which fails to include some reference to Jesus Christ as a particular person. Yet in his transcendental Christology, Rahner does in fact strive to define 'that which is significant for salvation' without any reference to Jesus Christ as a particular person; the idea of 'an absolute saviour' is *heilsbedeutsam* on the strength of its fitness to be the object of a universal, *a priori* human quest for ultimate meaningfulness and fulfilment.

As I have indicated, it seems that given Rahner's basic procedure, the definition and justification of 'that which is significant for salvation' *must* proceed without reference to Jesus Christ as a particular person. This is simply because the grounds upon which the ultimate meaningfulness and significance of 'an absolute saviour' are to be established (namely, an *a priori*, transcendental orientation) by nature fail to include any identifying reference to Jesus Christ, or, for that matter, to any particular person. That is, our transcendental orientation to an absolute saviour is not itself a personal historical experience or 'encounter', it is rather the prior condition of an unspecifiably diverse range of possible historical experiences. But Jesus Christ as a particular person, Rahner assumes, is accessible to us only through a personal historical experience which grasps the determinate pattern of features that constitutes his particular identity. In this way, Rahner's Christology fails to include, and indeed seems inevitably to exclude, Jesus Christ as a particular person from the domain of 'indispensable significance for salvation'; that domain is defined by a type of criterion, and a specific orientation, in which Jesus Christ as a particular person (again by definition) can have no place. Viewed in this light, 'absolute saviour' would seem not, strictly speaking, to apply to Jesus Christ as a particular person, in that Jesus Christ and his particularizing features are excluded by definition from the domain of saving significance defined by our transcendental orientation.

In none of this have I maintained that Rahner is attempting to 'prove' or 'deduce' that Jesus Christ is the absolute saviour. Rather, I have argued that, contrary to his own assumptions, the method and structure of his Christology fail to include Jesus Christ as a particular person among the elements which define 'that which is of indispensable significance for salvation'. Consequently, Rahner's rejection of any effort to prove that Jesus Christ is the absolute saviour does not seem to constitute a germane reply to our charge that he is fundamentally inconsistent.

2   Rahner sometimes treats the general relationship between transcendental and categorial experience as though it were the basis of an argument for an 'indissoluble bond' in his theology between our orientation to an absolute saviour and Jesus Christ as a particular person. For example, he characteristically insists that both the fact and the meaning (*Sinn*) of the resurrection of Jesus, as a feature of his particular life, are accessible to us only within the purview of a transcendentally necessary hope for our own resurrection. At the same time, however

> in this account, it is precisely not excluded, but included, that in the circle which exists between all transcendental and historical experience, the secure (*sichere*) objectification of the transcendental hope for resurrection is conditioned by the experience of Jesus' resurrection. Thus we can and must say: because Jesus was raised, I believe in and hope for my own resurrection.[6]

It can be assumed for the sake of argument that transcendentalists like Rahner are able to give a plausible account of this 'mutual conditioning' as a general epistemological axiom.[7] The specific 'bond' which Rahner is striving to articulate theoretically by his appeal to a 'circle between transcendental and categorial experience' is one in which the categorial element ('Jesus Christ'), precisely in its particularity, is logically indispensable for the transcendental element ('is the absolute saviour'). However, no particular, that is, no specific object, is logically indispensable to the transcendental conditions in the human subject (supposing that there are such things) which allow it to be experienced and known. Rather, this 'mutual conditioning' exists between our transcendental constitution and categorial objects under a certain common aspect, without regard to the particularity of those objects.

A well-known Kantian example of a 'transcendental condition' serves as a good illustration here: 'In all change of appearances substance is permanent.'[8] All possible objects, Kant says, conform to this rule, irrespective of their particular features. The changes of appearance under different lights which occur to the little Arabian dish on my desk and other features which mark it as a particular object, are irrelevant to the fact that I am transcendentally constrained to experience it as a substance (although this particular dish, of course, might conceivably serve as the occasion for making that constraint explicit). In fact, as far as its substantial permanence goes, I know everything I need to know or can know about it without experiencing it at all, which is not to deny (recalling a phrase Rahner applies to Jesus in a similar connection) that such knowledge is 'no substitute' for experiencing the little dish.

If the general reciprocal relationship between the transcendental and the categorial applies to the matter at hand, then the features which mark Jesus as a particular person will not be indispensable but, rather, irrelevant to our experience and knowledge of him as an absolute saviour, as these latter are conditioned by our transcendental *Ausschau* for a figure conforming to an *a priori* rule. This is precisely the kind of relationship between Jesus Christ and belief in a saviour which, according to his assumptions, Rahner wants to avoid in his Christology. Thus the appeal to a general relationship of 'mutual conditioning' to support the contention that the 'indissoluble bond' between these two is preserved in Rahner's Christology seems to do nothing to close the gap which his basic procedure has opened.

In the two related arguments I have just considered, Rahner's effort to ensure that Jesus Christ maintains a logically indispensable place and function in Christology could be summed up in the conviction (and admonition) that Jesus is, and must be, 'presupposed'. In both cases, Jesus Christ must be presupposed with respect to the idea of an absolute saviour in that his particularity cannot be 'derived' from that idea, but must be 'encountered'. According Jesus this kind of priority over against the concept which is supposed to express his ultimate significance does not, it appears, preserve the logical indispensability of Jesus Christ in Rahner's Christology. But Rahner's language suggests another way in which Jesus might be 'presupposed', and correlatively a somewhat different kind of argument in defence of the procedure he employs. Rahner sometimes points out that a believing encounter with Jesus' particular life constitutes a global experience and conviction which is both logically and temporally prior to any Christological theory as a whole. 'Faith precedes theology', so we need not and should not think 'that theological reflection must first construct . . . faith from out of nothing as it were, or must recapture completely (*adäquat einholen*) a faith which ultimately after all is based on grace and free decision.'[9] Here Jesus Christ is not simply presupposed in that he cannot be 'derived' from the significance we attribute to him, but in that his particular life and faith in him have precedence over any effort to give a theological account of that faith.[10] In this vein Rahner maintains that the point of departure for all Christology 'is the simple experience of the man Jesus, and of the Resurrection in which his fate was brought to conclusion'.[11] In light of this kind of remark, another argument against the charge that Rahner's Christology fails to preserve the indissoluble bond between Jesus Christ and his saving significance would run as follows: Jesus Christ, and a believing encounter with him, is the point of departure for the argument which attempts to establish that an absolute saviour is a credible possibility. By that very fact, so Rahner argues, Jesus Christ is logically necessary and indispensable for any belief in such a saviour. This argument demands closer inspection.

By maintaining that Jesus Christ is the presupposition and point of departure for the kind of Christology he undertakes, Rahner apparently has two things in mind. A believing encounter with Jesus is the one occasion for explicit reflection upon the general conditions under which 'absolute saviour' can signify something which is *heilsbedeutsam*. But this by itself is too weak to express Rahner's point. It is furthermore presupposed, as has been seen, that the idea of an absolute saviour justified by this reflection must be ascribed to Jesus Christ, who inspired the attempted justification, and to no one else.[12] In line with this presupposition, Rahner insists, for example, that the faith which would grasp in Jesus the absolute saviour cannot be uninterested *a priori* in the history (*Geschichte*) of Jesus before the resurrection and in his self-understanding. Otherwise, 'faith' would create the Christ of salvation 'on the occasion of' Jesus of Nazareth (*'gelegentlich' des Jesus von Nazaret*). This Christ would then be mythological, sustained by 'faith' rather than sustaining and empowering faith.[13]

The *process* of reflection which displays the credibility and meaningfulness of the idea of an absolute saviour always remains intelligibly tied to Jesus Christ as a particular person; he is its origin and goal, and not merely its 'occasion'. Since that process never leaves the circle of belief founded upon the life, death and resurrection of Jesus Christ, it is specious to question the coherence of applying the fruit of such reflection (namely, the idea of an absolute saviour) to Jesus. This is the *nervus probandi* of Rahner's frequent claim that a specifically transcendental Christology does not abandon or subvert the logical necessity and indispensability of Jesus Christ.[14]

Clearly though, the fact that an account of the possibility of salvation and a saviour originates in and aims at an encounter with Jesus Christ and faith in him as the absolute saviour does not establish that the account in question preserves the distinctive logic of that encounter, in which Jesus Christ, and he alone, can be the object of belief in salvation and a saviour. That must be manifest (or fail to be manifest) in the account itself. The fact that an encounter with Jesus Christ prompts the process of theological reflection does not ensure, as a general principle, that the formal structure and the method of a theology will actually preserve and recapitulate the distinctive logic which it strives to make at least partially explicit.[15]

Moreover, there is a specific difficulty with Rahner's attempt to carry out this reflection in an explicitly transcendental way. I am not contending, of course, with Rahner's stress upon the fact that theology cannot adequately 'synthesize' or conceptualize either the content or the structure of that living encounter. But it seems as though Rahner's own account actually falsifies the logic or structure of the encounter. Rahner appears to hold that because for Christians, Jesus is in fact the particular 'occasion' which prompts transcendental reflection upon the meaningfulness and credibility of the idea of an absolute saviour, the transcendentally justified idea of a saviour can logically apply only to him. In this way, he apparently maintains, a transcendental Christology is quite consistent with his assumptions about the logical structure of Christian belief. But this is a *non sequitur*. It would be like arguing that if my little Arabian dish were the occasion upon which one deduced the transcendental notion of substance, then the transcendental notion of substance could apply only to that initial datum. Like any transcendental construct, 'the idea of an absolute saviour' does not specify the particular or particulars to which it might apply; regardless of the occasion upon which it becomes reflectively explicit, it could apply to an unspecifiably diverse body of particulars. Even if Rahner can successfully argue that there can only be one 'absolute saviour', the logic of the matter is not altered.[16] Even if there can only be one absolute saviour, it is not logically necessary that that saviour be Jesus, any more than if there could only be one substance, it would be logically necessary that that substance be my Arabian dish. Therefore, although Jesus may be the occasion upon which we transcendentally deduce the ultimate meaningfulness of 'an absolute saviour', that idea, precisely as transcendentally justified, could logically apply to some other person. Therefore, on Rahner's own assumptions, it is not a genuinely Christian notion of 'an absolute saviour', or, more broadly, of 'that which is significant for salvation'. Conversely, since *per assumptionem* only Jesus can be the absolute saviour, it seems that his particular life must in some way be ingredient in an acceptably Christian idea of salvation or a saviour.

Although Rahner's conviction is clearly that only Jesus can be the saviour, his christological account of that conviction seems only to allow him to assert that Jesus is 'the occasion of' our faith in an absolute saviour, who might as well be someone else. Despite some possible responses to our line of criticism, therefore, it seems that where the logical indispensability of Jesus Christ as a particular person for faith in him as the saviour of the world is concerned, Rahner's transcendental Christology falls short of preserving the distinctive logic of Christian belief.

Excursus on 'anonymous Christianity'

It may be worth noting that Rahner's notion of 'anonymous Christianity' presents a curious and perhaps not wholly coherent

counterpoint to the arguments he seems to present in defence of
the claim that his transcendental Christology does not forfeit the
logical indispensability of Jesus Christ as a particular person. As
has been seen, these arguments all appeal in one way or another
to the fact that Jesus Christ is 'presupposed' in any attempt to
show that 'an absolute saviour' is significant for salvation. I have
maintained that none of these arguments succeeds in showing
that Rahner's Christology is actually consistent with his assumption that only Jesus can be the absolute saviour. However, the
suggestion of plausibility in those arguments seems to rest on the
claim that, at the very least, Jesus Christ, known to us as a
particular person through a concrete historical encounter, is the
sole 'occasion' upon which reflection concerning the *Heilsbedeutsamkeit* of an 'absolute saviour' takes place. This claim, in turn,
seems to imply that 'an absolute saviour' is in fact accessible to us
as an ultimately significant, saving reality only through a concrete
historical encounter with Jesus of Nazareth. Otherwise, even if
our access to and acceptance of an 'absolute saviour' were initially
only pre-thematic, there could presumably be any number of
occasions besides 'Jesus of Nazareth' for making reflectively
explicit in the form of 'the idea of an absolute saviour' that which
we have already realized and accepted implicitly and pre-
thematically.

In order to make this more clear, it may be helpful to recall that
the 'orientation towards an absolute saviour', as Rahner
understands it, aims at two distinguishable goals. One is the
actuality of the absolute saviour in history. This is the *object* with
which we seek to come into contact in virtue of our orientation,
which, Rahner assumes, can only be Jesus Christ as a particular
person. The other goal of our transcendental orientation is our
own *Wesensvollzug* as human subjects, or, more precisely, the
initiation of our own *Wesensvollzug* through a free decision, which
can only become definitive in death. This is the *condition* of the
human subject at which the orientation towards an absolute
saviour aims, and is equivalent to the subject's salvation, in so far
as the latter can be realized in this life. Now in Christology,
Rahner seems thoroughly committed to saying that realizing the
condition of salvation requires grasping the object of this orientation – in other words, that the *Wesensvollzug* of any individual
human life can only occur through a free decision which accepts

an actual historical saviour. If the human *Wesensvollzug* requires faith in an absolute saviour, and an absolute saviour is presumed to be actually accessible to us only through a concrete encounter with Jesus of Nazareth, one would expect Rahner consistently to affirm that the *Wesensvollzug* of all persons requires faith in (that is, a free decision for and commitment of one's whole self to) Jesus of Nazareth. This seems to cohere with the argument that Jesus Christ is the sole occasion for making explicit 'the idea of an absolute saviour' and its ultimate meaningfulness, an argument Rahner appears to rely upon in defence of his transcendental Christology. It also seems quite consistent with remarks to the effect that 'transcendental Christology allows one to search for, and in his search to understand, what he has already found in Jesus of Nazareth'.[17]

Yet, as is well known, Rahner sometimes asserts that a concrete encounter with Jesus Christ is not necessary for the *Wesensvollzug* of human reality in any individual case, at least in so far as that *Wesensvollzug* can be achieved in a preliminary way in this life. The notion of 'anonymous Christianity' as a way of understanding the salvation of non-Christians explicitly involves asserting the initiation of individual salvation or unsurpassable fulfilment without any encounter with Jesus Christ.

> According to the Catholic understanding of the faith, as is clearly expressed in the Second Vatican Council, there can be no doubt that someone who has no concrete, historical contact (*Verbindung*) with the explicit preaching of Christianity can nevertheless be a justified person who lives in the grace of God. He then possesses God's supernatural self-communication in grace not only as an offer, not only as an existential of his existence; he has also accepted this offer and so he has really accepted what is essential in what Christianity wants to mediate to him: his salvation in that grace which is objectively the grace of Jesus Christ.[18]

It is this sort of remark which is rather curious, in light of the cautions and limitations Rahner imposes upon our access to 'the idea of an absolute saviour' in an explicitly christological context. If the initiation of our *Wesensvollzug* requires faith in a saviour (that is, in God's definitive self-offer) who can only be 'encountered' and not 'deduced', and if, moreover, Jesus is the sole 'occasion' upon which we can make that faith reflectively explicit, it seems odd to acknowledge that whatever is 'essential' in Christianity can be accepted unto salvation, at least in a preliminary way, without any 'encounter' with Jesus of Nazareth. This means, as Rahner explicitly acknowledges in this non-christological context, that an unspecifiably diverse variety of things or persons, and not only Jesus of Nazareth, could function as the occasion for pre-thematic but saving faith in God's definitive self-offer (that is, in an 'absolute saviour'), and presumably also (although this he does not acknowledge) as the occasion for becoming explicitly and conceptually (or 'thematically') aware of that self-offer.[19]

The curiosity can be put even more sharply. In his Christology, Rahner seems to maintain that explicit Christians, who know Jesus Christ as the absolute saviour, exercise saving faith in God's self-offer precisely through an 'encounter' with Jesus Christ and not simply through their *a priori* orientation, or through the mere idea of an absolute saviour, to which that orientation gives rise. Yet when treating the salvation of non-Christians, he maintains that persons who have not 'encountered' Jesus Christ as a particular person can yet exercise saving faith on the basis of the orientation alone (given some occasion for accepting it). Indeed, he seems further to say that this 'pre-thematic' faith establishes a saving relationship precisely to Jesus Christ as a particular person, in that he is the assumed objective source of that orientation.[20] In other words, the 'anonymous' Christian seems to have the same subjectively efficacious saving relation to Jesus Christ as the explicit Christian; the encounter wherein the explicit Christian knows Jesus Christ as a particular person seems in this context to have no essential bearing on the character of the relation one has to Jesus Christ.[21]

To be sure, Rahner supposes that when a person has efficaciously accepted God's self-offer in the absence of an encounter with the particular life of Jesus Christ, he or she will necessarily seek such an encounter.[22] He also maintains that anonymous Christians become explicit Christians in and through death.[23] Rahner has a good reason, of course, for proposing the notion of anonymous Christianity, namely to offer an account of the possibility of the salvation of non-Christians, pursuant to the teaching of the Second Vatican Council.[24] But this particular way of accounting for the salvation of non-Christians seems to fit rather poorly with those features of his Christology upon which he relies, at least implicitly, in an attempt to ensure that his transcendental method is consistent with the assumption that only Jesus Christ as a particular person can be the absolute saviour. If the argument in the first section of this chapter is correct, Rahner's appeal to the presupposition of an encounter with Jesus Christ, not only as the sole occasion for explicit reflection upon the ultimate meaningfulness of an 'absolute saviour', but also, if less clearly, for the exercise of efficacious faith in an absolute saviour, is unsuccessful; it fails to show that his Christology is consistent with some of his own basic dogmatic commitments. But in his account of the possibility of salvation for non-Christians, such an appeal is not only absent; it appears at times explicitly to be countermanded.

THE MATERIAL DECISIVENESS OF JESUS CHRIST: RAHNER'S DEFENCE

I have so far looked at the 'indissoluble bond' of all that is of universal significance for salvation to Jesus Christ under the aspect of 'logical necessity and indispensability'. This label simply indicates the assumption that because Jesus Christ is the redeemer of the world precisely in his particularity, whatever we take to be of saving significance must be ascribed to him as a particular person and only to him. As yet a positive characterization of this 'necessity and indispensability' has not been given; it will be the business of later chapters to suggest a theological account of it, with attention to different kinds of 'saving significance' attributed to Jesus. The concern rather has been a more negative and preliminary one, namely to identify the kind of theological method or procedure in which this bond of logical necessity and indispensability cannot coherently be maintained. I have called this procedure, of which Rahner is one instance, the second way. By attempting to establish the credibility and meaningfulness of a saving reality (specifically, of an 'absolute saviour') by an appeal to general criteria for such a reality, without reference to Jesus Christ, Rahner makes it impossible actually to maintain his assumption that whatever is *heilsbedeutsam* must be ascribed only to Jesus Christ as a particular person. In this way, I have argued, Rahner's basic methodological decision in Christology (the second way), and more specifically his transcendental execution of it, ineluctably forfeit the 'logical indispensability' of Jesus Christ for belief in an absolute saviour. His several belated efforts to rebuild the bridge which his method demolishes at the outset are not only unsuccessful but seem not to recognize the gravity of the loss. However, it is now necessary to look in a different way at the indissoluble bond of 'that which is *heilsbedeutsam*' to Jesus Christ, namely with regard to what I have called the material decisiveness of Jesus Christ as a particular person. Rahner may be more successful in maintaining the indissoluble bond at this level and, even if he is not, the character of the bond and of the leading assumption involved in asserting it may become more clear in light of Rahner's attempt.

My argument up to this point has considered 'Jesus Christ as a particular person', and therewith the concept of 'particularity', primarily in contrast to the notion of 'positivity'. As a 'positive' reality, an individual is simply a single instance of a class or nature, irrespective of the particular 'when', 'where' and description under which that individual actually exists. All individuals of a given kind have this positivity in common apart from any particularizing or identifying descriptions, as opposed to those describable features which particular individuals may in some fashion have in common. By concentrating on the contrast between Jesus' concrete particularity and his abstract positivity in the discussion and criticism of Rahner, I have tacitly been considering Jesus' particular life as a whole and thus considering it in terms of the sum total of ostensible and describable features in virtue of which he is the particular person 'Jesus Christ'. Correlatively, I have treated Rahner's leading characterization of Jesus' redeeming significance (namely, 'absolute saviour') as one which is assumed to apply to his particular life as a whole and thus at any given point; he himself often treats the notion in this comprehensive way.

However, Jesus' particular life clearly has specific and prominent features which most sharply define his particular identity and serve as the primary basis upon which he is identified and known by us.[25] In these specific features, Jesus' particularity is most clearly focused and consequently his difference and distinctness from us is there most pronounced. This distinction between the particular identity of Jesus Christ 'as a whole', and the 'specific features' which are especially central to his particularity, lies at the heart of the difference between what I am calling the 'logical indispensability' and the 'material decisiveness' of Jesus Christ for the Christian belief in redemption and a redeemer. Jesus Christ is the unique redeemer or absolute saviour, so both the first and second ways assume, precisely as a particular person. Some specific features of his identity as a whole are especially definitive of his particularity, principally his death by crucifixion on Golgotha and his resurrection on the third day following his death. This means that he is the unique redeemer especially in virtue of these specific, distinguishing features of his particular life. According to the assumption shared by both ways, in other words, it is precisely these specific, particularizing features of Jesus' own identity which are significant for salvation. Therefore, any adequate characterization of 'that which is significant for salvation', and hence ultimately meaningful for us, must include some reference to these specific features of Jesus' identity and not simply to his particular life as a whole. Correlatively, given that only Jesus Christ can be the absolute saviour, any appropriate account of 'saving death' and 'resurrection' should apply only to Jesus Christ. A Christology which asserts, as Rahner's does, an 'indissoluble bond' of that which is 'significant for salvation' to Jesus' particular life as a whole, should do so especially by reference to the salvifically dominant features of that particular life. It ought, in other words, to find Jesus Christ 'materially decisive' as well as 'logically necessary' in its account of redemption and a redeemer.[26]

Rahner is explicitly aware of the need for a Christology which assumes that only Jesus Christ can be the absolute saviour to locate his redeeming significance especially in those specific features which are primarily constitutive of his particular identity.

> The death and resurrection of Jesus must be universally significant for salvation as such (*als solche*), and may not be made to appear merely as ultimately indifferent individual events of a life which is universally significant for salvation only because it was the life of the eternal Logos . . .[27]

Rahner's insistence upon the redemptive significance of these specific features of Jesus' life is simply an extension of his assumption that Christian faith and theology are 'indissolubly bound up not only with the historical existence of Jesus of Nazareth, but also with the historical events of a specific kind which took place during his life'.[28]

Rahner in fact has two different approaches by which he attempts adequately to accommodate the salvifically dominant features of Jesus' particular life while maintaining his primary methodological assumption that it must be general criteria which define that which is ultimately meaningful and significant for us (in his case, transcendental ones). One approach is to refine and extend the idea of an absolute saviour, on the basis of these general criteria, until it seems a fit description of the very salvific features which are ingredient in Jesus' particular identity. The other approach, which proceeds for the most part in the opposite direction, is to begin with Jesus' death and resurrection as central features of his particular identity and to try to give an account, again in light of general criteria, of what is *heilsbedeutsam* about these features of Jesus' particularity. In either case, Rahner will be consistent with his own assumptions if he can give an account of the saving significance of Jesus' death and resurrection which necessarily includes reference to those features, and so can only apply to Jesus himself.

I indicated at the end of the last chapter that one would expect a Christology structured like Rahner's, if the method were applied consistently, to have a difficult time honouring this assumption of Jesus' 'material decisiveness' in practice. Whether that is in fact the case, however, can only be seen by examining these two approaches in some detail.

The first approach: specifying the idea of an absolute saviour

The idea of an absolute saviour, in so far as it indicates the fit object of our basic orientation to unsurpassable fulfilment, marks the boundaries of what can possibly be 'significant for salvation'. An 'absolute saviour', as has been seen, must have two primary and complementary aspects. On the one hand the saviour must be a person who freely accepts God's loving offer of himself in his or her own life, a person who '*is* just the question about the mystery utterly given over to the mystery'.[29] On the other hand, the saviour must be God's definitive and tangible pledge of himself to us and not merely an external and unsurpassable sign or indication of that pledge. If we reflect on these two components of the idea of an absolute saviour, Rahner supposes, we can develop further the idea of the appropriate object of our *Ausschau* for salvation. It seems that the saviour's free acceptance of God's self-offer must be sustained particularly in that person's death, since human death in general is the event in which persons definitively accept or reject at once the whole course of their own lives and God's offer of blessing through communion with him.

> In our human situation as it is in fact, this salvation achieved in the person sought [that is, in the absolute saviour] cannot be understood as occurring otherwise than by death, since it is only here that history is completed, freedom becomes definitive, man surrenders himself freely and finally to the mystery of God and thus man's transcendence into God's incomprehensibility and his history reach their definitive unity.[30]

Moreover, it seems that the finality of God's pledge of himself in an absolute saviour must be manifest to us in an event which confirms that person's total and irrevocable acceptance of God's love. This means, Rahner is willing to say, that we are on the lookout not simply for an absolute saviour but for what can be called the 'resurrection' of that person. So Rahner says of a possible absolute saviour, not yet encountered in history,

> since it must be the effective promise of salvation for us . . . the death rescuing the person for salvation, as achieved and saved for us into God, even though in an absolutely once-and-for-all experience, must also become tangible: that is, the death of this person must be capable of being understood as passing into what we describe in traditional Christian terminology as the resurrection of this person.[31]

In sum, Rahner argues, 'the categoriality of God's irreversible offer of himself to the world as a whole [namely, an absolute saviour] can only be a man who on the one hand surrenders every inner-worldly future in death, and who on the other in this acceptance of death is shown to have been accepted by God finally and definitively.'[32]

When Rahner turns from the '*a priori* idea of an absolute saviour' to the focal features of Jesus' particular life, he finds, as indicated earlier, a quite striking fitness or correspondence between the two.[33] Jesus' teaching and preaching imply that he understood himself to be the 'absolute saviour', even if 'pre-thematically' rather than explicitly. This means that he understood his own life and proclamation to be one in which 'God's closeness to all men has now come to be in a new and irrevocable way ... grounded in his person'.[34] Jesus fully preserves this pre-thematic understanding of his own relation to God and his significance for other persons by his comportment in death. 'For, in the first place, by freely accepting the fate of death Jesus surrenders himself precisely to the unforeseen and incalculable possibilities of his existence; and, secondly, Jesus maintains in death his unique claim of an identity between his message and his person in the hope that in his death he will be vindicated by God with respect to this claim.'[35] And in fact '*this* Jesus with his *concrete* claim and his history is experienced in the resurrection experience as of permanent validity and as accepted by God.'[36]

The content of the idea of an absolute saviour and the central describable features of Jesus' particular identity seem almost perfectly matched. Noticing the apparent mutual fitness of the two does not, presumably, amount to actual belief in Jesus Christ as the absolute saviour, which requires a personal encounter and commitment of one's whole life. But, Rahner suggests, this correspondence does narrow the field of possible absolute saviours to one. Given our *Ausschau* for an absolute saviour (whether it is explicitly thematized or not), 'it is not so difficult to recognize (*erkennen*) precisely in Jesus this final and unsurpassable concretion of the encounter with God. For where else is there a person with a luminous, readily available history, who has laid claim at all to this event as having occurred in him? Where ... besides precisely the biblical Jesus?'[37] This mutual fitness, Rahner seems to maintain, clearly upholds the assumption that only Jesus Christ can be the 'dying' and 'rising' saviour: we ascribe the status and significance of 'absolute saviour' to him precisely because it accords so well with the focal events of his particular life.

At this point, even the most sympathetic reader is likely to grow uneasy with the suspicion that Rahner (to borrow a phrase from Austin Farrer) is covering a logical hiatus with verbal plaster. This first approach to maintaining the material decisiveness of Jesus Christ amounts to saying that the central redeeming events of his particular life are anticipated in our orientation towards an absolute saviour, with sufficient definiteness that we can match them up with what we anticipate and see the evident correspondence. As has been demonstrated, though, a basic assumption of Rahner's Christology, one which he repeats and defends frequently, is that Jesus Christ as a particular person is not and cannot be anticipated in our transcendental orientation towards an absolute saviour. This means that the decisive features of his particular life, namely his crucifixion 'under Pontius Pilate' and his resurrection 'on the third day', and thereby the identifying descriptions of him in which these features play such an important role, fall outside the sphere of our orientation to a saving reality. In so far as we necessarily anticipate them (and so can find them *heilsbedeutsam*), 'self-surrender in death' and 'vindication in resurrection' are not, on Rahner's own account, slightly generalized but wholly fitting descriptions of Jesus' particular life. Despite what he seems to suppose here, they are not identifying descriptions at all but rather characterizations of what could be *heilsbedeutsam* about an absolute saviour, irrespective of that person's particularity. They could, by their very nature, be applied to someone else, such as, to use our earlier examples, Socrates or Martin Luther King.

By contrast, in so far as 'death' and 'resurrection' are ingredient in an identifying description of Jesus Christ ('crucified under Pontius Pilate . . . the third day he rose') they are not anticipated in our orientation to salvation and hence are not included in the domain of 'indispensable significance for salvation' which that orientation defines. Indeed, since they are not anticipated by the orientation which constitutes the ultimate criterion of 'significance for salvation', they would seem not, properly speaking, to be redemptive 'as such' (to use Rahner's phrase) – that is, precisely as particular features of Jesus' own life. When 'death' and 'resurrection' function to characterize that which can have redemptive significance, they cannot describe a particular person; when they function to describe Jesus Christ as a particular person, they appear to be excluded by definition from the arena of redemptive significance. Using the same language in both cases does not resolve for Rahner the antinomy his basic procedure creates.

The second approach: 'resurrection'

As I have indicated, Rahner's treatment of 'resurrection' will be consistent with his own assumption of the 'material decisiveness' of Jesus Christ only if his characterization of 'resurrection' as a decisive redemptive event includes with the force of necessity some reference to Jesus' own resurrection. By contrast, it will be inconsistent with this assumption if he takes it to be the decisive redemptive event, but does so only in so far as 'resurrection' does *not* necessarily denote the climactic particularizing event of Jesus' life.[38] Not surprisingly, Rahner finds it necessary to insist that 'resurrection' can only be soteriologically intelligible to us if the transcendental anticipation of such a thing is lodged in our concrete human nature: 'The transcendental experience of the expectation of one's own resurrection, an experience man can reach by his very essence, is the horizon of understanding within which and within which alone something like a resurrection of Jesus can be expected and experienced at all.'[39] This hope for our own 'resurrection' is in fact 'completely identical' with a hope for 'definitive validity' (*Endgültigkeit*) or 'eternity'.[40] The eternity at which we necessarily aim is not endless time but the fulfilment of our orientation to immediacy with God, a fulfilment realized only through the free acceptance of God's self-offer, especially in death.[41] As beings who are the subjects of both transcendental and categorial experience, we necessarily seek to have this *a priori* hope for our own 'definitive validity' mediated to us by some categorial reality or realities. We seek, in other words, some manifest and irrevocable categorial confirmation of the fruitfulness of our own hope for *Endgültigkeit*.[42] Saying that we have a transcendental orientation to resurrection thus means, more precisely, 'that we have the right and the obligation at least to look and see whether this transcendental experience in grace of our eternal validity as moral persons has not become concrete and tangible in salvation history.'[43] What are we on the lookout for as 'resurrection', and so can find to be the decisive event of redemption, could simply be called 'the manifestation of eternal validity'. Or, since we anticipate 'eternal validity' in connection with some individual life, we can be said to be on the lookout for 'someone who is manifestly eternally valid'. This is precisely what resurrection means, in so far as it is, or could be, a redemptive event, namely, one which is meaningful, intelligible and existentially assimilable for us.

The assumption here, to recall, is that the resurrection of Jesus Christ is in fact the decisive redemptive event; it is supposed to have this significance, Rahner stresses, *in itself (als solche)*.[44] An expression like 'there is someone who is manifestly eternally valid', however, does not by itself include any reference to or description of the resurrection of Jesus Christ. A clear logical barrier prevents it from being taken as an identifying description of any stamp: it does not introduce a particular person into discourse. It includes no demonstrative elements, definite features or proper names.[45] The resurrection of Jesus Christ, by contrast, is a specific event which takes place at a definite point in time and space, involves individuals and circumstances which admit of identifying description (even if the resurrection itself cannot be directly described), and is the culmination of a particular life and identity. The assertion, 'there is someone who is the manifestation of eternal validity' enables us neither to locate the specific event of Jesus' resurrection in time and space nor does it assist us in describing that event and its circumstances. Consequently, such an assertion contributes nothing to an identifying description of the particular person to whom and in whom this decisive, specific redeeming event occurs.

Because of this lack, this kind of assertion fails to be a characterization of Jesus' resurrection as a specific event, indeed the event in which his particular identity is most clear. Therefore, since it is precisely Jesus' own resurrection as a particular event which is taken to be ultimately significant for salvation, 'the manifestation of eternal validity' fails to be a characterization of 'resurrection' as a redemptive event.[46] If 'resurrection' precisely as the climactic feature of Jesus' particular life is the decisive redemptive event, then 'the manifestation of eternal validity' has redeeming significance only in so far

as it is something which is true to say about the resurrection of
Jesus Christ.

This is, it would seem, the opposite of Rahner's procedure. In
his treatment of 'resurrection' he continues to follow the pattern
of his basic approach to Christology. As a result, 'Jesus' resurrection' becomes so attenuated and abstract that it ceases to have the
particular reference ingredient in what Rahner himself would
take to be an adequately Christian notion of 'resurrection'. He can
say, as the second way induces him to, that the phrase 'there is
someone who is manifestly eternally valid' adequately specifies
the content of 'resurrection' as a redemptive event, which seems
wholly inconsistent with the conviction that Jesus' own resurrection is alone and *als solche* the decisive redemptive event. Or, he
can follow the lead of his basic assumptions about the shape of
Christian belief, where the resurrection of Jesus Christ is *als solche*
the decisive redemptive event. But this would mean that the
notion that 'there is someone who is manifestly eternally valid' is
by itself simply unfit to be an account of 'resurrection' as a
redemptive event, since by itself it is too abstract to count as, or
include, an identifying description of Jesus Christ.

This analysis of the way Rahner handles 'resurrection' brings to
the fore the distinctive issue which is at stake when we speak of
the 'material decisiveness' of Jesus Christ for the Christian belief
in salvation and a saviour. Both the first and the second ways of
showing how Jesus Christ can be significant for salvation hold in
common the assumption that he is so precisely as a particular
person and consequently that the central events of his particular
life are of decisive redemptive significance *in themselves*. As has
been noted, some characterizations of Jesus' redemptive
significance are meant to apply to his life as a whole, without
special attention to any specific feature of that life. At times
Rahner uses 'absolute saviour' in this comprehensive way
(namely, when it means simply 'historical irreversibility of God's
self-offer'). As will be seen in chapter 5, the notion of 'the
incarnation of the Logos' is an especially clear and distinctive
example of the kind of account of Jesus' redeeming significance
which is not 'feature specific'. There has already been occasion to
observe at some length that such characterizations of Jesus'
redeeming significance are inappropriate and inadequate,
according to the governing assumption of both sides, if they fail to

include in some way an identifying reference to Jesus Christ and, correlatively, if they are applicable to other individuals.

When turning to accounts of Jesus' significance which are applied to him in virtue of specific features of his life, the force of this assumption for Christology, along with that of the two-fold requirement of reference and exclusivity it involves, becomes more clear. 'Feature-specific' characterizations of Jesus' significance for salvation must not only include some exclusive reference to him; they must in some way be capable of functioning as descriptions of that particular feature of his life, the significance of which they are attempting to characterize. This requirement follows from the assumption that the focal features of Jesus' life are significant for salvation 'as such', and thus in so far as they are ingredient in his particular life. Given this assumption, remarks which aim to be characterizations of a given redemptive event (such as an account of 'resurrection') must at the same time be able to serve as descriptions of the relevant feature in Jesus' own life (and hence as identifying descriptions), since it is precisely this feature of this particular person which is taken to be redemptive.

The second approach: 'redemptive death'

As his discussion of 'resurrection' indicates, Rahner will try to justify not only 'feature-neutral' but also 'feature-specific' accounts of Jesus' redeeming significance by appeal to general criteria of significance for salvation. Taken simply as the object of a transcendental anticipation, 'the manifestation of eternal validity' is inappropriate as a characterization of Jesus' redemptive significance for the same reason the global notion of 'absolute saviour' is: by itself, it includes no reference to Jesus Christ and the particular features of his life. Congruent with this logical status, the specific account of 'resurrection' Rahner develops in conformity with the notion of a universal *Ausschau* for unsurpassable fulfilment is bound to come out as a general pattern, at least potentially applicable to all persons and thus of no value in describing a particular person. As a result, 'the manifestation of eternal validity' inevitably fares quite badly as an account of the universal redeeming significance of Jesus' own resurrection. This would seem to be the case, in fact, even if there were no appeal to a transcendental anticipation of this event as that which secures its ultimate significance. 'Resurrection' is somewhat ambiguous on this score, however, both because Rahner does 'transcendentalize' it rather extensively, and because the resurrection of Jesus Christ does not seem to admit of direct description.[47] The death of Jesus Christ, by comparison, is a redemptive event which can be directly described and which Rahner does not specifically transcendentalize.[48] It will therefore enable us to see to what degree, when he is simply trying to elucidate the redemptive meaning of a specific event in Jesus' life, Rahner follows the lead of his overall theory and offers an account of 'redeeming death' which is too general to count as a description of Jesus' own death.

Rahner stresses that the event of Jesus' death is decisive for the redemption of the world: 'The death of Jesus and consequently his passion as a whole is a necessary constitutive element in the eschatological word of God's self-promise to the world as its absolute future.'[49] It is taken to be so *als solche*: 'Redemption is for the Christian redemption through Jesus Christ. Through his death and resurrection. This, the Christian cannot doubt.' 'But', he hastens to add, 'what that more precisely means (*besagt*), and eventually also does not mean, is not easy to say.'[50] The crucial issue for the present purposes is the way Rahner explains just what it is that makes the death of Jesus Christ a redemptive event. Human death in general, and thus in every individual instance, is that 'self-realization of creaturely-human freedom in which man faces God and disposes of himself completely and finally for or against God: this he does in [a] final state of creaturely powerlessness'.[51] It is the very essence of human death to be the point at which a person finally accepts or rejects God's self-offer. In discussing the death of Jesus Christ, as when he treats other aspects of Jesus' life, Rahner assumes that redemption can only occur through a person who freely and unreservedly accepts God's offer of himself.[52] Given this assumption, it is the general character of human death which stipulates that Jesus Christ, if he is to be significant for salvation, must be so above all in his death. 'If then the final and definitive acceptance of God's offer of himself is supposed to take place in Jesus and he is thus to be the eschatologically victorious word of God to the world, this can come about only through his death.'[53]

More importantly, the specific way in which Jesus' own death has redemptive significance is already clear from, and in fact defined by, the nature of human death in general. The death of Jesus Christ is redemptive because of his bearing towards God in it, because of his 'free acceptance of his death'; thus his death is redemptive '*as* entered into in free obedience and *as* surrendering life completely to God'.[54] As human death generally is the point at which all persons ultimately accept or reject God's love, so Jesus' death is the point at which he accepts God's love without reservation. That is its redemptive significance. Or, as Rahner says, that is its 'success', which becomes clear to us in Jesus' resurrection.[55]

Not only can this pattern of death in which God's self-offer is resolutely accepted be recapitulated in our own lives; our salvation is contingent upon that recapitulation, whether or not the latter is bolstered by an awareness of Jesus' own death. 'Many die the death of Jesus, who do not know him by name in faith, but who allow themselves to be taken by death in a final submission, but without cursing existence.'[56] Consequently, the peculiar redemptive significance of the death of Jesus Christ lies not simply in the general pattern evinced by his death, which the redeemed share with him, but specifically in the fact that he is the first instance of that pattern, the one who brings it into historical realization. 'In the cross of Jesus the transcendental and the historical dimension of man are finally and irrevocably reconciled: the absolute reference of man to the self-giving mystery of God becomes [an] historical event, and indeed in successful death as such, without which this would not be possible.'[57]

Nowhere in this account of the saving import of Jesus' passion and death does Rahner appeal directly to a transcendental anticipation in virtue of which his kind of death could be experienced by us as *heilsbedeutsam*. Yet even when an explicitly transcendental procedure has receded into the background, the demands of the second way continue to exercise a powerful, indeed decisive, influence over Rahner's Christology. For he can only find redeeming significance in the death of Jesus Christ by emptying it of everything which makes it Jesus' own death, and distinguishes it from 'successful' human death in general. At least in his later writings Rahner is remarkably candid about this: 'Death – and only it – is the event in which the decision of freedom becomes definitively valid.'[58] Such is the universal and essential character of human death, as has been observed. With regard to the death of Jesus Christ, then, 'even though the concrete manner in which Jesus dies may in essence belong entirely to salvation history, fundamentally Jesus' death is of salvation-historical significance because it is the final validity of the acceptance of God's self-offer to Jesus (and in him, to all humanity).'[59]

The death of Jesus Christ is a particular historical event ('in essence belong[s] entirely to the history of salvation'), which happens in a certain way and at a definite place and time: Jesus died by crucifixion under Pontius Pilate. As a particular historical event, Jesus' death can in no way be located, identified or described simply by invoking the general rubric of successful 'becoming definitively valid' through 'the decision of freedom'. Consequently, since the first instance of this general rubric signals the event of redeeming death, the particular features of Jesus' own death, the 'concrete manner' in virtue of which his death can be located, identified and described, has no essential bearing upon the event of redemptive death.[60] On the contrary: Jesus' death as an event in salvation history has redemptive value only on account of what can be assumed to have taken place in it, namely 'the final validity of the acceptance of God's self-offer'. The death of Jesus Christ is redemptive, in other words, only in so far as it is the first instance of a general pattern of 'successful' human death which not only may but must be repeated by others. Jesus' passion and death are not redemptive, by contrast, in so far as they constitute a unique and unsubstitutable pattern of events in which his particular life culminates, and which bring his particular identity most sharply into focus. In Rahner's actual account of the matter, despite his stated assumptions, the death of Jesus Christ is not redemptive *als solche*, that is, as *Jesus'* own death, which supremely distinguishes him as a particular person from all others.

This exploration of Rahner's 'feature-specific' characterizations of Jesus' redeeming significance reveals a noteworthy logical peculiarity. Despite his initial insistence that the particular pattern of events which constitutes the passion, death and resurrection of Jesus Christ is redemptive *als solche*, 'in itself', Rahner persistently finds redemptive significance not in this particular pattern of events but in general patterns of 'death' and of 'resurrection'. At least with respect to his account of 'redemptive death', this seems to be true even where he is not constrained by an explicitly transcendental element. Correlatively, he consistently avoids giving an account of 'redemptive death' or 'resurrection' which is definite and specific enough to describe these particular events, rather than being simply a general characteristic which does not distinguish one person from another. When the question explicitly arises, in fact, Rahner seems to reject any notion of Jesus' redeeming significance which would locate that significance in a describable difference between Jesus and us, that is, in something which distinguishes Jesus from all other persons. This is especially clear in his discussions of *Stellvertretung*.

To characterize the redemptive significance of the passion and death of Jesus Christ as *Stellvertretung* (both 'representation' and 'substitution') is to say, among other things, that in that particular pattern of actions and events, Jesus does for other persons what they cannot do for themselves. Or better, following a helpful suggestion of Hans Frei, it is to say that Jesus redeems by enacting the good of others on their behalf, in complete obedience to God.[61] Rahner emphatically rejects this way of understanding the redemptive import of Jesus' passion and death. 'A conception of substitutionary redemption (*stellvertretenden Erlösung*) in which Jesus does something in my place, which I really should do, but cannot, and which is then "reckoned" to me, I hold to be false. Or at least it is a misleading formulation of the dogmatic truth that my redemption is dependent upon Jesus and his cross.'[62]

Rahner has several reasons for rejecting *stellvertretende Erlösung*, a full discussion of which cannot be undertaken at this point. Two of these, however, together deeply illuminate the final fate of Jesus Christ as a particular person in Rahner's treatment of redemption. On the one hand, Rahner refuses to construe redemption as *Stellvertretung* because in principle the notion cannot serve to characterize a general pattern of activity of which Jesus is only an instance, albeit the original instance. My redemption cannot be dependent 'upon Jesus and his cross' in that he there enacts my ultimate good on my behalf. No. It is dependent in the sense that 'through Jesus it is precisely possible . . . that I can really do the highest thing which can be expected at all from a human being under the highest presuppositions' – that is, in the sense that I too can realize the pattern first realized by Jesus.[63] On the other hand, in striking contrast to his initial assumption,

Rahner seems to reject *Stellvertretung* precisely because such a conception would too readily locate the redemptive significance of Jesus' passion and death in the specific events themselves, rather than in the essential, repeatable pattern which, he supposes, they manifestly evince.

> Normal preaching tends to concentrate in the case of the death of Jesus, despite its crucial significance for salvation, too much upon the particular categorial event which takes place alongside many others on the world stage and has its own specific character (*Eigenart*). But the particular character of this death does not make plain much of the innermost being of the world and of human existence, or bring it to fulfilment. One moves too quickly to a consideration of the external causes and the violent nature of this death and treats it in the context of a theory of satisfaction as the purely external and meritorious cause of . . . redemption. But in a theology of death the event of Jesus' death can be more closely related to the basic structure of human existence.[64]

This is a rather startling admission. When he explicitly faces the alternative, Rahner would rather eviscerate his basic conviction that Jesus' passion and death are redemptive *als solche* than reconsider the theoretical premise that only a general pattern of events repeatable by us really can be *heilsbedeutsam*. 'The particular character of [Jesus'] death', he has said, 'does not make plain much of the innermost being of the world and of human existence, or bring it to fulfilment . . . But in a theology of death [in general] the event of Jesus' death can be more closely related to the basic structure of human existence.'

By rejecting *Stellvertretung*, Rahner refuses to accept what his convictions manifestly require: a feature-specific characterization of redemption which involves binding reference to the particular events that constitute Jesus' passion and death and is definite enough fitly to describe them. 'In complete obedience to God, he enacts the ultimate good of all persons on their behalf' is not only a characterization of a sequence of events with universal redemptive scope, but also seems materially fit to count as at least a partial description of Jesus' passion and death, precisely as particular actions and events which distinguish him from all other persons.[65] Not so with the only sort of characterizations of redemption which Rahner's method allows, namely those which denote general patterns or classes of events, of which the first instance is *eo ipso* the redemptive one. The definition of a class, like 'acts of willing self-surrender to God in death', does not count as or include a description of any particular instance of the class in its distinctiveness from all others. The qualification that the redemptive instance of the class is, properly speaking, only the first one does not compensate for this lack of descriptive force; 'the first instance of willing self-surrender in death' does not describe that instance as a particular event distinguished from all others, but only places it in a series of instances of the same class or pattern. Thus, if 'the first instance of wholly willing self-surrender to God in death' is taken to express the redemptive significance of Jesus' own passion and death, then that particular sequence of events is not redemptive *als solche*, but only on account of its *location* in a series of events of the same kind.

The second way, it seems, has exacted a heavy toll, even in a form which foregoes any appeal to specifically transcendental criteria of ultimate meaningfulness. In spite of his express intentions, Rahner appears unable to give a theological account of either the logical indispensability of the particular life of Jesus Christ as a whole, or the material decisiveness of the prominent features of that particular life, for the Christian belief in redemption and a redeemer.

CONCLUSION

In his *Religion Within the Limits of Reason Alone*, Kant proposed a view of redemption which has haunted the second way, then in its infancy, ever since.

> In the appearance of the God–man, it is not that in him which strikes the senses and can be known through experience, but rather the archetype, lying in our reason, that we attribute to him (since, so far as his example can be known, he is found to conform thereto), which is really the object of saving faith.[66]

Kant, of course, assumes that this is the right way to understand redemption. Rahner does not; he assumes that Jesus Christ, in all his particularity, is 'really the object of saving faith' in a redeemer. Yet despite all of the important differences in detail and execution, and despite his strenuous efforts to the contrary, the position Rahner reaches in his theological argument on the place of Jesus Christ in an account of redemption and a redeemer, as distinguished from the convictions and dogmatic commitments he brings to that argument, is essentially the same as the one evinced in this Kantian remark.

What I have called the 'second way' of answering the question 'how can Jesus Christ be *heilsbedeutsam?*', proposes that a reply to this question is logically possible only after the character of 'that which is *heilsbedeutsam*' has been adequately defined. Consequently, the logical basis upon which the second way proceeds is some definition of 'redemption' or 'significance for salvation' as a generality, a universally accessible patttern, or what Kant calls an 'archetype'. The second way always presupposes that Jesus alone can be the ultimate subject of any notion of 'that which is *heilsbedeutsam*'. At the same time the general definition of 'significance for salvation' is taken to be a fit criterion for, or itself to function as, both feature-neutral and feature-specific characterizations of that which has redemptive significance. This analysis of Rahner indicates that these two assumptions are incompatible. It seems as though there is no coherent way to honour both (1) the conviction that only Jesus Christ as a particular person can be the unique redeemer; and (2) the methodological assumption that the ideas of redemption and a redeemer are only credible, meaningful and intelligible for us as, or on the basis of, general criteria or patterns.

The second way, as Rahner's case illustrates, seems finally to be an unsuccessful attempt at a compromise between these two incompatible assumptions. A theology of this kind (as opposed to a position which cuts the tie to Jesus altogether) will always make some distinction between grasping the conformity of a saving predicate to the general criteria and grasping redemption through Jesus Christ (for Rahner, it is the non-deducibility of Jesus). But the line which distinguishes these (for Rahner, the positivity of the absolute saviour) will, it seems, also be the outer limit of what conforms to or is included in the sphere of ultimate meaningfulness and significance established and governed by the general criteria. As a result, the domain of ultimate meaningfulness and significance will be defined without reference to the specific events which cumulatively constitute Jesus' particular identity and which are assumed to *be* 'that which is significant for salvation'. In so far as it honours its methodological assumption that redemption, in order to be meaningful for us, must be susceptible of definition in general terms, the second way is not, it appears, a genuine alternative to the sort of position so tellingly articulated by Kant.

It will be recalled that Rahner is lead to adopt the overall christological strategy that I have called the second way primarily by a desire to conceive and present the Christian message to the modern world, indeed, in the first instance, to modern Christians, in a meaningful and intelligible way. This strategic or methodological decision is radically inconsistent with his own most basic commitments about the place of Jesus Christ as a particular person in the Christian belief in redemption and a redeemer. Yet Rahner's desire to conceive and present the Christian message in a meaningful way is entirely legitimate and necessary.

So Rahner, or anyone who wants to follow the second way, seems finally, as indicated in the Introduction, to be confronted with a choice. On the one hand, he can consistently maintain that 'redemption' can only be meaningful and intelligible in the modern world if it has the logical status of a generality; this would be explicitly to deny that belief in redemption, and even in a redeemer, has any indissoluble bond to Jesus Christ as a particular person. Kant cuts the tie to Jesus in this way, and others (Marx, for example) have taken up his suggestion in various ways, sometimes with powerful effect. On the other hand, he can consistently maintain that only Jesus Christ as a particular person can be the redeemer and the realization of redemption. This, however, will involve finding a different strategy or method for answering the question 'how can Jesus Christ be *heilsbedeutsam*?', and thus a different strategy for defining 'that which is significant for salvation' in a meaningful and intelligible way. One way in which an alternative strategy might be pursued is the subject of the next chapter.

NOTES

1   Karl Rahner, *Theological Investigations* (hereafter *TI*), tr. Cornelius
    Ernst et al. (20 vols, New York: 1961–83), vol. 6, p. 131. This is a
    translation of Rahner's *Schriften zur Theologie* (hereafter *SzT*), (16
    vols, Einsieldeln: 1954–84), vol. 6, p. 160. On the practice I will
    follow in citing Rahner and the use of the standard English transla-
    tion, see the Preface.
2   On the first way and the second way as divergent strategies for
    answering the question, how can Jesus Christ be *heilsbedeutsam*? cf.
    chap. 2, pp. 21–2.
3   Rahner views the impossibility of 'deduction' and the necessity of
    'encounter' as strictly complementary, and usually invokes both in
    the same breath. For relevant texts, cf. chap. 2, nn. 81–2, 94, 103.
4   Karl Rahner, *Foundations of Christian Faith: An Introduction to the Idea of
    Christianity* (hereafter *Foundations*), tr. William V. Dych (New York:
    1978), p. 206. A translation of Karl Rahner, *Grundkurs des Glaubens:
    Einfürung in der Begriff des Christentums* (hereafter *Grundkurs*) (Freiburg:
    1976), p. 206.
5   For a detailed treatment of Rahner's account of Jesus' death and
    resurrection, cf., below, pp. 95–8 and pp. 98–104.
6   *SzT*, vol. 12, p. 347; *TI*, vol. 17, pp. 18–19. Similar appeals to the
    christological relevance of a universal 'circle' between the transcen-
    dental and the categorial are especially frequent in the *Foundations*.
    Cf. pp. 242–3, p. 269, pp. 275–6, p. 282; *Grundkurs*, pp. 239–40, p.
    264, pp. 270–1, p. 276.
7   Cf. the brief remarks in chap. 2, pp. 17–18.
8   Immanuel Kant, *Critique of Pure Reason*, tr. Norman Kemp Smith, 2nd
    edn rev. (London: 1933), p. 212 (A 182 = B 224).
9   *Foundations*, p. 204; *Grundkurs*, p. 203. Cf. Karl Rahner, 'Jesus Christ,
    IV: History of Dogma and Theology', in *Sacramentum Mundi: An
    Encyclopedia of Theology*, ed. Karl Rahner et al. (6 vols, New York:
    1969) vol. 3, p. 193, col. 2: 'In fundamental theology a Christology
    may not and need not proceed as if it had to synthesize faith in
    Christ (*fides qua* and *fides quae*) in the retort of scholarship by means
    of pure reflection.'
10 The distinction between these two ways of presupposing Jesus
    Christ is not always clear in Rahner's text, since he uses much the
    same terminology (*Begegnung, personale Verhältnis, unableitbar*) to
    indicate both the priority of Jesus Christ over the idea of an absolute
    saviour *within* Christology, and the priority of belief in Jesus Christ
    as the absolute saviour over the entire *enterprise* of showing how that
    belief is credible.

11 *TI*, vol. 13, p. 215; *SzT*, vol. 10, p. 229. The cited remark refers
    specifically to 'ascending' or *heilsgeschichtliche* Christology, but this is
    in turn presupposed in the contrasting 'descending' or *metaphysische*
    Christology. Cf. *TI*, vol. 13, p. 220; *SzT*, vol. 10, p. 234.
12 Cf. chap. 2, n. 108.
13 *Foundations*, pp. 235–6. *Grundkurs*, p. 233.
14 The sort of objection against which Rahner brings this argument
    based upon an appeal to the presupposition of a 'concrete encoun-
    ter with Jesus' is quite different from that which I am developing
    here. The charge Rahner explicitly faces is that he is too meta-
    physical, that he obviates the need for a personal involvement with
    the historical content of the Christian mysteries by absorbing the
    mysteries into an *a priori* transcendental scheme. Rahner's rejoinder
    seems to meet this kind of objection, since, as I have pointed out, he
    not only acknowledges but insists that the historical content of the
    Christian mysteries 'encounters us underivably and therefore
    cannot be obtained surreptitiously by speculative means'
    (*Grundkurs*, p. 207; *Foundations*, p. 207. Cf. *SzT*, vol. 15, pp. 232–5,
    where he replies to critics like Küng, whom he takes to question or
    ignore the need for and legitimacy of a distinctively transcendental
    Christology on such grounds.) My argument, by contrast, is not that
    Rahner has failed to distinguish a personal encounter with Jesus
    from a 'speculative' justification of his significance but that the
    structure and aims of his Christology prevent him from successfully
    uniting the two.
15 Rahner here appears to have conflated a logical relation of depen-
    dence with a psychological and genetic one, from which the former
    is in fact quite distinct, and in which it is not entailed.
16 Cf. chap. 2, pp. 35–6, on the contention that there can only be one
    'absolute saviour'.
17 *Foundations*, p. 212; *Grundkurs*, p. 211.
18 *Grundkurs*, p. 178; *Foundations*, p. 176. Cf. the similar summary
    remark in *SzT*, vol. 9, p. 249; *TI*, vol. 11, p. 237: 'There can thus be
    such a thing as anonymous Christianity, in which grace, forgiveness
    of sins, justification and salvation occur, without the person in
    question being explicitly related, in his or her objective
    consciousness, to the historical event of Jesus of Nazareth.' Cf. also
    TI, vol. 5, p. 132; *SzT*, vol. 5, p. 155.
19 Rahner's three favourite examples are the call to love of neighbour,
    to preparation for death and to hope in the future. This trio appears
    frequently in Rahner's later writings; cf. *TI* vol. 13, pp. 197–200;
    SzT, vol. 10, pp. 211–14; *TI*, vol. 16, pp. 222–4; *SzT*, vol. 12, pp.
    279–82; *Foundations*, pp. 295–7; *Grundkurs*, pp. 288 – 91; 'Jesus
    Christ', p. 194, cols 1–195, col. 2.

20 Cf., e.g. *Foundations*, passage cited above, n. 18; also *TI*, vol. 4, p. 119; *SzT*, vol. 4, pp. 153–4.

21 Rahner tempers this in some of his later remarks on anonymous Christianity by recognizing that the 'objective' provenance of the offer of grace in Jesus Christ is not equivalent to the subjective realization of a relation to Jesus Christ in one who accepts the offer anonymously. 'The universal significance for salvation of the cross of Jesus', he writes, 'is . . . only given and understood by all humanity when the relation is *mutual*, when not only does Jesus have a relation to humanity, but humanity also has one to him' (*SzT*, vol. 12, p. 272; *TI*, vol. 16, p. 216). He continues to maintain, however, that the *Ausschau* in history, conceived as a 'questing Christology' and anonymously realized (cf. n. 19), constitutes a saving relationship to Jesus himself, 'even if a man does not know how to call him by his proper name' (*TI*, vol. 16, p. 222; *SzT*, vol. 12, p. 279).

22 So Rahner says of the term 'anonymous Christianity', for example, that it 'signifies precisely the fact that while it is true that Christianity is already present in an incipient state it has not yet developed to the true fullness of its nature, not yet come to be expressed in its historical and social modality and visibility', which is presumably supposed to include the otherwise absent recognition and acceptance of Jesus Christ as a particular person (*TI*, vol. 12, p. 164; *SzT*, vol. 9, p. 501). Cf. also *TI*, vol. 6, p. 395; *SzT*, vol. 6, p. 550–1.

23 Human death is either 'a personal repetition and confirmation of the sinful emancipation of the first human being and so the culmination of sin, definitive mortal sin, or it will be the personal repetition and appropriation of Christ's obedient death (Phil. 2:8) by which Christ inserted his divine life into the world itself.' Karl Rahner, 'Death', *Sacramentum Mundi: An Encyclopedia of Theology*, vol. 2 (New York: 1969), p. 62, col. 1. Here again, however, the significant difference between explicit and anonymous Christians is not entirely clear, since this definitive 'personal appropriation of Christ's obedient death' is necessary for both.

24 Cf. chap. 2, pp. 24–5. For an alternative suggestion regarding the salvation of non-Christians which is sympathetic to Rahner's motives but critical of 'anonymous Christianity', cf. George A. Lindbeck, *The Nature of Doctrine: Religion and Theology in a Postliberal Age* (Philadelphia: 1984), pp. 55–63.

25 This distinction between 'Jesus Christ' and his most prominent 'specific features' (which would, of course, be applied to any particular life) does not imply at this point any claims about the way the relation between the two ought to be understood anthropologically or metaphysically. It leaves open the question of

whether this relation is best thought of as one of agent to intentional acts, of subject to self-expression, of substance to accidents, simply of whole to parts, or as some combination of these. In other contexts (e.g., an exegetical and theological account of Jesus' redeeming significance) it might indeed be important to make a decision about this matter.

26   This is not to prejudice the issue (which will be looked at more closely in chap. 5) of precisely how those characterizations of Jesus' redeeming significance which are applicable to him specifically in virtue of his crucifixion and resurrection are related to those which are applicable to his particular life as a whole ('incarnation' is perhaps the historically dominant paradigm for the latter). Rahner, as will be seen momentarily, clearly expects the properly qualified notion of an 'absolute saviour' to serve both functions.

27   *SzT*, vol. 12, p. 266; *TI*, vol. 16, p. 211.

28   Cf. chap. 2, n. 107.

29   *TI*, vol. 4, p. 111; *SzT*, vol. 4, p. 144.

30   *TI*, vol. 18, pp. 146–7; *SzT*, vol. 13, p. 176.

31   *TI*, vol. 18, p. 147; *SzT*, vol. 13, p. 176. In this characterization I am still dealing with the content of our transcendental orientation, that is, as Rahner expressly indicates, with the idea of an absolute saviour who is 'still being sought'. Cf. in a similar vein *Grundkurs*, p. 278; *Foundations*, p. 284: 'God's word of promise is therefore only completed when man's affirmative answer to it appears historically (precisely in what we call "resurrection") . . .'

32   *Foundations*, p. 211; *Grundkurs*, p. 210.

33   Cf. chap. 2, pp. 49–50.

34   *Foundations*, p. 254; *Grundkurs*, p. 250.

35   *Foundations*, p. 255; *Grundkurs*, p. 251.

36   *Foundations*, p. 279; *Grundkurs*, p. 274. Cf. *SzT*, vol. 15, p. 214 – 5: 'But Jesus raises the claim of being in an unconditional and irreversible way God's definitive promise of himself, and his self-interpretation and claim are confirmed by God through the final validity of his existence in death and resurrection.'

37   *Ich Glaube*, pp. 33–4. Our orientation precisely to a dying and rising 'absolute saviour' finds what it seeks in Jesus Christ, Rahner points out, 'at least because such an offer has been made (*erfolgt*) nowhere else in the religious history of humanity' (*SzT*, vol. 13, p. 184; *TI*, vol. 18, p. 153). Cf. chap. 2, nn. 102, 104.

38   The important question of *how* the resurrection of Jesus Christ is constitutive of his particular identity is left open here, and thus the question of precisely how it can be described and how it functions to identify him in relation to the whole pattern of his particular life. I will assume, with Rahner, only *that* it does so.

39 *Foundations*, pp. 273–4; *Grundkurs*, p. 269. The phrase 'an experience man can reach by his very essence' (*vom Wesen des Menschen her erreichbare*) is rather odd in light of Rahner's more typical (and apparently opposed) position 'that *a posteriori* experience first brings our transcendentally given *a priori* horizons of hope reflexively to consciousness'. In either case, the meaningfulness and intelligibility of the '*a posteriori* experience' depends upon the presence of the '*a priori* horizons of hope'; when the latter do become explicit, they are recognized as 'the ones which are always already given, even if perhaps very inexplicitly' (*SzT*, vol. 9, pp. 219–20; *TI*, vol. 11, p. 207).

40 *Foundations*, p. 273, p. 271; *Grundkurs*, p. 268, p. 267.

41 Cf. *TI*, vol. 11, p. 209; *SzT*, vol. 9, p. 221: 'We know nothing of the eschata beyond the fact that we are and that we receive the history of our own reality and free decision and our relationship to God as something that is permanently definitive (*als Endgültigkeit*).'

42 The argument here is highly reminiscent of that by which Rahner attempts to establish the need for a categorial 'saviour' in general; it is simply focused upon a specific aspect of our orientation to salvation and hence of the idea of an absolute saviour.

43 *Foundations*, p. 273; *Grundkurs*, p. 268. Cf. *TI*, vol. 11, p. 207; *SzT*, vol. 9, p. 219.

44 Cf. Rahner's remark on the first disciples' experience of resurrection as 'strictly related to the crucified one with his entirely determinate individuality and fate, in such a way that *this one* is experienced as valid and saved' (*Grundkurs*, p. 271; *Foundations*, p. 277).

45 Rahner says that 'the resurrection has an entirely distinctive (*eigentümliche*) and unique, but nevertheless real availability (*Greifbarkeit*) in history' (*SzT*, vol. 13, p. 201; *TI*, vol. 18, p. 168). But he never indicates what this *Greifbarkeit* amounts to, beyond 'the manifestation of eternal validity'.

46 This is not to deny, of course, that 'the manifestation of eternal validity' might be a true predicate of Jesus Christ. But Rahner evidently takes a phrase like 'the manifestation of eternal validity' to be substitutable for 'raised from the dead on the third day and appeared to Cephas, then to the twelve', precisely as a description of the decisive redemptive event. As I have pointed out, however, the former phrase cannot possibly enable us to locate Jesus' own resurrection and identify him in it (unlike 'on the third day and appeared to Cephas ...'). Moreover, since it includes no identifying reference to Jesus Christ, it can only be applied to him once he has been identified on other grounds. And *per assumptionem*, it is precisely these grounds – namely the specific climactic

sequence of Jesus' own life – which are significant for salvation *als solche*. Consequently, it cannot be the applicability of a non-identifying phrase which makes Jesus *heilsbedeutsam*; on the contrary, he must be 'significant for salvation' as a particular person *before* we can apply such a phrase. This means that 'the manifestation of eternal validity' cannot be substituted for 'Jesus' resurrection', and that, while it may be a true predication regarding Jesus Christ, is the most (not, as Rahner would have it, the least) remote, general and uninformative kind of thing we can say about him as the unique redeemer.

47 This latter fact, one would suppose, is largely responsible for the seeming plausibility of 'the manifestation of eternal validity' as an account of Jesus' own resurrection.

48 The saviour's death is, of course, included in the general anticipation of an 'absolute saviour'. Cf. above, nn. 30, 32. Rahner does not always allude to this, however, when he is discussing Jesus' own death.

49 *TI*, vol. 18, p. 140; *SzT*, vol. 13, p. 168.

50 *SzT*, vol. 15, pp. 243–4. As this remark indicates and Rahner frequently emphasizes, the death and resurrection of Jesus Christ bear a necessary and ordered relation to one another as redemptive events. 'The resurrection of Christ [is] not another event *after* his suffering and death, but . . . the appearance of what has occurred in the death of Christ' (*SzT*, vol. 4, pp. 165–6; *TI*, vol. 4, p. 128).

51 *TI*, vol. 18, p. 139; *SzT*, vol. 13, p. 167.

52 'God's promise of himself, if it is to be not merely words but also deeds, can only be given in a person who has accepted this self-promise in freedom and with final validity' (*SzT*, vol. 13, p. 165; *TI*, vol. 18, p. 138).

53 *TI*, vol. 18, p. 140; *SzT*, vol. 13, p. 168.

54 *Foundations*, p. 284; *Grundkurs*, p. 278.

55 Jesus dies 'in such a way that the success (*Geglücksein*) of this acceptance [of God] in the powerlessness of death also becomes available for us in faith, and thus together with his resurrection' (*SzT*, vol. 13, p. 168; *TI*, vol. 18, p. 140).

56 *SzT*, vol. 7, p. 144; *TI*, vol. 7, p. 143. Similarly, Rahner distinguishes between death as 'the beginning of redeemed finality in God', which occurs through the acceptance of death 'as the dawn and approach of . . . silent infinity', and death as 'the event of final perdition', in which 'the subject in the last resort culpably refuses to accept any freely bestowed love from another person' (*TI*, vol. 18, p. 164; *SzT*, vol. 13, p. 196). The death of Jesus Christ is of the former variety. In death, despite the 'trackless dark in which everything fell away from him', Jesus 'nevertheless calmly surrendered himself as to eternal

love and not to the hell of futility. In that sense his death is the same as ours, even though the concrete circumstance[s] of death vary' (*TI*, vol. 18, p. 165; *SzT*, vol. 13, p. 198). Thus Rahner can say that 'the most distinctive thing' which can be said about the death of Jesus is 'that in this absolute nadir (*Nullpunkt*) of our life and our experience true life first occurred' (*SzT*, vol. 7, p. 143; *TI*, vol. 7, p. 142–3).

57 *SzT*, vol. 13, pp. 169–70; *TI*, vol. 18, p. 141. Rahner calls Jesus' 'successful' death (which, precisely as 'successful', is death 'into resurrection') 'really the productive model (*Vorbild*) of our death' (*SzT*, vol. 13, p. 199; *TI*, vol. 18, p. 167). However, the 'productive' character of this *Vorbild*, and thus the distinction between it and the repetitions or images of it in the deaths of believers, lies simply in its temporal priority, viewed with Rahner's characteristic ontological stress. Before Jesus' resurrection (i.e., his 'successful' death), 'the drama of world history as a whole was still open and ambivalent. Since the resurrection it is otherwise', in that 'on account of the one reality, which is already given, there is given a presumption for the real success of other possibilities' (*SzT*, vol. 13, p. 202; *TI*, vol. 18, p. 169).

58 *SzT*, vol. 15, p. 223.

59 Ibid.

60 Here again Rahner is quite frank. The essential character of human death implies that it is 'fundamentally indifferent, in what concrete way the death of a person occurs'. Instead, the crucial issue is whether or not death is accepted, however it occurs. So, with regard to the death of Jesus Christ,

it is not forbidden to a theologian, even if it is not enjoined, to reflect on why and how the concreteness of Jesus' death (its violence in conflict with the political and religious powers, the utter God-forsakenness of this death, etc.) is also essential and significant for the saving significance (*heilshafte Bedeutsamkeit*) of this death for Jesus himself, and all the more for us.

The reason why such considerations are only optional is by now familiar. 'But it remains decisive that death also in Jesus' case is to be conceived fundamentally as the highest act of freedom in radical powerlessness, with the simultaneous aim of final validity' (*SzT*, vol. 13, p. 168; *TI*, vol. 18, p. 140).

61 Cf. Hans Frei, *The Identity of Jesus Christ: The Hermeneutical Bases of Dogmatic Theology* (Philadelphia: 1974), p. 104, p. 111.

62 *SzT*, vol. 15, pp. 244–5. In a parallel discussion, Rahner stresses that *Stellvertretung*, in the sense of enacting the good of others in their

place and on their behalf, simply cannot be 'an act which is significant for, and effects, salvation' for us. On the contrary: 'In this sense, so we must now say, there is no *Stellvertretung*' (*SzT*, vol. 15, p. 261).

63   *SzT*, vol. 15, p. 245.

64   *TI*, vol. 16, p. 223; *SzT*, vol. 12, pp. 280–1. On the insistence that a theology of death in general, as opposed to any description of Jesus' own death, is the proper context in which to characterize the redemptive significance of Jesus' death, cf. *SzT*, vol. 7, p. 273; *TI*, vol. 7, p. 285:

> If [the Christian] is really supposed to understand what is said to him in the message [of the death of Christ], he should strive for an understanding of the essence of death in general. However much he can learn *from* the message of the death of Christ, what death is *at all (überhaupt)*, yet to the same degree he must also bring along a concept of death which is as fully realized and experiential as possible, in order to understand at all what it means to say: there one has *died* for all.

It is important to stress that I am not criticizing Rahner for rejecting those distortions in which *Stellvertretung* is construed as 'penal substitution', or as 'the purely external and meritorious cause of redemption' (to use Rahner's phrase). The difficulty rather lies in his inability to attribute ultimate redeeming significance to Jesus Christ in so far as Jesus differs from us, i.e., in virtue of his particular identity.

65   The way in which it might do so, and in which it and other characterizations of 'that which is significant for salvation' might involve binding reference to Jesus Christ, will be the subject of the next chapter.

66   Immanuel Kant, *Religion Within the Limits of Reason Alone*, tr. T. Greene and H. Hudson (New York: 1960), p. 110.

4

Jesus Christ as the Criterion of Meaningfulness in Barth's Christology

RETROSPECT AND PROSPECT

It has been shown that a theology structured like Rahner's is inconsistent, despite its undoubted intention to the contrary, with the basic conviction that only Jesus Christ as a particular person is the unique redeemer or absolute saviour. The inconsistency in which Rahner finds himself is on the one hand procedural or methodological. That is, the problem *originates* in a definite decision about the right way to answer the question, 'how can Jesus Christ be ultimately significant?' or 'significant for salvation?' In practice this basic methodological decision decisively controls the function and import of Rahner's theological discourse about both the significance and the particularity of Jesus Christ. On the other hand, the inconsistency evinced by Rahner's Christology constitutes a pressing material or dogmatic problem. Part of the business of theology, Rahner would agree, is to give an account of the logic and thereby the intelligibility of Christian belief. But it appears that for a theology which proceeds the way Rahner's does, the Christian belief that only Jesus Christ can be the absolute saviour is ultimately unintelligible; indeed, it seems that for this kind of theology the contrary belief is rather the intelligible one, namely that anyone could be the absolute saviour.

Since this dogmatic problem stems from a procedural decision, a more successful account of the logic and intelligibility of the Christian belief that Jesus Christ as a particular person is the unique redeemer will have to have a different method. It will, in other words, have to involve a fundamentally different way of handling the question, 'how can Jesus Christ be significant for salvation?' As an instance of a more successful procedure for answering this question, I will examine Karl Barth's theology of reconciliation. Before I can do that, however, some preliminary remarks are necessary regarding the character of my approach to Barth.

In the Foreword to his *Barth-Studien*, Eberhard Jüngel remarks that

> Barth research – and here everything shall be reckoned to be Barth research, which considers itself as such – has chiefly been engaged in reducing the unusual richness of Barth's theology to a few barren leading ideas (*einige dürre Konstruktionsprinzipien*), which allow the whole of this theology to seem readily comprehensible, and thereby either commendable or refutable.[1]

My treatment of Barth will attempt to heed the useful warning implied in this somewhat caustic remark. Few theological writers of any period resist independent attempts critically and informatively to state the logic of their actual procedure quite so effectively as does Barth.[2] This relative intractability to fruitful analysis makes an exceptionally daunting and perhaps misguided enterprise of the project of finding a *Konstruktionsprinzip*, a systematic or methodological principle or concept which governs the whole in all of its parts.

At a different level, it is rather simple to say what Barth's theology is all about, but he himself indicates that this involves abandoning the search for *Konstruktionsprinzipien*, even the most obvious and likely of them:

> I have no christological principle and no christological method. Rather in each individual theological question I seek to orientate myself afresh – to some extent from the very beginning – not on a christological dogma but on Jesus Christ himself (*vivit! regnat! triumphat!*).[3]

The aim of my treatment of Barth is to articulate the logic of this orientation on Jesus Christ in a single respect: its bearing on characterizations of his significance. This is clearly an important theological question for Barth, to which he devotes frequent and occasionally explicit attention. But it is not at all the whole of his theology, nor is it necessarily the key to his whole theology. This discussion is therefore not an attempt to say what Barth's theology, or even his Christology, is all about, or to find for it a comprehensive *Konstruktionsprinzip*.[4] For just this reason, while I shall argue that Barth gives a relatively successful account of the issue with which I am concerned, that argument does not at all amount to an endorsement of Barth's theology or Christology as a whole, nor does it necessarily bear upon a variety of critical questions which might arise in connection with the general area of Barth's theology towards which my attention will primarily be directed. Rather, as was the case with Rahner, the overriding interest here is quite specific. I am concerned with the clarification and assessment of his distinctive procedure in answering the question, 'how can Jesus Christ be *heilsbedeutsam*?'

As I indicated at the beginning of the discussion of Rahner, there seem to be two basically different ways of handling this question, one which has so greatly preoccupied modern theology.[5] I took Rahner to be one important example of what I have called simply the second way of showing how Jesus Christ can be significant for salvation. As I begin to investigate the opposite procedure at work in Barth's theology, it may be useful to recall the decisive feature of the second way. An analysis of Rahner's central christological argument shows that the heart of the second way is a methodological decision or rule. Any attempt to answer the question, 'how can Jesus Christ be *heilsbedeutsam*?', so the reasoning goes, presupposes the answer to a logically distinct question. This independent and prior question asks about general criteria for, and thereby the most general features of, any reality which could possibly count as ultimately significant or 'significant for salvation'. In Rahner's case, the criteria are generated by a transcendental anthropology.

The practical implications of this procedure are most clearly in evidence when a theologian who follows it attempts to articulate the significance for salvation of the focal events of Jesus' life, especially his death and resurrection. The logic of the method, which can find something significant for salvation only in virtue of its conformity to general criteria, requires that 'death' and 'resurrection' be characterized as saving events by excluding any

identifying or particularizing descriptions of Jesus from the characterization.[6] In practice as well as in principle, I have argued, the
second way proves unable to account for the intelligibility of its
own assumption that only Jesus can be the redeemer or saviour;
on the contrary, it would seem to make this belief unintelligible.
Thus the losses involved in the second way appear to overwhelm
its intended apologetic benefits.

I have already sketched very briefly the outlines of a different
way of treating the question about how Jesus Christ can be
significant for salvation.[7] The distinctive feature of the first way,
to recall the language I have already used in describing this
alternative procedure, is the argument that Jesus Christ is
heilsbedeutsam in virtue of his own life, death and resurrection. I can
now be more precise about the central argument of the first way.
Accounts of redemption and a redeemer, so this argument goes,
are themselves finally meaningful, intelligible and existentially
accessible *because* and in so far as they are appropriately applied to
Jesus Christ as a particular person. Here, the significance for
salvation of any concept or explanation of what Jesus Christ is
(such as 'the absolute saviour') depends upon its predication of
and reference to this particular subject. The criterion for that
which is *heilsbedeutsam* is therefore its conformity and applicability
to the particular life of Jesus Christ. Since Jesus' particular
identity is the measure of all 'significance for salvation', it is
logically impossible that the question, 'how can Jesus Christ be
heilsbedeutsam?', be answered by an appeal to any kind of general
criteria for that which is *heilsbedeutsam*. Rather, because the
criterion of 'significance for salvation' itself has the logical status
of a particular, this question can only be answered by a sufficiently comprehensive description of that particular.

Similarly, the question about how Jesus Christ can be
heilsbedeutsam cannot for the first way be governed by a logically
distinct and prior question about how any reality can be
heilsbedeutsam. Since the criterion of significance for salvation is the
distinctive life of a particular person, 'that which is *heilsbedeutsam*'
cannot denote, as the latter question assumes, a class of possible
realities with certain general features (even when, as a writer like
Rahner insists, there is in fact only one instance of this general
class). Construed in this way, so the argument goes, the criterion
of 'significance for salvation' permits an account of redemption

and a redeemer in which it is actually intelligible and meaningful that Jesus Christ is *heilsbedeutsam* precisely as a particular person. By proceeding along these lines, the first way tries to answer the question, 'how can Jesus Christ be *heilsbedeutsam?*', in a manner consistent with an assumption both ways take to be basic and indispensable.

THE CONTEXT OF BARTH'S ARGUMENT

Barth's theology evinces the pattern and procedure I am calling the first way with exceptional clarity. This is due in no small measure to the fact that he deliberately parts company on this issue with the tradition that has dominated Protestant theology since the late eighteenth century, and Catholic theology with increasing pervasiveness in the last two generations.[8] Barth's purposive methodological departure rests in part simply on a recognition of the distinctive character of the modern question about how Jesus Christ can be significant for salvation, to which the second way seems so well-suited. But at the same time it constitutes a deliberate reversal of the assumptions and decisions of the second way. His commitment to the first way is one in a network of related methodological or procedural decisions, many of them bearing on peculiarly modern problems, which enter his theology with varying degrees of explicitness and scope.[9]

One of these, to which Hans Frei has drawn particular attention, is an especially close cognate to Barth's preference for the first way. With increasing clarity as the work progresses, Frei maintains, Barth's *Church Dogmatics* is informed by a decision that 'the relation between the self-description of Christianity and all *autonomously* conceived human, cultural quests for ultimate meaning is indirect, that they are logically diverse even when they are existentially connected, that is to say, even when they reside in the same breast'.[10] Consequently, 'autonomous anthropology and Christian theology cannot be understood as mutually implicated, nor is there any one specific conceptual framework that must be the precondition for making theological discourse meaningful'.[11] In relation to the christological issue which is my concern here, Barth's contention that Christian theology need not and should not appeal to logically independent and external criteria of meaningfulness would seem to be incompatible with the second way. This is not to say, however, that in Barth the first way is simply the christological application of this decision about the autonomy and comprehensiveness of Christian theology. While congruent with this latter argument in ways I cannot explore in detail here, the christological decision has its own distinctive character and logic. My project is to articulate the logic of that specific decision.

The broadest and most comprehensive form of Barth's decision to treat the particular identity of Jesus Christ as the sole criterion of 'significance for salvation' is the sort of remark most typically found in the context of his theology of election. 'The general (the world and man) exists for the sake of this particular [Jesus Christ]. In this particular the general has its meaning (*Sinn*) and fulfilment.'[12] This contention that the particular is in theologically decisive ways prior to the general has a negative form, which Barth enunciates with the tenor of a warning: danger lurks in generalities (*Latet periculum in generalibus!*).[13] With regard to the present concern, the place of Jesus Christ as a particular person in an account of redemption and a redeemer, the crucial point in Barth's contention is not simply that the general 'exists for the sake of' the particular, but especially that the general 'has its meaning and fulfilment' in the particular. Or, as Barth reverses the point in a somewhat different context: 'Precisely this particular [Jesus Christ] as such, and only it, aims at the general and includes the general in itself.'[14] Barth's deliberate reversal of the second way, stated in relatively abstract fashion, consists in this contention that the general is accessible only as that at which the particular 'aims', and correlatively that the general finds its meaning in the particular.

Barth's insistence that the general has its meaning in the particular, with specific reference to Jesus Christ, does not function as a premise or axiom in his theology, from which specific conclusions could be derived. Consequently, Barth devotes no attention at all to articulating a relation between the particular and the general as such or in principle, that is, independently of specific theological contexts in which this priority of the particular over the general may serve as an appropriate clarification. For example, Barth argues in his theology of election that the primal decision in which God determines himself and all his works *ad extra* is the election of Jesus Christ, that is, the decision to enact the particular history or story (*Geschichte*) of that person as his own. Just at this point he adds the observation that the general (here meaning all human and world history) finds its meaning and fulfilment in the particular (here meaning the life or history of Jesus Christ).[15] Consistently, it is in fact Jesus Christ himself (or his 'history') who is the 'particular' in which something 'general' finds its meaning and fulfilment, or has rightly to be understood.[16] For the issue with which I am concerned, the 'general' is any account of redemption and a redeemer. In order to see how the particular has priority over the general in this specific case, it is necessary to look to the theological contexts in Barth where Jesus Christ and his significance are treated most explicitly. This means attending above all to the christological sections of Barth's theology of reconciliation.

Throughout the *Church Dogmatics*, and especially in the concluding volumes which make up 'The Doctrine of Reconciliation', Barth draws frequent attention to the common conviction which both ways of answering the question, 'how can Jesus Christ be *heilsbedeutsam*?', strive to articulate appropriately. Barth's ways of formulating the shared assumption that Jesus Christ is the unique saviour precisely as a particular person typically accentuate a basic methodological posture, the lineaments of which have just been seen. The right way to honour this conviction, he maintains, is consistently to accord its particular side a complex priority over its general side.

One way he puts the assumption is to stress the real and also epistemological identity of the comprehensive event of reconciliation with the particular life of Jesus Christ. 'The atonement (*Versöhnung*) is, noetically, the history about Jesus Christ, and ontically, Jesus Christ's own history.'[17] But the real or ontological identity of Jesus Christ as a particular person with his universal significance (for which *Versöhnung*, with its presupposition, *Erwählung*, is probably the most comprehensive designation) is only available to us noetically if the right order between the two is consistently maintained. So Barth does not simply stress the shared conviction that Jesus' significance is really identical with his particularity but expresses the conviction in terms which already imply a decision for the first way. For Barth, the Christian message of the event or history of reconciliation has a distinctive logic, which (as Rahner would agree) a theological account of that message must maintain. The Christian message 'recounts this history and speaks of its inclusive power and significance (*Bedeutung*) in such a way that it declares a name, binding the history (*Geschichte*) it recounts strictly and indissolubly to this name and presenting it as the story (*Geschichte*) of the bearer of this name.'[18] This means though,

> that all the concepts and ideas used in this report (God, man, world, eternity, time, even salvation, grace, trangression, reconciliation and any others) can receive their meaning (*Sinn*) only from the bearer of this name and from his history, and not the reverse. They cannot have any independent significance or role grounded in a quite different pre-understanding (*Vorverständnis*). They cannot say what has to be said here with some meaning of their own or in some context of their own abstracted from this name. They can serve only to describe this name – the name of Jesus Christ.[19]

Attention to the way Barth actually proceeds in his theology of reconciliation will enable the reader to see the argumentative shape that this ringing affirmation of the first way takes in practice.

Excursus: reconciliation and election

The precise relation between reconciliation and election, a point I have just mentioned in passing, is a complex and problematic issue in Barth's theology.[20] It raises an important question, although not the one which is my primary interest here: precisely what significance is in fact to be attributed to Jesus Christ as a particular person? As has just been seen, Barth insists that the history of Jesus Christ is really identical with the reconciliation of the world. This implies that the conquest of sin must be part of the significance attributed to Jesus Christ. Yet, as will be seen (below, pp. 126–30), Barth insists with equal vigour that God's original decision, which is indeed God's determination of his own identity, is to bear the name 'Jesus Christ', and in the particular life of Jesus Christ to have covenant fellowship with human beings. This seems to create a dilemma. (1) If fellowship with human beings in the particular life of Jesus Christ is God's original purpose, and the particular life of Jesus Christ is identical with the reconciliation of the world, then it would seem that in willing the particular life of Jesus Christ, God must necessarily will sin in his original decision, as that which is to be conquered in reconciliation. (2) This undesirable result can be avoided, it seems, only by discarding either 'election' or 'reconciliation' as an essential and necessary characterization of Jesus' significance; they cannot, it seems, both be necessarily true of the same person.

Barth, however, thinks it is not only possible, but theologically indispensable, to characterize Jesus' significance both in terms of 'election' and of 'reconciliation', when the latter are properly distinguished and related. In a more extensive discussion of the way Barth views the place of Jesus Christ in an account of his significance, his solution to this problem would have to be treated in detail.[21] For the more limited purpose here, however, I can leave this question unanswered. The way Barth handles the logic of ascribing significance to Jesus Christ, as will be seen, is distinguishable from the complex account of that significance which Barth himself actually proposes. Therefore, although I will not argue the point in detail here, it would seem that the basic logic of the ascription of ultimate significance to Jesus Christ need not change, even if Barth's harmonization of election and reconciliation were unsuccessful. With the issue of its relation to election noted, I will use the term 'reconciliation' as the most comprehensive designation of Jesus' significance in Barth's theology.[22]

THE ELEMENTS OF RECONCILIATION

The first way in Barth consists in the ordering and relation of three elements in his theology of reconciliation, in so far as that ordering establishes which of these elements or aspects is the criterion of significance for salvation. These three aspects are (1) descriptions of Jesus Christ as a particular person; (2) characterizations of the event of reconciliation, which are applied to Jesus; and (3) descriptions of the immediate action and presence of God in Jesus Christ, that is, of the incarnation. It will be useful to point out a few crucial features of each of these elements before considering the way Barth treats their mutual ordering and relation.

1   The name 'Jesus Christ' denotes a particular person, who can be referred to and described in his concrete individuality.[23] Barth not only likes to stress that the name invokes a particular person; he also maintains a definite conception of what constitutes Jesus' particular identity. 'Whoever says *"Jesus"* thereby says immediately and unavoidably: *history (Geschichte)* – his history – the history in which he is who he is, and does what he does.'[24] Jesus' particularity consists in his 'history', as the sequence of intentional acts, in interaction with specific circumstances, of which he is the free subject.[25] Because it is constituted by a pattern of situated actions, Jesus' particular identity is accessible to us primarily in the form of a distinctive kind of description, namely a story or narrative.[26] The particular identity of Jesus, conceived as his history, has two distinguishable aspects. These correspond to what I have called 'ostensibility' and 'describability' in the discussion of the concept of particularity.[27] To say that Jesus' history is ostensible means simply that it can be pointed to or designated with demonstratives, because it has a specific location in space and time. Barth can put this specific point quite sharply:

> 'Jesus Christ for us', the incarnation and the crucifixion, do not exist or come to pass in an abstract always and everywhere in which our here and now are at once included, but in a concrete and singular then and there which as such cannot be taken away (*nicht aufzuhebenden*) and thus cannot be exchanged – outside our here and now and contrasted with it.[28]

Jesus' history is describable in so far as it is constituted by a coherent sequence of actions and events, a pattern of definite features culminating in passion, crucifixion and resurrection.[29]

In both its ostensible and describable aspects, Jesus' history or particularity is 'the dramatic way of conflict from Bethlehem to Golgotha', as this is depicted primarily in the synoptic Gospels.[30] Barth sees 'the way from Bethlehem to Golgotha' as naturally falling into two parts, corresponding basically to Jesus' public ministry and his passion, with the prayer in Gethsemane as the decisive turning point between the two. The resurrection is a third part of Jesus' history and thus its culmination, but it stands in a

peculiar noetic and ontic relation to the whole 'way from Bethlehem to Golgotha', a relation to which Barth devotes great
attention but the details of which are outside the scope of this
study.[31] In sum, the particular identity of Jesus Christ is the
ostensible and describable history, that of the one who went the
way from Bethlehem to Golgotha, and rose on the third day.

2   Barth's various characterizations of reconciliation can be
understood as attempts to depict in conceptual and thus relatively general terms the universally significant event which takes
place in the history of Jesus Christ. The most comprehensive
characterizations of reconciliation are simply the three main
divisions of the fourth volume of the *Church Dogmatics*: 'The Lord
as Servant' (IV/1), 'The Servant as Lord' (IV/2) and 'The True
Witness' (IV/3). Within the opening christological section of each
division, Barth works out in detail a conceptual account of the
event of reconciliation suited to the perspective of that division.
So, reconcilation is 'the judge judged in our place' (IV/1, §59.2),
the life of 'the royal man' (IV/2, §64.3), and the triumph of 'the
victor' over evil (IV/3, §69.3). These characterizations and their
detailed explication are all necessary, Barth maintains, for a fully
appropriate account of reconciliation and a reconciler.
   It is very important to notice, however, that these expressions
by themselves are not identifying descriptions of Jesus Christ, or
of anyone else. In fact, they could be unfolded in considerable
detail (as in Barth's pages they regularly are) and still lack the
kind of ostensive and descriptive definiteness needed to identify a
particular person. In the language of the earlier discussion, they
are positivity introducing expressions, they may introduce an
individual into discourse, but not a *particular* individual. It is
important to stress in this connection the role of the demonstrative or ostensive element in distinguishing an identifying or
particularizing description of an individual from both a conceptual characterization and a classification of that same individual.
As the case of concepts like 'the unique redeemer' or 'the reconciler' seems to indicate, a specific location in space and time is
indispensable to an actual identifying description of this person
(namely, of Jesus Christ). That is, the concepts used in the
description may be entirely appropriate to Jesus (for example,
'teacher', 'worker of miracles', 'crucified'), and they may be

worked out with some precision. But as long as the element of spatio-temporal reference is lacking (for example, 'in the days of Tiberius Caesar', 'a place called Golgotha', 'between two thieves'), the conceptual description alone need not identify Jesus; it is always possible and conceivable that the merely conceptual description applies to someone else, in a different place or time. The demonstrative element alone, of course, does not constitute an identifying description. It is this element, however, which definitively distinguishes an identifying description of 'the redeemer' from a general conceptual characterization of what it is to be 'the redeemer', even when such a characterization is materially quite complex and detailed (as is, for example, Rahner's conception of an 'absolute saviour', or Barth's idea of 'the judge judged in our place').[32] The non-identifying nature of these conceptual characterizations means that they are not by themselves adequate to serve as accounts of reconciliation, although they are, of course, necessary to such accounts. Any account of reconciliation, it seems, must in some way include an identifying description of Jesus Christ, some element (especially a demonstrative one) which introduces his particular history. Only in this manner, Barth will maintain, can theology honour the pre-systematic assumption that 'reconciliation is Jesus Christ's own history'.

Barth himself is clear that no conceptual characterization of redemption or reconciliation can serve as an identifying description of Jesus Christ. At the outset of his entire theology of reconciliation, he points out that his own preliminary characterization of reconciliation as 'God with us', does not speak 'with the concreteness with which it ["God with us"] is said at the heart of the Christian message . . . and with which it must also be said at the heart of dogmatics'.[33] This preliminary characterization is insufficiently concrete precisely because it does not introduce Jesus Christ as a particular person, to whose name, as I have shown, every concept pertinent to reconciliation is 'strictly and indissolubly' bound. Barth also stresses the lack of identifying force in this kind of characterization when he insists that no concept or principle can be a legitimate *substitute* for the name and description of Jesus Christ in talk about reconciliation.[34]

3   Descriptions of the divinity of Jesus Christ, the incarnation or immediate presence of God in him, bear a peculiar relation to the

other two elements in Barth's theology of reconciliation which are central to the issue at hand. At first glance, these might seem to be simply further characterizations of Jesus' significance, logically no different from those considered under point 2 above. That is, the immediate presence of God is a predicate of Jesus as a particular subject, which aims to signal something significant for salvation. He is the obedient Son of God, gone 'into the far country' for the sake of sinners (IV/1, §59), and in that very obedience he is 'true man', exalted into fellowship with God (IV/2, §64). Here as before, Barth maintains that these predicates (*vere Deus* and *vere homo*), in their irreversible order and material relation, are in reality identical with and therefore properly knowable 'only as the being and the history of the one Jesus Christ'.[35] The predicate 'truly God', however, has a distinctive function in relation to the particular identity of its subject, Jesus Christ, and also in relation to the characterizations of redemption and a redeemer which are applied to him:

(a)   The human history in which Jesus Christ has his particular identity is God's own history. Precisely in its particularity, in its distinctive shape and unique location in space and time, 'the way from Bethlehem to Golgotha' is God's own way. 'God Himself is the One who lives here, who is engaged in the actualization (*Verwirklichung*) of His being, who is the free Subject of this occurrence. But it is God Himself as this one man, as the Bearer of his definite human name, and as the free subject of his human decisions, resolves, and actions.'[36] This is not, to be sure, self-evident. That this story of human suffering, humiliation and obedience is also the story of God's own suffering, humiliation and obedience is the mystery or secret (*das Geheimnis*) of the existence of Jesus Christ.[37] But recognition of that mystery is necessary on Barth's account in order to appreciate the history itself. For Jesus' history, and thus his particular identity, is the history of God in a radical sense: it comes to pass precisely as the enactment of God's original, eternal and free decision about who he is, about what it is to be God. The very meaning of the term 'God' is not available in an abstract conceptual description; it necessarily includes and is determined by reference to the history of Jesus Christ.

The primal history [namely, of Jesus Christ], and with it the covenant, are . . . the attitude and relation in which by virtue of the decision of his free love God wills to be and is God. And this relation cannot be separated (*nicht zu lösen ist*) from the Christian conception of God as such.[38]

God's being and identity, Barth holds, are self-determined, and God's primal self-determination (*Selbstbestimmung*) is to be this particular person, or to 'posit' this human history as his own.[39] 'The way from Bethlehem to Golgotha' is God's original self-determination and self-definition, which cannot be separated or abstracted from his being as God. He is the ultimate subject of this history, although not its only subject. For this reason, that particular history can be properly appreciated only when it is recognized as God's own.[40]

(b) Descriptions of the immediate presence or incarnation of God in Jesus Christ also have a special function with regard to the characterizations of redemption or reconciliation which are applied to him. As has just been seen, descriptions of Jesus' divinity serve for Barth to indicate the ultimate subject of the history in which Jesus' particular identity consists. This history, in turn, has the universal significance which Christians ascribe to it because it is, in its very particularity, God's own history. 'The way from Bethlehem to Golgotha', which culminates in Jesus' resurrection, can be 'ontically and noetically' identical with the reconciliation of the world to God because this history is constitutive not only of Jesus' particular identity, but also of God's. Reconciliation must be characterized, of course, in a variety of different ways and Jesus' divinity will have a different function in each case, depending upon what aspect of reconciliation is under consideration. In each case, however, the immediate presence of God as the ultimate subject of his history will be an indispensable condition of the application of these characterizations to Jesus Christ as a particular person. Barth rarely says this in so many words. But the basic relation between (a) Jesus' particular identity, (b) reconciliation and (c) incarnation is succinctly, if not runically, stated when he writes '[a] He becomes and is real man, he is *there* as man, in that [b] God as the helper of each every man [c] is *there* in him.'[41] Thus both of the following statements are true for Barth; indeed, the first implies the second: first, the history in which Jesus Christ has his particular identity is the reconciliation of the world because God is its primary subject. Second, God reconciles the world to himself by becoming the subject of this particular history.[42]

Thus, on Barth's account, the immediate presence of God in Jesus Christ is integral to both Jesus' particularity and his universal significance. It is ingredient in each, however, in the order and relation they have to one another; descriptions of Jesus' divinity confirm the priority of his narrated particularity and the dependence of concepts of his significance in accounts of reconciliation. The primary task of an attempt to articulate the argument of the first way is therefore to examine this relation of priority and dependence in detail, since it is the means by which Barth attempts to give an account of reconciliation consistent with the conviction that Jesus is the reconciler or redeemer as a particular person. More specifically, how Barth uses Jesus' particular history as the one criterion of 'significance for salvation' will have to be examined. It is precisely by doing this that Barth frees himself consistently to ascribe various characterizations of redemption and a redeemer to Jesus as a particular person, and only to him.

Excursus: 'God fully defined in Jesus'

This maximalist construal of the idea that who and what God is, 'is fully defined in Jesus', first assumes a central position in Barth's theology of election (II/2).[43] This centrality will not only be retained, but amplified, in the further development of the *Dogmatics*. It is, of course, anticipated before II/2, and indeed before the *Dogmatics* itself:

> The Word of God does not just come to us through the man Jesus of Nazareth, as though we could later have heard it and known it in itself and apart from him. The Word of God is this man as man, and always and inescapably it is spoken to us as the reality of this man and not otherwise. This is God's mercy, that precisely in the reality, no, as the reality of this man, God is Immanuel, God with us, God among us.'[44]

Once he began the *Church Dogmatics*, Barth stopped commenting on further changes of direction in his theology, although he continued to remark often on those which preceded the onset of the *Dogmatics*. It might be argued, however, that 'The Doctrine of Election' marks a material relocation in Barth's theology commensurate in magnitude to the breaks with liberalism and dialectical theology, which were more methodological in character. Only when he begins to apply consistently in a wide variety of contexts (especially in the doctrine of God) the sort of contention already found in the *Ethics* lectures, so the argument would go, does he rigorously practice the 'method' upon which he later insists – to orientate oneself afresh in each question on the person Jesus Christ, rather than on a systematic principle or concept (as 'revelation' may have functioned earlier, even in parts of II/1).

BARTH'S ACCOUNT OF 'REDEMPTIVE DEATH'

The best way to trace the distinctive logic of the first way, especially in a theology as little interested in building theories as Barth's, is to look at a salient example of the way Jesus' particular identity functions in an account of his significance. Barth's discussion of Jesus' passion and death, in the context of his account of 'the judge judged in our place' (IV/1, §59.2), is especially well suited for this purpose. There are two reasons for this. On the one hand, the logic of Barth's procedure on the issue with which I am concerned is perhaps at its clearest here. For that reason, I have preferred to direct my attention primarily to this section, rather than to his characterizations of Jesus Christ as 'the royal man' and 'the victor', although the argument is basically the same in each case. On the other hand, it is in his characterization of 'redemptive (or reconciling) death' as 'the judge judged in our place' that the difference between Barth's procedure and Rahner's is most readily apparent. Rahner's account of reconciling or redeeming death, to recall, is the point in his Christology which seems to hold the greatest promise for remaining consistent with the assumption that Jesus' own life and death are redemptive *als solche*, since he there foregoes any explicit appeal to a transcendental reading of 'redeeming death'. But even at this point, I have argued, Rahner does not proceed in a way consistent with that assumption in that, still adhering to the argumentative structure of the second way, he gives an account of redeeming death which fails to include identifying reference to, or description of, Jesus Christ.[45]

The task here cannot be to examine in detail what Barth means when he calls Jesus Christ 'the judge judged in our place', although I will try to make the outlines of this characterization plain. Rather, the guiding question is, how does this become a genuine characterization of reconciliation or redemption and thus of that which is 'significant for salvation'? On what basis does 'the judge judged in our place' indicate a reality or event which is *heilsbedeutsam*?

Barth begins his account of 'the judge judged in our place' by issuing a reminder: the history of Jesus Christ is an event which took place at a specific place and time in the past. We must speak of the reconciliation which occurs when the judge suffers 'in our place and for us' as something which 'came to pass'; we must speak 'as we do when we tell the story (*Geschichte*) of something that happened in the world at a definite (*bestimmter*) place and a definite point in time'.[46] Jesus' history (that is, his particular identity), especially its ostensible aspect, is not the 'beginning' of Barth's account in the sense that he opens his presentation with it, but in the sense that it is logically presupposed in all of the account. Only that which can be said to have happened there and then (*illic et tunc*, as Barth unfailingly puts it), 'before the gates of Jerusalem in the days of Tiberius Caesar', is logically capable of being included in an account of 'redemptive death'.[47]

Jesus' history is not only capable of being pointed to, it is capable of being described. It is the cumulative sequence of actions and events which make up 'the way from Bethlehem to Golgotha', and constitute Jesus' particular identity. This sequence exhibits a variety of patterns, Barth maintains, one of which is especially important for the characterization of reconciliation as 'the judge judged in our place'. As it is presented in the synoptic Gospels, the initial and largest part of this history is that of 'the sayings and acts of Jesus Christ in His entry into and life in Galilee within the wider and narrower circle of his disciples, the multitudes and the spiritual and (on the margin) political leaders of the people'.[48] It is characteristic of this part of 'the way from Bethlehem to Golgotha' that Jesus 'stands out in marked contrast (*Gegensatz*) to this whole world of man'.[49] In the actions and events of this part of Jesus' history, 'there has passed through the midst of all these men one

who is absolutely superior to them, exalted above them, and
fearfully alone'.[50] Indeed, where Jesus' words and works confront
and bring to light a 'world of man' which is 'blind and deaf and
lame . . . even dead', there 'the Lord has been among them', and
'has shown himself their Judge, the One for whom not one of them
was a match'.[51] Beginning around the entry into Jerusalem, Barth
sees a striking change of direction in Jesus' history. Jesus' own
words and works cease to dominate his history; it is now characteristic of 'the way from Bethlehem to Golgotha' that 'Jesus no
longer seems to be the subject but the object of what happens. His
speech is almost exclusively that of silence and his work that of
suffering'.[52]

In a separate exegetical excursus, Barth holds that the decisive
point of transition to this unexpected second part of Jesus' history
is the prayer in the garden of Gethsemane. Jesus' prayer is 'the
establishment of his definitive willingness (*Bereitschaft*) for the real
passion which comes upon him immediately after'; Jesus here
remains obedient to God, accepting the radical change of direction in which his history now aims at imminent suffering and
death.[53] When this suffering and death actually come to pass in
Jesus' trial, passion and crucifixion, Barth concludes, 'there is, in
fact, a complete reversal, an exchange of roles. Those who are to be
judged are given space and freedom and power to judge. The
judge allows himself to be judged.'[54] On Barth's account, this is
one pattern clearly exhibited by Jesus' history: in willing
obedience, the judge of all persons becomes judged by them.[55]

I have quoted Barth at some length in order to help make plain
the logical status of the notion of 'the judge who is judged'. It is a
description of Jesus' particular history, in a straightforward and
obvious sense: applied to Jesus as a predicate, it characterizes him
in an appropriate way. The precise nature of its descriptive force
must be carefully noted. A phrase like 'the judge judged in our
place' can indeed function as a description of the history or particular identity of Jesus Christ but it necessarily does so in a
derivative way. Its force as a description of Jesus depends upon the
ostensive and descriptive elements by which Jesus can be
identified as a particular person and to which the characterization
can be appropriately applied. When the judge of all accepts judgement in our place, Barth writes, 'we are dealing with an act which
took place on earth, in time and space, and which is indissolubly

linked with the name of a certain (*bestimmten*) man'.[56] Thus at each point in his development and application of the idea of 'the judge judged', Barth appeals to a particularizing feature of Jesus' life which warrants the ascription of the predicate. Jesus 'judges', is 'obedient' and 'suffers judgement' when he preaches, teaches and works miracles in Galilee, prays in Gethsemane and dies on the cross at Golgotha. In each case, on Barth's account, the predicate clearly and straightforwardly applies to Jesus; in a derivative and dependent way, it describes his history, and thus an aspect of his particular identity.

So for Barth the history of Jesus Christ is in fact the history of the judge of the world, who allows himself to be judged by the world. Or, to put the same point from the opposite perspective, in a theology of reconciliation, 'the judge judged' characterizes a particular history, which took place at a specific place and time and under a definite description; it characterizes 'the way from Bethlehem to Golgotha'. As I have indicated though, the history of Jesus Christ in all its particularity is God's own history; it not only 'defines' who Jesus is but also who God is.[57] Since God is the primary and ultimate subject of this history, God himself is 'the judge judged in our place'. By defining himself in Jesus' way from Bethlehem to Golgotha, God 'willed to make good [our] affronting and disturbing of His majesty, this devastating of His work, not by avenging Himself on its author, but by Himself bearing the inevitable wrath and perdition (*Unheilsfolge*) . . . which, if it had fallen upon man, could only have obliterated and destroyed him'.[58] When the 'exchange of roles' took place on the way from Bethlehem to Golgotha and Jesus accepted suffering and death in obedience to the Father, 'what took place is that the Son of God fulfilled the righteous judgement on us men by Himself taking our place as man and in our place undergoing the judgement under which we had passed'.[59] The saving event which comes to pass when the Son of God accepts the judgement due to sinners is primarily negative in character and so constitutes only one aspect of the reality of reconciliation. The Son of God who identified himself with Jesus of Nazareth 'blocked the source of our destruction', not, Barth argues, 'by suffering our punishment as such, but in the deliverance of sinful man and sin itself to destruction, which he accomplished when he suffered our punishment'.[60]

For the present purposes, the crucial point in the way Barth unfolds the idea of 'the judge judged in our place' is that what this phrase describes would not be a saving event for us, in which sin is conquered and our destruction blocked, if it could not be truly and properly ascribed to God himself, and if God were not the primary and ultimate subject of this event. Here, as in different ways throughout the theology of reconciliation

we have to do with a definite (*bestimmtes*) action of the Son of God. It has been carried through (*vollzogen*) by Him in His unity with the man Jesus of Nazareth, in our midst and as one of us, but it has been carried through also in the power of God and therefore effectively. And (because in this power it applies to all men) it is in force and effective for all men.[61]

THE LOGICAL INDISPENSABILITY OF JESUS CHRIST

The place of Jesus Christ as a particular person in an account of redemption and a redeemer stands out clearly in the way Barth handles 'the judge judged in our place'. With important material variations, Barth follows essentially the same procedure throughout his theology of reconciliation. That procedure can be summarized as follows. (1) 'The judge judged in our place' qualifies as a description of reconciliation and a reconciler, and so of that which is *heilsbedeutsam*, because it is true of God. (2) 'The judge judged' is true of God because it is true of the particular person (a) whose history is God's own, and (b) of whom 'the judge judged' is a fit but derivative and dependent description. (3) That person is Jesus Christ. (4) Therefore, an identifying description of Jesus Christ is not only included in, but is logically indispensable to, this account of reconciliation and a reconciler (and, *mutatis mutandis*, to any such account).

The specific question with which we are here concerned, it will be recalled, is that of the basis upon which 'the judge judged in our place' succeeds in being a characterization of reconciliation. Or, to put the question a bit more broadly, how does any concept or idea succeed in designating that which is *heilsbedeutsam*? The heart of Barth's answer to this question is already clear. As his treatment of 'the judge judged' indicates, Jesus Christ as a particular person is in practice necessarily ingredient in any account of reconciliation. Jesus Christ is logically indispensable to such accounts in a precise way. A concept or pattern like 'the judge judged' can count as a characterization of reconciliation, or, more generally, of a saving reality, because and in so far as it can be applied to Jesus Christ, that is, because and in so far as it can be an apt characterization of his particular history, which is as such God's own history. Jesus Christ as a particular person is therefore logically indispensable to an account of reconciliation in a radical sense: only because of him, as the subject to whom it is applied, can any concept function as a characterization of reconciliation. It is by being fitly applied to Jesus Christ that 'the judge judged in our place', or any potential characterization of reconciliation, actually succeeds in being *heilsbedeutsam*. In order to see the force of this conclusion the way in which Barth arrives at it must be examined more closely.

As I have shown, Barth shares with Rahner the assumption that Jesus Christ as a particular person is *heilsbedeutsam*, and with it the requirement that any theological explication or justification of 'that which is *heilsbedeutsam*' must be consistent with this assumption. To be sure, Barth uses the language of 'significance' (*Bedeutsamkeit*) relatively infrequently and unprogrammatically, preferring to speak instead simply of 'reconciliation'. But 'reconciliation' (including its background in 'election') often has basically the same role in his theology as 'significance for salvation' has for Rahner. It denotes the function which any conceptual characterization of Jesus Christ (for example, 'absolute saviour', 'the judge judged in our place') aims to serve – namely to designate a universally significant saving reality. The precise sense of the shared assumption that Jesus Christ 'as a particular person' is *heilsbedeutsam* needs special emphasis. As was indicated in connection with Rahner, it means that only Jesus Christ, and no one else, can be ultimately significant or *heilsbedeutsam*. This follows from the perhaps more manifest assumption that any specific characterization of redemption and a redeemer can apply only to Jesus Christ. If these characterizations (for example, 'absolute saviour') are distinguished from other concepts by the fact that they signify something *heilsbedeutsam*, and they can only apply to Jesus Christ, then only Jesus Christ can be *heilsbedeutsam*. The crucial question, of course, is on what grounds an 'absolute saviour', or any cognate notion, can be itself *heilsbedeutsam*.

No concept of redemption and a redeemer, Barth points out, can possibly constitute an identifying description of Jesus Christ. No matter how great the detail in which they are elaborated, such concepts lack the demonstrative or ostensive element by which we can definitively locate or identify a particular person. As I have shown, it is precisely the presence of this demonstrative element which primarily distinguishes an identifying description of Jesus Christ from those conceptual characterizations of his significance which, while perhaps materially fit for him, could always in principle apply to someone else.[62] Concepts of redemption and a redeemer, like 'the judge judged in our place', also lack sufficient descriptive definiteness to allow us to identify Jesus Christ. The line between a general concept and an identifying description is more difficult to draw in a satisfactory way here, where it is only a matter of the relative definiteness of concepts, than it is where the demonstrative aspect of particulars and their identification is invoked. This is because concepts ordinarily can be made 'definite' enough to describe a particular (assuming, of course, that the requisite demonstrative elements are already present or implied). For purposes here, however, it is sufficient to recall that Barth could only apply the concept of 'the judge judged in our place' to Jesus Christ on the basis of various more definite descriptions of actions and events, by which Jesus was actually identified. For this reason, 'the judge judged in our place' is a derivative and dependent, rather than a primary and identifying, description of Jesus Christ. Barth is well aware that by itself 'the judge judged' cannot function as an identifying description of Jesus Christ, due to its lack of demonstrative force and descriptive definiteness. It could logically apply to another individual. 'The history of religious and cultic speculation knows of other suffering and dying gods, and the similarity of "the judge judged" with these pictures forces itself upon our attention.'[63]

The assumption shared by the first and second ways, and specifically by Barth and Rahner, is that only Jesus Christ can be ultimately significant for salvation. Jesus Christ is *heilsbedeutsam*, in other words, precisely as a particular person and thus as the subject of an identifying description. As it stands, Barth argues, 'the judge judged in our place', or any conceptual characterization of redemption and a redeemer, is logically excluded from functioning as a description of Jesus Christ as a particular person, that is, as an identifying description. Therefore, a concept like 'the judge judged', standing by itself, cannot possibly signify something 'significant for salvation'. Only that which in some way describes Jesus Christ as a particular person can be *heilsbedeutsam*, but the mere concept of 'the judge judged', or 'the absolute saviour', does not describe Jesus Christ. It can describe him, of course, but it only does so when it is actually applied to him, ostensively and descriptively identified, in a proposition. A concept like 'the judge judged' therefore becomes *heilsbedeutsam* by being applied to Jesus Christ. Or, more broadly, general, non-identifying concepts can signal something significant for salvation only because and in so far as they are applicable to Jesus Christ. This means that any reality is significant for salvation only on account of its being, in some respect, included or ingredient in the life, death and resurrection of Jesus Christ. So Barth says

> That it took place at this time and place as this history is what distinguishes the passion, crucifixion, and death of this one Jew [that is, 'the judge judged'] from all other occurrences in time and space with which the passion of Jesus Christ is otherwise similar in every respect. Distinguished in this way, it [that is, the passion as the event of 'the judge judged'] is the subject of Christian faith and proclamation.[64]

Thus Barth rejects the idea that the reality of reconciliation, or of that which is *heilsbedeutsam*, can be expressed in a concept alone. It can be expressed only in a proposition, of which Jesus Christ as a particular person is the logical subject. Concepts of redemption and a redeemer, by contrast, express and describe a saving reality only as predicates of Jesus Christ.[65] Barth seldom bothers to state this explicitly. Early in I/2, however, he clearly summarizes the position he will take in practice throughout the *Church Dogmatics*, especially in 'The Doctrine of Reconciliation'. The sorts of concepts the New Testament writers apply to Jesus Christ, Barth contends, 'would be but marginal and transient, if interpreted as the proclamation of a principle, idea, or general truth – but ... literally everything is central and fundamental and eternal, the moment it is interpreted as the predicate in an utterance about Jesus Christ.'[66]

THE MATERIAL DECISIVENESS OF JESUS CHRIST

General concepts and characterizing expressions, Barth argues, successfully denote that which is *heilsbedeutsam* in virtue of their application, explicit or implied, to Jesus Christ. Not every concept, however, is a fit and appropriate predicate of Jesus Christ. In various ways, concepts can fail to be materially fit for application to this particular subject, even when there is no strictly logical barrier to such application. Or, to put the point in grammatical terms, a predication can be syntactically possible while being semantically inappropriate. Barth's theology of reconciliation, and especially his treatment of 'the judge judged in our place', includes at least two criteria of material fitness for concepts which are to be *heilsbedeutsam*, that is, for predicates of Jesus Christ. They are essential to his way of accounting in theology for the 'material decisiveness' of Jesus Christ for the Christian belief in redemption and a redeemer (as I put the issue in my discussion of Rahner). They complement his argument that the 'logical indispensability' of Jesus Christ is best maintained in theology by making application to Jesus Christ the condition or criterion of significance for salvation.

1 In order for a concept of redemption and a redeemer to be materially fit for application to Jesus Christ, and so to be *heilsbedeutsam*, there must first of all be some specific feature or pattern of features in Jesus' particular identity which warrants the · application or ascription. I will call this simply the criterion of 'descriptive aptness'; that is, to use language employed earlier, such concepts must contribute something to a description of Jesus Christ as a particular person, even though they cannot be counted on to identify him on their own. 'The judged judged in our place' is a striking example of this criterion in action. There is, so Barth argues, a distinctive, prominent and central pattern of specific actions and events in Jesus' history which can be aptly described as a transition from judging to suffering judgement. A concept like 'the judge judged' is especially 'apt' as a characterization of recon-

ciliation or redemption precisely because of the clarity and force with which it describes a pattern of Jesus' particular life, passion and death. A concept of reconciliation is materially fit, as this example indicates, in so far as it captures and summarizes the features, or patterns of action and event, which particularize Jesus Christ and distinguish him from all other persons.[67] The better suited a concept is to Jesus, and thereby (typically, if not with necessity) the less readily it fits other persons, the more apt it is as a predicate of him, and therefore as a designation of that which is *heilsbedeutsam*.

To be sure, the concepts alone (including 'the judge judged') do not identify Jesus; it is always logically possible for them to apply to someone else.[68] In this case, that logical possibility may seem remote and perhaps somewhat forced, since 'the judge judged' seems so well suited to Jesus' distinctive history or particular identity.[69] However, the more general concepts which aim to signal something 'ultimately meaningful' become and the less distinctively they are suited to Jesus as distinguished from other persons, the more obvious the logical possibility of their application to someone else becomes. To that same degree, Barth argues, they become less appropriate as characterizations of reconciliation or redemption. As I have shown, this was the peculiar difficulty of Rahner's attempt to conceptualize the saving significance of Jesus' crucifixion and resurrection. His accounts of crucifixion as 'complete self-surrender to the mystery of God in death', and of resurrection as 'the presence of eternal validity' *could* be applied to Jesus as saving predicates in a Christology structured like Barth's (though not, I have argued, in Rahner's own). They are so general and abstract, however, that they could just as readily apply to another person as to Jesus. Indeed, they are constructed with just the aim of achieving such a high level of generality; it is only by conforming to and realizing the general pattern evinced in Jesus' death that other persons can achieve salvation. Consequently, although it is logically possible for such characterizations to be applied to Jesus Christ, their lack of descriptive aptness renders them at best, even given such application, only minimally useful and appropriate accounts of 'that which is significant for salvation'.[70]

2 At least some of the characterizations of redemption and a redeemer will have the force of 'logically individuating' char-

acterizations.[71] A characterization is logically individuating when it bears some mark (such as 'the first . . .', 'the last . . .', 'the only . . .', or simply 'the') which signals that it has a single, unique application, even though it is not intrinsically capable of actually identifying the subject to which it applies. Such characterizations, when appropriately applied, will logically distinguish their bearer or subject from all other persons. 'The judge judged in our place' is manifestly a logically individuating characterization, in two senses. The definite article alone announces its uniqueness of application. More importantly though, the characterization itself is logically individuating in content: it at once distinguishes 'the judge judged' from all other persons, in whose 'place' he accepts judgement and suffering, and it relates him to all others in a specific way.[72] While 'the judge judged in our place' is by itself insufficiently definite to identify Jesus Christ, when it is applied to Jesus as a characterization of his significance, it distinguishes him as the bearer of that significance from all other persons with exceptional clarity. For just this reason, it is especially appropriate as a conceptual characterization of that which is significant for salvation.

For Barth, application to Jesus Christ makes any characterization of redemption and a redeemer actually *heilsbedeutsam*. Thus applicability to Jesus Christ as a particular person is the decisive criterion for that which is significant for salvation. 'Jesus Christ as a particular person', however, means 'Jesus Christ in so far as he is distinguished from all other persons'. Accordingly characterizations of redemption and a redeemer which not only are descriptively apt for predication of Jesus Christ, but which also logically distinguish their bearer from all other persons, are especially well-suited to express the nature of that which is significant for salvation in general, conceptual terms. It is this kind of characterization, Barth argues, which enables one to give a theological account of reconciliation that not only honours, but maximalizes, the conviction that Jesus Christ is ultimately significant for salvation precisely as a particular person.[73]

A comparison with Rahner is again instructive. Rahner rejects *stellvertretende Erlösung* as a characterization of Jesus' redeeming significance because it cannot possibly be a general pattern, applicable to many individuals, of which Jesus can be said to be the first. Obviously, Rahner's contention that only a general pattern with a series of instances can be *heilsbedeutsam* excludes any logically individuating concepts from the domain of significance for salvation; such concepts have only one application or 'instance'. Of course, Rahner can and does qualify the general pattern so that it counts as a logically individuating conception. Thus, *'the first* act of complete self-surrender to the mystery of God in death' has unique redeeming significance for all subsequent instances of the same pattern. While any expression qualified by 'the first . . .' is formally a logically individuating one, on Rahner's account such an expression can signify something *heilsbedeutsam* only if the pattern it contains is repeatable. With 'the first instance of self-surrender to God in death', as opposed to 'the judge judged in our place', the pattern itself is not logically individuating, but only the qualification of the pattern.[74]

By taking applicability to Jesus Christ as the decisive criterion of significance for salvation, Barth clears the way for the use of logically individuating concepts (such as those which involve notions of 'substitution', 'representation', 'exchange', or 'satisfaction') in characterizing redemption and a redeemer. There is at least no logical barrier to the intelligibility of such concepts in Christology. Rahner, by contrast, inevitably finds such concepts unintelligible in a christological context (that is, not possibly *heilsbedeutsam*) regardless of the specific content they might have, because he has erected a logical barrier to their use. The decisive criterion of significance for salvation lies in the anthropological claim that persons are by concrete nature transcendentally oriented towards ultimate fulfilment in God. Only the various patterns by which this fulfilment is achieved can be *heilsbedeutsam*. Since these are precisely the patterns by which human nature comes to fulfilment in any given case, they are necessarily general and repeatable. Therefore no saving pattern can be instrinsically logically individuating; the peculiar significance which attaches to the first instance of these patterns (that is, to the 'absolute saviour') cannot alter their essential generality and repeatability.

Not all materially fit characterizations of redemption need be logically individuating, and on that account applicable only to Jesus Christ (although they are significant for salvation only in that application). It is sufficient for them to be descriptively apt; thus Barth develops characterizations of reconciliation which

apply not only to Jesus Christ but to all who have been transform-
ed by his reconciling work. For example, Barth detects in the
particular history of Jesus Christ a pattern of faithfulness and
obedience to God which prompts him to characterize that history
and, therefore, reconciliation, as 'the exaltation of the Son of
Man'. As a redemptive event, of course, 'the exaltation of the Son
of Man' happens only on the way from Bethlehem to Golgotha and
in this sense can be said only of Jesus Christ. 'Exaltation means
the history in which this movement [of faithfulness and
obedience] takes place, in which this man is man. When we say
"Jesus Christ", we can say only "the humiliation of the Son of
God", but this is also to say, "the exaltation of the Son of
God", but this is also to say, "the exaltation of the Son of Man"'.[75]
However, not only Jesus is 'exalted'; we are as well. In the redemptive exaltation which is his history, 'our own has already taken
place'.[76] Yet for Barth 'exaltation' does not, as similar notions
clearly do for Rahner, denote a class of like instances, of which the
redemptive instance is simply that which is first in the series and
unsurpassable in degree. While both Jesus and we are 'exalted',
we are not exalted in the same sense as Jesus is. The difference
between Jesus' exaltation and ours is not simply that ours depends
upon his, nor does it lie simply in the fact that his faithfulness and
obedience to God are perfect and complete, while ours are
inevitably imperfect and incomplete (in both cases Rahner would
agree). For Barth, 'exaltation' stands for a redemptive event
precisely on account of its application to Jesus Christ. Consequently, the particular history of Jesus Christ, the actions and
events on the way from Bethlehem to Golgotha, perfectly coincide
with the redemptive sense of 'exaltation', and thus with the notion
of 'complete faithfulness and obedience'. As Barth says, the
concepts we apply to Jesus Christ ultimately 'derive their meaning
(*Sinn*) only from the bearer of this name and from his history, and
not the reverse'.[77]

The concept of 'complete faithfulness and obedience to God' is
not, of course, wholly meaningless in abstraction from its application to Jesus Christ. But the concept has the full contours of its
meaning only in that application, that is, in connection with the
subject whose particular identity perfectly instantiates the
concept. It is, in other words, not only part of the theological
grammar of concepts like 'exaltation' that they apply to us only in
an imperfect and derivative sense, but that they *describe* their con-

tent (precisely in its perfect and primary sense) only in so far as they are simultaneously *ascribed* to a particular person, namely Jesus Christ. It is in this way that the particular identity of Jesus Christ is ultimately inseparable from the sense or meaning of 'complete faithfulness and obedience'. Our own faithfulness and obedience, and thus our 'exaltation', are consequently not a matter of fitting a general pattern, but of being conformed in our own way to the particular life of Jesus Christ. 'Exaltation' as a characterization of redemption is an analogical term rather than a class name. It has its primary sense in its application to Jesus Christ, its secondary and dependent sense in its application to us. In the exaltation of Jesus Christ, in other words, 'there is proto-typically modelled (*exemplarisch vorgebildet*) and dynamically grounded what occurs and is to be known as exaltation in the reconciliation of man with God'.[78]

CONCLUSION: BARTH AND RAHNER ON 'SIGNIFICANCE FOR SALVATION'

Barth's argument about how any reality can be 'significant for salvation' is now before us, at least in its basic outline. It is a remarkably consistent version of the first way. For just that reason, it seems especially successful at answering the question, 'how can Jesus Christ be *heilsbedeutsam?*', in a way which is consistent with the assumption that the status and significance of the unique redeemer can belong only to Jesus Christ as a particular person. Barth argues that a concept can successfully characterize redemption and a redeemer, and thus 'that which is ultimately significant', only by being fitly applied to Jesus Christ. Or, to put the point in more ontological terms, something can be significant for salvation only when it is in some way included in, or a part of, the particular identity of Jesus Christ.

Not every concept can be *fitly* applied to Jesus Christ, or designate a genuine aspect of his particular identity. Identifying descriptions of Jesus Christ provide the criteria of descriptive aptness for potential characterizations of redemption and a redeemer. Such characterizations as are not only descriptively apt but also logically individuating are especially well suited to expressing Jesus' significance, since they distinguish their bearer from all other persons, and *per assumptionem* Jesus is the unique redeemer precisely in so far as he is distinguished from all other persons. Thus on Barth's account applicability to Jesus Christ is both formally and materially the criterion of significance for salvation. Therein lies his success at showing how Jesus Christ can be *heilsbedeutsam* while honouring (indeed, maximalizing) the assumption that he and Rahner share. If Jesus Christ himself is the ultimate *criterion* of significance for salvation, it is logically impossible for any account of redemption and a redeemer to honour the criterion of significance for salvation without also honouring the assumption that Jesus Christ has this status and significance precisely as a particular person, and that characterizations of redemption and a redeemer can apply only to him.

Rahner, together with the second way generally, proceeds in the opposite fashion. For Rahner, the fact that a concept is fitly predicated of Jesus Christ is not a sufficient basis for it to designate something 'significant for salvation'. The only sufficient basis of significance for salvation is conformity to general, non-identifying criteria. In his case, the notion of a universal transcendental orientation to ultimate fulfilment serves this function, but the criteria need be neither anthropological nor transcendental.[79] It is their generality, as the logically necessary basis of their putative universality, which is decisive on the issue of significance for salvation. Only by conforming to a criterion of this kind can a concept of redemption and a redeemer (like 'the absolute saviour') succeed in being significant for salvation. Neither such concepts nor the criteria that validate their significance actually identify and describe Jesus Christ as a particular person.[80] Therefore, a notion like 'absolute saviour' will be unfolded and its saving significance accounted for without including reference to, or an identifying description of, Jesus Christ. This omission is not accidental but necessary. Since general terms alone cannot constitute an identifying description, any account of that which is significant for salvation in general terms alone will fail to include Jesus Christ as a particular person.

This, however, seems directly opposed to the assumption with which both sides are working. If Jesus Christ is significant for salvation as a particular person, there can be no account of that which is significant for salvation that fails to include his particularity. To be sure, Rahner insists that whatever is taken to be significant for salvation on the basis of general criteria should be applied only to Jesus. But because such characterizations of redemption and a redeemer lack identifying or particularizing force, they *could* equally well be applied to an indefinite number of other persons, real or imaginary. The assumption, however, is that only Jesus Christ can be the absolute saviour, or can have ultimate redeeming significance. It is therefore logically impossible for an account of that which is significant for salvation which is justified on the basis of conformity to general criteria to be consistent with this conviction.[81]

The question with which I began this attempt to come to grips with Rahner's Christology, and to which Barth gives an answer contrary to Rahner's, is, 'how can Jesus Christ be *heilsbedeutsam?*'. Barth's way of handling this question, I have argued, is basically successful: it is both internally coherent and consistent with the assumption that only Jesus Christ, this particular person, is ultimately *heilsbedeutsam*. I have not, of course, argued that Barth's answer is the only one or even the best one, but simply that, exemplifying the first way, it is a successful one. Rahner's, I have argued, is not: it is internally coherent only at the price of being inconsistent with that basic assumption, to which he is as committed as Barth. But Rahner, or anyone committed to the second way, might well wonder whether Barth has really answered the question at all.

Heilsbedeutsam means, as I have pointed out, 'meaningful', 'intelligible' and 'existentially accessible'. By making Jesus Christ himself the ultimate criterion of significance for salvation, Rahner might argue, Barth has paid an unacceptable price for honouring the conviction about Jesus' particularity. As I have analysed his Christology, Barth deliberately avoids grounding his explication of how Jesus Christ can be *heilsbedeutsam* in a description of our subjective appropriation of Jesus' particular story as something which is ultimately meaningful for us. But for Rahner, such a description is indispensable at this point. Any viable explication of Jesus' meaningfulness or significance for us must proceed precisely by giving a general description of what human subjects find ultimately meaningful and thus by isolating the subjective conditions for our appropriation of an 'absolute saviour'. In a modern world which has grown tired of the Christian story, people will never take belief in Jesus Christ seriously, Rahner assumes, **unless it can be made plausible to them that they are already 'on** the lookout' for what Christians claim Jesus brings – quite apart from whether they are convinced that he actually brings it. It is just this assumption which leads Rahner into a Christology which is fundamentally inconsistent with his convictions about the unique and exclusive significance of Jesus Christ. But even granted this fundamental problem, Rahner might argue, the confrontation between the first and the second ways is at best a standoff. The second way may lose the particularity of Jesus in an attempt to make him meaningful and intelligible for us, but the first way presents a particular person who is the answer to a question no one asks; who is, along with the significance we ascribe to him, meaningless and inaccessible to us.

Barth in fact devotes the greater part of 'The Doctrine of Reconciliation' to describing various aspects of our subjective appropriation of Jesus Christ and his ultimate significance. The event of reconciliation, as the particular life of Jesus Christ *extra nos*, is itself *pro nobis*; it effects and includes our justification, sanctification and calling. And it is capable of realizing itself *in nobis*, both corporately (in the gathering, upbuilding and sending of the Christian community) and individually (in the faith, love and hope of the Christian). The details of all this, that is, of the exceedingly complex (and sometimes needlessly obscure) description of the set of relations between Jesus Christ *extra nos*, *pro nobis* and *in nobis*, is not our concern here; a full discussion of the process by which we appropriate Jesus' particular identity and thereby his ultimate significance, is beyond the scope of this study.

It is, however, essential here to point out that for the first way, workable accounts of our subjective appropriation of redemption and a redeemer as that which is ultimately significant for us, while they may vary in quite important ways, will evince a distinctive logical structure which clearly marks them off from treatments of this issue which conform to the second way. In a Christology structured like Barth's, what makes Jesus Christ ultimately significant and meaningful, and what finally makes him intelligible and existentially accessible for us, is his own history or particular identity. As the ultimate criterion of all that is significant for salvation, Jesus' particular identity is itself *heilsbedeutsam* in Rahner's comprehensive sense of the term. When questions of the meaningfulness or intelligibility of redemption through Jesus

Christ arise, his particularity is logically basic; it is to this that one finally appeals in answering such questions.

The second way also makes an appeal to something logically basic, namely a general principle of meaningfulness (whether or not ingredient in a transcendental anthropology, as with Rahner) which is assumed as that upon which all further explanation depends. Although Rahner never explicitly raises the issue, his answer to any questions about what makes our desire for ultimate fulfilment itself 'meaningful' can only be that this desire is logically basic, and that there is nothing further to which one can appeal when faced with questions of 'meaningfulness' and 'ultimate significance'. In a logically similar way, Barth's answer to the question, 'what makes Jesus *himself* "ultimately meaningful"?' is clearly to point out that Jesus' particularity is logically basic in this matter, so that there is nothing more basic to which one could turn to answer such a question further.

This logical feature of the first way has an important implication for accounts of the subjective appropriation of Jesus Christ and his redemptive significance. On Barth's view, since Jesus' own history is the criterion for the ultimate significance and meaningfulness of all that we attribute to him, these attributes or 'significances' can only become 'existentially accessible' to us through an acquaintance with and appreciation of Jesus' history or particular identity.[82] That which is existentially appropriated is 'redemption' in the Christian sense and signals something ultimately significant, only on account of its binding reference and exclusive application to Jesus Christ. Therefore the subjective appropriation of 'redemption', whatever form it may take, depends upon an appreciation of the Christian story and specifically of Jesus' own history. Contrary to Rahner, who designs his account of our subjective appropriation of redemption precisely in order to meet the christological exigencies of the second way, there can be no subjective access to 'that which is *heilsbedeutsam*' which is independent of access to the particular identity of Jesus Christ.

Barth is clearly aware that there is a certain loss involved in an explicit decision for the first way, although obviously he thinks this loss is preferable to that which the second way involves. If Jesus Christ himself is the criterion of that which is ultimately significant for us, then the meaningfulness of redemption and a redeemer will never be directly accessible to us through a grasp of our own subjective aims. So Barth remarks that we cannot turn the question of the content of God's act for us in Jesus Christ, including its ultimate significance, into a question concerning 'the determination of the being of man which takes place when the passion is proclaimed to a man and believed by him'.[83] This means that the direct fit at which Rahner aims between general descriptions of the human condition or goal, which strive to be persuasive to anyone who can understand them, and a unique redeemer as that which is ultimately meaningful for us, is simply unavailable on the first way. The link between the basic aims of the human subject and any general account of that which is ultimately significant in human life is indirect, even if those aims are taken to be universal. As I have described, on the first way 'redemption' and 'a redeemer' can only be appropriated by the human subject as something ultimately meaningful by grasping the particular person to whom this significance is ascribed. So for the first way, in clear contrast to the second, the question to which I have devoted my attention, namely what makes Jesus Christ ultimately 'significant' and 'meaningful', cannot be resolved by an appeal to conditions for the subjective appropriation of his significance, and therefore is logically and irreducibly distinct from the question of how we are able to appropriate him along with his ultimate significance.

As the example of Rahner indicates, such an appeal ordinarily involves using the conditions for subjective appropriation as general criteria for the meaningfulness and significance of Jesus Christ as a particular person. If my argument is correct, there can be no such criteria. Therefore, whatever subjective conditions there may be for the appropriation of redemption through Jesus Christ, they cannot be the basis upon which he has the function of ultimate meaningfulness and significance.

But this logical feature of the first way makes no stipulation regarding the form this subjective appropriation actually takes, that is, about the best way to describe the process or event by which we assimilate redemption through Jesus Christ. Specifically, the first way leaves open the question of whether or not this process or event has one basic form or pattern, and hence of whether there is a single universal subjective condition for (or anticipation of) belief in Jesus Christ and his ultimate significance. One could answer this question in the negative (as

Barth seems to do). Just as Jesus Christ himself is inexhaustibly rich, the paths by which people come to appropriate that richness are irreducibly and unsystematizably diverse. There is, one might argue, no single common pattern which includes them all, no matter what the experiential or epistemic depths of the subject at which one might look. On this view, it makes no essential difference to the logic of our existential access to 'that which is ultimately meaningful' whether we are 'on the lookout' for something like 'redemption', perhaps in a way thoroughly shaped by Christianity (as, for example, Luther was), or whether we are not on the lookout for such a thing at all (as, it appears, Paul was not). The first way allows for an irreducible cultural and historical diversity of patterns by which people appropriate Jesus as ultimately significant. This diversity is held together by its common binding reference to Jesus Christ as a particular person rather than by any common denominator in the human subject.

However, the first way does not exclude the view that there is in fact a single basic pattern for the subjective appropriation of Jesus' saving significance, or that all human beings anticipate redemption through Jesus Christ in essentially the same way. For example, one could maintain, as Catholic theologians have often done, that a desire for the vision of God (or for happiness, which finally can come only through the vision of God) is the subjective basis upon which people lay hold of Jesus' death and resurrection as our way to the vision of God. Or one could maintain, as Luther did (in some moods), that a longing for deliverance from the terrors of the conscience under the law of God has this function.

For my purposes, it is not necessary to decide whether these patterns of subjective appropriation are single or manifold, and the first way does not compel me to do so. The crucial point here is rather that even if there is a single universal pattern of appropriation (such as that signalled by 'the desire for the vision of God'), what makes this pattern a genuine anticipation of 'that which is ultimately significant' is not its universality or subjective indispensability but its binding and exclusive reference to Jesus Christ (as the one who alone brings the vision of God). For the first way, in other words, 'the vision of God' (to continue with one example) can only function to characterize 'that which is ultimately significant' because it can be tied to Jesus Christ as its exclusive and permanent source; it does not have this function simply because it fulfills the deepest human longing, unless the latter is described precisely as a longing for Jesus Christ as a particular person. This means that contrary to what theologians of the second way typically maintain, there can be no Christological necessity, rooted in the presumed need to display the meaningfulness of redemption through Jesus Christ by an appeal to general criteria of 'significance for salvation', for the subjective assimilation of redemption through Jesus Christ to take a single form. Even if there is assumed to be such a universal mode of subjective appropriation, it cannot be used, in Rahner's fashion, to generate criteria of ultimate meaningfulness and significance.

How can Jesus Christ be *heilsbedeutsam*? The question seems to beg for an answer in general terms. In this sense, Barth's answer obviates the question. That, I have argued, is why it is a successful answer.

NOTES

1 Eberhard Jüngel, *Barth-Studien* (Zurich–Cologne and Gütersloh: 1982), p. 12.

2 Hans Frei perceptively identifies some of the reasons for this in 'An Afterword: Eberhard Busch's Biography of Karl Barth', in *Karl Barth in Re-View: Posthumous Works Reviewed and Assessed*, ed. H.-Martin Rumscheidt (Pittsburg: 1981), pp. 109 – 16.

3 This remark of Barth's is found in a letter to B. Gherardini of 24 May 1952, cited in Eberhard Busch, *Karl Barth: His Life From Letters and Autobiographical Texts*, 2nd edn, tr. John Bowden (Philadelphia: 1976), p. 380. Cf. Jüngel's remark in *Barth-Studien*, p. 234: 'There can be no talk of a "Christomonism" – at the very least because the christological concentration does not involve a principle, nor a system to be deduced from such a principle, but only a concentration on the concrete being of Jesus Christ.'

4 Neither did I try to do this with Rahner. However, Rahner's theology does lend itself somewhat more readily than Barth's to the kind of analysis I am undertaking here.

5 Cf. chap. 2, pp. 21–2.

6 For a detailed account of this unwanted paradox in his theology, cf. the discussions of Rahner on 'resurrection' and 'redemptive death', chap. 3, pp. 95–8 and pp. 98–104.

7 Cf. chap. 2, p. 21.

8 It could be argued that something like the first way was taken for

Meaningfulness in Barth's Christology

151

granted in most Christian theology prior to the first intimations of an explicit alternative in the late seventeenth century. Yet just because a basically different approach had not been proposed explicitly, the presence of the first way is likely to be less prominent and more diffuse there than in a theology like Barth's, in which a decision is intentionally made on this point.

9 I am speaking here of decisions made within Barth's theology about how to proceed on specific, often basic, points. Of these there is a rich, perhaps unsystematizably rich, diversity. By contrast, the determination always to 'orientate afresh on Jesus Christ' is more a pre-theological conviction than a technical or methodological decision.

10 Frei, 'An Afterword', p. 103.

11 Ibid., p. 105.

12 Karl Barth, *Kirchliche Dogmatik* (hereafter *KD*) (Munich and Zurich: 1932–68), II/2, p. 8. The English translation is Karl Barth, *Church Dogmatics* (hereafter *CD*) (Edinburgh: 1956–75), II/2, p. 6. As with Rahner, references to all citations of Barth's works will be given for both German and English editions, whenever the latter are available (see the Preface).

13 Cf. *KD*, II/2, p. 51; *CD*, II/2, p. 48.

14 *KD*, II/2, p. 54; *CD*, II/2, p. 51. Cf. also *KD*, II/2, p. 56; *CD*, II/2, p. 53: 'He [God] does everything general for the sake of this particular [Jesus Christ], and conversely: through this particular, indeed in and with it, God does everything general. This is God according to his self-revelation.'

15 Cf. *CD*, II/2, pp. 7–8; *KD*, II/2, p. 6. Barth can make similar remarks about the particular and the general in the course of discussions of the object of election (*CD*, II/2, pp. 41–2; *KD*, II/2, pp. 43–4), the divine government of the world (*CD*, II/2, pp. 48–51; *KD*, II/2, pp. 51 –5), and the human capacity for the knowledge of God (*CD*, III/2, pp. 402–3; *KD*, III/2, p. 483).

16 Jüngel's observation is especially pertinent: 'The beginning, with which theology constantly has to begin anew, has a name. The beginning is called Jesus Christ, and is as such uniquely concrete, distinguished without confusion from every general *arche*.' *Barth-Studien*, p. 336. Jüngel alludes to Barth's *Latet periculum in generalibus!* frequently in these essays; cf. pp. 13, 18, 35, 50. The remarks of two other commentators on this notion are also useful. Cf. Walter Sparn, '"Extra Internum": Die christologische Revision der Prädestinationslehre in Karl Barths Erwählungslehre', in *Die Realisierung der Freiheit: Beiträge zur Kritik der Theologie Barths*, ed. Trutz Rendtorff (Gütersloh: 1975), p. 50; and Walter Kreck, *Grundentscheidungen in Karl Barths Dogmatik: Zur Diskussion seines Verständnisses von*

Offenbarung und Erwählung (Neukirchen–Vluyn: 1978), p. 189.

17 *CD*, IV/1, p. 158; *KD*, IV/1, p. 172. Cf. also *KD*, IV/1, pp. 21–2; *CD*, IV/1, p. 21: 'The peace between God and us, and the salvation which comes to us, is here not something general, but this particular as such: the concrete reality which is to be designated with the name of Jesus Christ, and with no other name. For he who bears this name *is* himself peace, *is* himself salvation.' Barth can also state the identity of Jesus and his significance in logico-grammatical terms, although such language seems to have a purely heuristic function for him. So the saying 'Jesus is Victor', he notes, 'in some degree . . . analyses the name of Jesus and it gathers up this analysis in the simple equation: Jesus=Victor' (*CD*, IV/3, p. 172; *KD*, IV/3, p. 196).

18 *KD*, IV/1, p. 16; *CD*, IV/1, p. 16.

19 Ibid. Barth's insistence upon what I am calling the first way becomes both more prominent and more determinative as the *Dogmatics* progresses (in connection, as I have observed, with a host of related material and methodological developments). It is, however, unmistakable at a fairly early point. Illustrating by reference to the Pauline phrase, 'whom God made our wisdom, our righteousness and sanctification and redemption' (I Cor. 1:30), Barth suggests that we imagine such a clause

> without the subject Jesus Christ on which it depends, dependent upon some other subject. For the writers of the New Testament it would have become a totally meaningless (*bedeutungslosen*) statement in spite of the high content of its predicates. For them wisdom, righteousness, sanctification and redemption are not relevant conceptions in themselves, but only as predicates of the subject Jesus. (*CD*, I/2, p. 10; *KD*, I/2, p. 12).

20 On election and covenant as the 'presupposition' of reconciliation, cf. *CD*, IV/1, § 57, 1.

21 For a balanced presentation of the problem and Barth's response, cf. Kreck, *Grundentscheidungen*, pp. 236–44, esp. 241f.

22 There is, it may be worth noting, at least this formal similarity between Barth's conception of the election of Jesus Christ and Rahner's notion of an absolute saviour: each wants their global idea to *include* the conquest of sin but not to be *defined* by it.

23 On the concept of a 'particular person' or 'particular individual', cf. the discussion in chap. 2, pp. 42–7.

24 *KD*, IV/3, p. 205; *CD*, IV/3, p. 179. Cf. *KD*, III/2, p. 65; *CD*, III/2, p. 56: 'He is . . . who and what he is utterly in the continuity of this *history (Geschichte)*.'

25 This insistence that a person's particular identity is equivalent to his or her history is only one aspect of Barth's larger view of personal being. The latter is nicely summed up in Barth's remark that personal being is that which 'does not subsist of itself, but only in a specific doing (*Handeln*) on the part of the subject' (*CD*, I/2, p. 369; *KD*, I/2, p. 406. The personal being under consideration in this passage is specifically that of Christians.). As is typical for him, Barth makes no attempt to give a detailed account of the notion that persons have their being in their acts independently of its theological applications. He does, however, use this notion for a variety of purposes; in this context it simply serves to give explanatory backing to the assumption that Jesus' particular identity is identical with his history.

It would be possible, of course, to provide a detailed account of personal being congruent with this Barthian dictum. Such an account could well be a wholly non-theological one; thus, David H. Kelsey suggests (following Hans Frei) that there are strong affinities between the anthropology which might be implied in Barth's remark, and the developed positions of P. F. Strawson and Stuart Hampshire (and, one might add, Austin Farrer). Cf. D. Kelsey, *The Uses of Scripture in Recent Theology* (Philadelphia: 1975), p. 46. For Barth, it is important to stress, the theological points which might be made by using an independent, non-theological account of personal being would not be logically dependent upon that account.

26 In Jesus Christ, 'a history (*Geschichte*) is taking place; a drama is being enacted; a war (*Kampf*) waged to a successful conclusion. If from the very first there can be no doubt as to the issue of the action, there can also be no doubt that there is an action, and that it is taking place, and can thus be described only in the form of narration' (*CD*, IV/3, p. 168; *KD*, IV/3, p. 192). Barth's native tongue allows him to introduce both Jesus' particular identity and its narrative description in the same breath, since *Geschichte* can mean both 'history' and 'story'. Cf. his exploitation of this usage, above, n. 18, below, n. 46.

27 Cf. chap. 2, p. 44.

28 *KD*, IV/1, pp. 316–7; *CD*, IV/1, p. 288. On the specifically ostensible aspect of Jesus' history, cf. also *CD*, I/2, p. 51, p. 209; *KD*, I/2, p. 56, p. 229; *CD*, IV/1, pp. 167–8; *KD*, IV/1, pp. 182–3; *CD*, IV/2, p. 260; *KD*, IV/2, p. 288; *CD*, IV/3, p. 298; *KD*, IV/3, p. 343.

29 Cf. *KD*, I/2, p. 13; *CD*, I/2, p. 12. As the 'reality of revelation', the history of Jesus 'is single (*eine*), it is this entirely determinate *Geschichte*, which had not occurred before and will not occur again'.

30 On 'Bethlehem to Golgotha' as a summary of Jesus' history, cf. *CD*, IV/3, p. 181; *KD*, IV/3, p. 207; cf. also *CD*, IV/2, p. 75; *KD*, IV/2, p.

81. Barth draws attention to the fact that 'in these [synoptic] Gospels there is relatively little express mention of the significance of the Christ event which took place then and there', and correlatively greater stress upon the 'stimulating singularity' (*aufregenden Seltsamkeit*) of Jesus' history itself (*CD*, IV/1, p. 224; *KD*, IV/1, p. 246).

31 Barth's most succinct retelling of the story of Jesus Christ, and his division of that story into three parts, is found in *CD*, IV/1, pp. 224–8; *KD*, IV/1, pp. 246–50. I will return to this passage in more detail later.

32 Some mention of the notion of the 'identity of indiscernibles', much discussed in analytic philosophy, is unavoidable at this point (Cf., for example, the articles on this topic by Max Black, A. J. Ayer and D. J. O'Connor, collected in *Universals and Particulars: Readings in Ontology*, rev. edn, ed. Michael J. Loux (Notre Dame, Ind: 1976), pp. 250–80).

There is no unanimity about exactly what the notion involves. But for my purposes, I have taken it as the claim that particulars which have exactly the same conceptual description are not really distinct, or, perhaps more germane to the point, the claim that for any one conceptual description, there *can be* only one particular in reality. By arguing that a demonstrative element is ultimately indispensable to our identification of, and further discourse about, particulars, the foregoing remarks imply a criticism in principle of the identity of indiscernibles, at least in this form (Strawson's detailed arguments on this score seem persuasive; cf. P. F. Strawson, *Individuals: An Essay in Descriptive Metaphysics* (London: 1959), pp. 119–32; and *Subject and Predicate In Logic and Grammar* (London: 1974), pp. 15–16). However, the theological argument of this chapter does not depend upon rejecting the identity of indiscernibles in principle. Rather, with regard specifically to Jesus Christ, the assumption shared by Rahner and Barth is that no characterization of the status and significance of 'the unique redeemer' alone is capable of bringing about acquaintance with him, i.e., knowledge of him as a particular person (on some of the theological reasons for this, cf. chap. 2, pp. 30–1). Since it seems to be precisely the spatio-temporal aspect which is peculiar to those sorts of descriptions which *are* capable of acquainting us with Jesus Christ as a particular person, I have framed my distinction between these (identifying) descriptions and more general characterizations of Jesus' significance in terms which are incompatible with the identity of indiscernibles. But this is not to say that that theologically necessary distinction could not be stated in a way which would be compatible with the identity of indiscernibles, although perhaps not with the same clarity and force.

33 *CD*, IV/1, p. 16; *KD*, IV/1, p. 15.

34 See here especially Barth's reaction to G. C. Berkouwer's contention that his theology is essentially (and misguidedly) one of 'the triumph of grace'. Such an expression is inevitably inadequate as an account of the relation between God and evil, Barth says, because it is not concrete enough to identify and describe the actual subject of this triumph.

> I am not trying unilaterally to think through the principle of grace to the point at which I reach 'the triumph of grace' in this relationship [viz., between God and evil]. I should regard such a procedure as quite illegitimate. My desire is that from the very first, at every point, and therefore in answering this question too, we should take with unconditional seriousness the fact that 'Jesus is Victor'. (*CD*, IV/3, p. 175; *KD*, IV/3, p. 200).

35 *CD*, IV/2, p. 21; *KD*, IV/2, p. 21.

36 *CD*, IV/3, p. 40; *KD*, IV/3, p. 42.

37 Cf. *CD*, IV/1, p. 163, p. 177; *KD*, IV/1, p. 179, p. 193.

38 *CD*, II/2, p. 9; *KD*, II/2, p. 7. Cf. *CD*, II/2, p. 99; *KD*, II/2, p. 106:

> We are not thinking or speaking rightly of God Himself if we do not take as our starting point the fact which should be both 'first and last': that from all eternity God elected to bear this name. Over against all that is really outside God, Jesus Christ is the eternal will of God, the eternal decree of God and the eternal beginning of God.

39 In Jesus Christ, 'God is self-determined (*er sich selber bestimmt hat*), so that the determination belongs no less to Him than all that he is in and for Himself' (*CD*, II/2, p. 7; *KD*, II/2, p. 6. Cf. also *CD*, II/2, p. 51, p. 91; *KD*, II/2, p. 54, pp. 98–9). On the importance of the notion of 'self-determination' as a way of explaining the logically basic function of Jesus' particular history in Barth's doctrine of God, cf. the suggestive remarks in Sparn, '"Extra Internum"', pp. 45–7.

40 In chap. 5, I will be concerned in more detail with the complex relation between Jesus' divinity and his particular identity or history. My concern at this point simply is to characterize Barth's maximalist reading, which is vital to the logic of his Christology, of the belief that the history of Jesus is the history of God.

41 *KD*, III/2, p. 80; *CD*, III/2, p. 69, my emphasis.

42 Chap. 5 will also discuss the relation between Jesus' divinity and his

significance in greater detail.

43 The apt phrase 'fully defined' (*vollständig definiert*) is Jüngel's; cf. *Barth-Studien*, p. 336.

44 Karl Barth, *Ethics*, tr. Geoffrey W. Bromiley (New York: 1981), p. 322. These lectures, which were first published posthumously in the Barth *Gesamtausgabe*, date from 1928. Cf. also Barth's first published attempt at dogmatic theology, the *Die christliche Dogmatik im Entwurf* of 1927: 'Whoever sees and hears this man, sees and hears the Lord – with the possibility not only of faith but of scandal, for otherwise the Lord is not to be seen and heard by us – but he sees and hears *him*, the Logos himself, and no second one next to him.' Karl Barth, *Die christliche Dogmatik im Entwurf, Erster Band: Die Lehre vom Wort Gottes, Prolegomena zur christlichen Dogmatik*, ed. Gerhard Sauter (Zurich: 1982), p. 357. Formulations very close to these are already present in Barth's earliest lectures on dogmatics in the summer of 1924, which were not published during his lifetime. Cf. Karl Barth, '*Unterricht in der christlichen Religion*,' *Erster Band: Prolegomena*, ed. Hannelotte Reiffin (Zurich: 1985), p. 194.

45 See the discussion in chap. 3, pp.98–104.

46 *CD*, IV/1, p. 223; *KD*, IV/1, p. 245.

47 *CD*, IV/3, p. 298; *KD*, IV/3, p. 343. This phrase occurs in the context of a discussion of Jesus' resurrection. As I have shown, though (cf. above, n. 28), for Barth the ostensible aspect is indispensable to every part of Jesus' history.

48 *CD*, IV/1, p. 224; *KD*, IV/1, p. 246.

49 Ibid.

50 *CD*, IV/1, p. 225; *KD*, IV/1, p. 247.

51 Ibid. On the way 'the Lord is among them' specifically in Jesus' words and works, cf. Barth's discussion of the 'analogy' between Jesus and God in *CD*, IV/2, p. 166f.; *KD*, IV/2, p. 185f.

52 *CD*, IV/1, p. 226; *KD*, IV/1, p. 248.

53 *CD*, IV/1, p. 264; *KD*, IV/1, p. 291.

54 *CD*, IV/1, p. 226; *KD*, IV/1, p. 248.

55 Barth is quite clear that there not only can but must be other patterns evident in this history. Jesus Christ, and therefore his history, 'is inexhaustibly rich, so that it is not merely legitimate but obligatory that believers should continually see and understand it in new lights and aspects' (*CD*, IV/1, p. 763; *KD*, IV/1, p. 853). So he devotes an excursus to several other cognate patterns which the New Testament sees manifest in Jesus' history, all of which focus upon the central 'reversal' and 'exchange of roles', but which employ concepts and images different from the forensic ones he prefers when discussing 'the judge judged in our place' (cf. *CD*, IV/1, pp. 273–83; *KD*, IV/1, pp. 301–11).

This synopsis of the way Barth sees the pattern of 'the judge judged' evinced in Jesus' history is indebted to Hans Frei's *The Identity of Jesus Christ. The Hermeneutical Bases of Dogmatic Theology* (Philadelphia: 1974), pp. 102–15. Barth's discussion is not obscure, but Frei's own reading of Jesus' history, which is structurally similar to Barth's, usefully highlights a number of points which might otherwise have gone unnoticed in Barth's account.

56 *CD*, IV/1, p. 245; *KD*, IV/1, p. 269.

57 For Barth the *knowledge* of Jesus' divinity, of the identity of his history with God's own, depends upon the knowledge of Jesus' resurrection, in which his history or particular identity culminates. Jesus Christ 'is revealed in His resurrection from the dead as the one He is, revealed and confirmed as the beloved and obedient Son of God and therefore as His Elect from all eternity . . .' (*CD*, IV/1, p. 350; *KD*, IV/1, p. 387). Barth attends to the ontic and noetic import of Jesus' resurrection in great detail, devoting a section in each christological paragraph of 'The Doctrine of Reconciliation' to just this set of issues. Here, I can only mention its importance for him.

58 *CD*, II/2, p. 166; *KD*, II/2, p. 182.

59 *CD*, IV/1, p. 222; *KD*, IV/1, p. 244.

60 *CD*, IV/1, p. 254; *KD*, IV/1, pp. 279 – 80. On the ordered relation between the negative and positive aspects of reconciliation (and also of God's eternal election), cf. *CD*, II/2, pp. 173–4; *KD*, II/2, p. 190. 'God wills . . . His own humiliation on man's behalf, that judgement might be taken way, all righteousness fulfilled, and the road trodden to the very end. But he wills [this] only in connection with and for the sake of . . . one thing: that by right man might be heir of His own glory, goodness and blessedness, entering into fellowship with Himself.'

61 *CD*, IV/1, p. 552; *KD*, IV/1, p. 616.

62 Cf. the discussion of identifying descriptions and non-identifying concepts, above, pp. 125–6.

63 *CD*, IV/1, p. 245; *KD*, IV/1, p. 269.

64 *CD*, IV/1, p. 248; *KD*, IV/1, p. 273. Similarly when he points out that there are many 'suffering and dying gods', Barth stresses that in this case,

> we are dealing with an act which took place on earth, in time and space, and which is indissolubly linked (*unauflösbar verknupfte*) with the name of a certain man . . . The Gospels do not speak of a passion which might just as well have been suffered in one place or another, at one time as another, or in a heavenly or some purely imaginary space and time. They indicate a very definite point in world history which cannot be exchanged for any other. (*CD*, IV/1, p. 245; *KD*, IV/1, p. 269. Cf. also above, n. 47).

65   It is possible, of course, for a conceptual characterization of redemption and a redeemer to be the grammatical subject of a sentence. But on Barth's view, sentences like this have a place in an account of reconciliation, and signify something *heilsbedeutsam*, only in so far as their grammatical subjects can serve as predicates in logically prior sentences of which Jesus Christ is the subject.

66   *CD*, I/2, p. 11; *KD*, I/2, pp. 12–13.

67   In calling 'the judge judged' and other accounts of 'reconciliation' 'concepts', I am using the latter term in an admittedly broad sense, which includes non-identifying characterizations as well as classes and properties.

68   They could logically apply to someone else in addition to Jesus, or instead of Jesus.

69   It is well to recall, though, that Barth himself insists upon honouring the logical possibility, even in this case. Cf. above, n. 63.

70   Cf. on this chap. 3, pp. 96–7, esp. n. 46.

71   The notion of a 'logically individuating characterization' is suggested by Strawson's account of 'logically individuating descriptions' in *Individuals*, p. 26. I speak of 'characterizations' rather than 'descriptions' here because, unlike Strawson, my primary concern is with expressions which are, in themselves, non-identifying, and which I have sought to distinguish clearly from those that do have identifying force (for which latter I have typically reserved the term 'descriptions'). But given this basic distinction, what I am calling 'characterizations' could also be called 'descriptions', as they regularly are in analytic philosophy. So, for example, what I am calling 'logically individuating characterizations' are closely parallel to what Russell calls 'definite descriptions', which carry 'the implication of uniqueness' (of application) without necessarily identifying (cf. B. Russell, *Introduction to Mathematical Philosophy* (London: 1919), p. 176).

72   Unfortunately, I have had to pass over in my discussion Barth's detailed account of the senses in which Jesus Christ acts and suffers 'in our place', as our 'representative' and 'substitute' (in Barth's term, as our *Stellvertreter*). As with Rahner's treatment of the same issue, I have had to limit my attention to the (bare) logic of the matter.

73   It should be remembered that the logical distinctions I have drawn, somewhat more sharply than Barth himself does, between (1) Jesus Christ as an ascriptive subject, (2) identifying or primary descriptions of him and (3) characterizations of his universal significance, are not meant to imply that these elements are separable in reality. Reconciliation, Barth insists, *is* 'ontically, Jesus Christ's own history' (cf. above, n. 17). But Rahner assumes essentially the same

thing. The purpose of the logical distinctions, therefore, is to achieve a certain amount of reflective clarity about the true structure of the unitary but complex phenomenon of 'reconciliation'; the aim, in other words, is to achieve an understanding of this complex phenomenon congruent with the shared assumption that all of its aspects are unified ontologically in the history of Jesus Christ. I have argued, by using such distinctions, that Barth does this more successfully than Rahner does.

74   Another way to put basically the same point is to say that 'the first self-surrender to God in death', which is a logically individuating characterization, lacks sufficient 'descriptive aptness' to be ascribed to Jesus as a saving predicate.

75   *CD*, IV/2, p. 29; *KD*, IV/2, p. 30.

76   *CD*, IV/2, p. 103; *KD*, IV/2, p. 114. Barth allows that even 'the judge judged in our place' has not only an effect, but a certain parallel in our own life and action. 'The great humility of the Son of God must and will make its impress on the lesser humility of the man who believes in Him. The faith of that man will be characterized by it' (*CD*, IV/1, p. 636; *KD*, IV/1, p. 711). This echo of 'the judge judged in our place' in the lives of believers does not mean, however, that such a logically individuating characterization can be applied to the believer as well as to Jesus Christ himself; in this it differs from a concept like 'exaltation'.

77   *KD*, IV/1, p. 16; *CD*, IV/1, p. 16.

78   *KD*, IV/2, p. 19; *CD*, IV/2, p. 19. A discussion of Barth's notion of analogy would be useful here, but would take me farther afield than I can go at this juncture. The primary point for present purposes has already been noted. For Barth, the 'prime analogate' for any analogical characterization of redemption (viz., one which applies in different ways to both Jesus and us) is not simply a concept but the particular subject to whom that concept uniquely applies. This seems to be the force of the sort of remark on analogy which is especially striking in Barth's doctrine of God. 'We can never expect to know generally what event or act or life is, in order from that point to conclude and assert that God is He to whom this is all proper in an unimaginable and incomprehensible fullness and completeness. When we know God as event, act and life, we have to admit that generally and apart from him we do not know what this is' (*CD*, II/1, p. 264; *KD*, II/1, pp. 295–6). The reason for this is that '*actus purus* is not sufficient as a description of God. To it there must be added at least "*et singularis*"', i.e., reference to the particularity of the one to whom the 'pure' sense of the concept applies (ibid.).

79   Cf. chap. 2, n. 29.

80   Rahner is clearly aware that conceptual characterizations by them-

selves do not have the force of identifying descriptions. He repeatedly emphasizes that we cannot 'deduce' the particular identity of Jesus Christ from the idea of an absolute saviour. But he seems not to realize the implications of this fact for his christological method.

81 For a version of this argument oriented in more detail to the specifics of Rahner's Christology, cf. chap. 2, pp. 53–60.

82 Two typical remarks may help give a sense of the way in which Jesus' particular identity, and therewith his redeeming significance, are existentially accessible for Barth. On the *pro nobis* aspect:

> He does not first become 'for us' when we come to some kind of discipleship and imitation (*Nach- und Mitvollzügen*), rather he is 'for *us*' in himself, independently of the answer we give to the question (which is certainly put to us) about such discipleship and imitation. The event of salvation occurs there, then, *in him*, and in this way, *for us*. (*KD*, IV/1, p. 252; *CD*, IV/1, p. 229).

On the *in nobis* aspect:

> Many human events and developments may have other origins and beginnings. The Christian life, fidelity to God as a person's free act and disposition, commences with what became real in the days of Augustus and Tiberius, on the way from the crib in Bethlehem to the cross on Golgotha, as that which is possible *para theo* (Mk. 10:22 Par), according to the measure (*Ermessen*) of God. (Karl Barth, 'Extra Nos – Pro Nobis – In Nobis', in *Hören und Handeln: Festschrift für Ernst Wolf zum 60. Geburtstag*, ed. Helmut Gollwitzer and Helmut Traub (Munich: 1962), p. 20).

83 *CD*, IV/1, p. 248; *KD*, IV/1, p. 273. Cf. *CD*, IV/1, pp. 223–4; *KD*, IV/1, p. 245.

5

Particularity and Incarnation

In the narrowest sense, the aim of this book has already been achieved. I have analysed two ways of understanding the place of Jesus Christ as a particular person in theological accounts of his significance, and I have argued that one of these ways is consistent with the relevant assumptions shared by both, while the other is inconsistent with those same assumptions. The issue I have striven to resolve can be viewed as primarily a methodological one. I have tried to show one way a theology might be constructed which honours the assumption that only Jesus Christ can be the unique redeemer, or, more generally, that only he can fulfill the function or have the role of 'that which is ultimately significant'. Given this assumption, I have argued, a theology should construe 'that which is significant for salvation' in a way which includes Jesus Christ; it should not suppose that it has actually described a reality (or possibility) which is *heilsbedeutsam* (such as an 'absolute saviour', or 'the judge judged in our place') until it has shown how Jesus Christ is that reality. In logico-grammatical terms, such a theology should (as Barth does) express 'that which is significant for salvation' in *propositions* of which Jesus Christ is the actual or implied subject, rather than (as Rahner does) in bare *concepts*, which are taken to be *heilsbedeutsam* on the strength of conformity to general criteria. The issue itself has been primarily methodological, but a material christological assumption has shaped my decision on that issue.

While the most limited goal of this book has been reached, I have only briefly alluded to some possible theological correlates and implications of an explicit decision for the first way. In fact, the norms I have articulated for a theology consistent with the conviction that Jesus Christ is the unique redeemer precisely as a particular person might bear upon a number of dogmatic issues in a potentially fruitful way. One such issue, however, has already suggested itself with particular clarity, especially in the discussion of Barth. That issue is the logical distinctiveness of 'incarnation' and its cognates among characterizations of Jesus' significance. This chapter will offer a preliminary treatment of the distinctive logic of 'incarnation' among the predicates of Jesus Christ, or more generally of the interaction of incarnation and particularity in a theology consistent with the rules of the first way.

I have already had occasion to note the distinctive role of the incarnation or immediate presence of God in Barth's account of the ascription of ultimate significance to Jesus Christ. It has been seen that 'the judge judged in our place', or any other concept or characterization of redemption, is actually capable of functioning as a description of that which is ultimately significant precisely because it can be applied to Jesus Christ. Moreover, this characterization is predicable of Jesus in two specific ways: it is descriptively apt and logically individuating, although only the feature of descriptive aptness is absolutely essential for a potential characterization of redemption. Predicability of Jesus Christ, however, while it is the criterion of that which is *heilsbedeutsam*, actually constitutes significance for salvation only in connection with a specific assertion about Jesus Christ. 'The judge judged in our place', for example, only becomes significant for salvation when, by being fitly ascribed to Jesus Christ as a particular person, it is ascribed to God as well. Barth is quite explicit about this, as I have indicated. 'What we men must suffer . . . can be suffered for us only by God Himself as man: if, that is to say, it is to take place validly and effectively for us all.'[1] Ascription to God, it seems, is a necessary condition for the predicates of Jesus Christ signalling a saving reality. 'The human speaking and acting and suffering and triumphing of this one man directly concerns us all, and his history is our history of salvation which changes the whole human situation, just because God Himself is its human subject in His Son.'[2] In at least this sense, namely that the ultimate subject of what we ascribe to Jesus Christ is God himself, the incarnation is logically indispensable for Barth in any account or analysis of 'that which is significant for salvation'.

These considerations suggest a distinctive relation between the particularity of Jesus Christ and the incarnation of God in a theology like. Barth's, or in any theology that clearly follows the first way, and also includes an appeal to something like 'incarnation'. As I have shown, Barth's theology is not only consistent with but tellingly exemplifies the procedural rule that Jesus Christ as a particular person is the norm for all that is ultimately meaningful or significant. At the same time, Barth seems fundamentally committed to the principle that the divinity of Jesus Christ functions as the *sine qua non* for all other significance we ascribe to him; if we could not ascribe the incarnation of God to him, nothing else we predicate of him would be ultimately meaningful or significant. Taken together, these two assumptions delineate the logically distinctive status of 'incarnation' among characterizations of Jesus' significance in Barth's theology. On the one hand, 'incarnation', like any characterization of Jesus Christ, only counts as something significant for salvation in virtue of its application to him. It must, in other words, conform to the two-fold requirement of reference and exclusivity implied in the conviction that only Jesus Christ can be *heilsbedeutsam*; 'incarnation' characterizes a saving reality only when it is construed in such a way that it includes reference to him and applies exclusively to him. On the other hand, a predicate like 'Son of God' (taken to involve a unique relation to God in which Jesus' history is God's own) is presupposed in the 'saving' application of a more obviously descriptive predicate like 'the judge judged' to Jesus Christ. How the appropriate application of such descriptive or 'feature-specific' predicates is governed by the norms of the first way has already been discussed.[3] But the place and function of specifically 'incarnational' predicates in relation to Jesus' particularity cannot be accounted for simply by appealing to those norms. 'Incarnation of God' is not an ordinary instance of the norms of the first way, because this predicate or its equivalent must already be in place in order for those norms to apply in any other case. Borrowing a phrase from P. F. Strawson, I can say that for Barth, 'incarnation' has a 'logically primitive' status among characterizations of Jesus' significance.

I will attempt here to give a preliminary account of the function of these predicates with regard to Jesus' particular identity, and thus of the distinctive relation of the incarnation to Jesus' particularity, in a theology of the first way. In this attempt to clarify the 'logical primitiveness' of 'incarnation' among the predicates of Jesus Christ, it is possible to distinguish two related questions, which may serve as guides in this inquiry. (1) What is being affirmed when we say that Jesus' history, precisely in its particularity, is God's own? (2) What specifically must be said about 'incarnation' if this pivotal assertion is to be maintained? Answering these questions will help us to see how 'incarnation' might be significant for salvation only on account of its exclusive reference to Jesus Christ as a particular person, and at the same time be the condition under which any other predicates can be applied to Jesus Christ with a genuinely 'saving' force. To this end, I will investigate in more detail Barth's way of answering these questions. I will also look at the way Thomas Aquinas construes the logical relation between the particularity of Jesus Christ and the incarnation of God in him. Ultimately, his answer to these questions is congruent with Barth's, but, I shall argue, the explicative power of his presentation is greatly enhanced by the way he answers them, especially by his purposive employment of logico-grammatical analysis as well as ontological description as a means of explicating the logical primitiveness of incarnation.[4]

There are several things I am *not* attempting to do in this chapter. Noting them may help further clarify the issue before I take it up in detail.

1   I can only treat one aspect of a theology of incarnation. This means that several complex and difficult issues which would be elaborated in a more comprehensive treatment of incarnation will have to be introduced here with little or no explanation.

2   While the place of the particularity of Jesus Christ is only one aspect of a theology of incarnation, it is not an inessential or secondary one. In focusing upon it, I will not attend at all to the conceptual problems which may be generated by the idea of incarnation and which are sometimes treated *in abstracto*, that is, as questions about a union of humanity and divinity apart from the realization of that union in Jesus Christ. Despite important differences in the aims and conceptuality of their theologies of incarnation, both Barth and Thomas assume that incarnation is a unique event which, if it is properly to be understood, must

always be tied to Jesus as its subject: only he can be the incarnation of God, since only he can be ultimately significant for salvation. This assumption is nicely stated by Thomas, in regard to whom its importance may be less obvious. In one of his anti-Eutychean arguments Thomas points out that the union of divinity and humanity does not constitute 'a kind of general class (*communis species*) . . . in which many could participate. It is obvious that this is false. For there is only one Jesus Christ (I Cor. 8:6), God and man'.[5] In consequence of this assumption, explication of the tie between incarnation and Jesus Christ as its unique and exclusive subject seems fundamental to a theology of incarnation and both Thomas and Barth deal explicitly with it, although in different ways.

By contrast, relatively abstract conceptual considerations about the union of divinity and humanity, such as whether and how apparently contrary divine and human properties are compossible, have a secondary and derivative status in their discussions of incarnation. Such questions are not illegitimate, but are useful only in so far as they further an explication of the union of humanity and divinity precisely in Jesus Christ as a particular person, and hence in so far as they do not contravene the assumption that only he can be the incarnate one.

3 The actuality of the incarnation, especially in so far as it is necessarily tied to the name of Jesus Christ, is usually taken to be insusceptible of proof. But here I am not attempting to prove even the possibility of 'an incarnation'. This is not to say that such a proof is wholly unavailable. However, were it part of my task to undertake a proof of the possibility of incarnation, I would argue that such a proof is available only in a limited and derivative sense. The reason for this can be inferred from what has just been said in point 2 above.

The subject matter of a theology of incarnation, at least one consistent with the first way, is not 'incarnation' *in genere*, but incarnation in Jesus Christ. As Thomas points out, the incarnation which is affirmed actually to have occurred in Jesus Christ does not constitute a general class of possible events, not even a class with only one member; rather, it is assumed that he is the only possible subject to whom that event can be ascribed. Since the relation of 'incarnation' to 'Jesus Christ' is *not* one of class to instance, any demonstration of the possibility of 'an incarnation', no matter how persuasive on its own terms, will fail to demonstrate the possibility of what has actually occurred in Jesus Christ.[6] Such a procedure would in effect constitute an equivocation on the term 'incarnation'; the latter would function as a class name in the proof of possibility, but it cannot do so in the affirmation for which the proof would be trying to account.

For this reason, I have not asked, 'how can it be' that God is the subject of Jesus' particular history? My primary concern here is more modest. I am attempting to specify and explicate what it *means* to affirm that Jesus' history is God's own, or more generally, to affirm that statements about the particular person, Jesus Christ, are precisely as such statements about God. As mentioned, this explicative procedure could include a limited demonstration of possibility. That is, in the course of explicating the sense of the conviction that Jesus' history is God's own, replies can be offered to objections against the possibility or conceivability of this conviction. Such replies logically presuppose the content and the truth of the conviction. Their aim is only to show, as Thomas puts it, that the objections do not have demonstrative force but, rather, admit of intelligible responses.[7] At least in the case of this christological conviction, such 'replies to objections' may be the most appropriate form of 'demonstration of possibility'.

BARTH'S ONTOLOGICAL EXPLICATION OF 'JESUS' HISTORY IS GOD'S OWN'

Commenting on Barth's theology of election, Walter Kreck makes a remark about the relation between Jesus Christ as a particular person and the being of God which states neatly an implied rule in all of Barth's discussions of incarnation: 'God is here [in Barth's theology] inseparable from the name and person of Jesus Christ; apart from him God has no shape or form (*kein Gesicht*) for us.'[8] There are, however, two different kinds of statement governed by this rule. In order to understand the way Barth explicates the indissoluble bond of Jesus' particularity and the incarnation, it is well to distinguish between these different kinds of statement.

On the one hand there are statements about *God*, which,

according to the rule, must ascribe to the being and activity of God an indissoluble link with 'the name and person of Jesus Christ', or at least imply such ascription. This kind of statement, and the issues it raises, Barth treats primarily (but by no means exclusively) in the doctrine of God, especially in his discussion of the election of Jesus Christ as God's primal self-determination. As is typical for him, Barth invokes technical distinctions from the history of theology in his discussions of what an indissoluble link with the name and person of Jesus affirms about God; these distinctions typically are used dogmatically both to illustrate Barth's own position and to further the explication of it. Among these, that between the Logos *asarkos* and the Logos *ensarkos* is especially important to Barth, because of its bearing upon the link between the being of God and 'the name of Jesus Christ', in so far as this link is an issue specifically in the doctrine of God.[9] On the other hand, the rule governs statements about *Jesus Christ* as a particular person, stipulating that such statements must imply or ascribe to him an indissoluble link with the whole being and activity of God. For the most part (but again not exclusively) the issues suggested by statements of this kind are handled in the explicitly christological sections of the *Church Dogmatics*. In his efforts to give an account of some of these issues, one technical distinction to which Barth repeatedly appeals is that between the *anhypostasis* in itself of the humanity assumed by the Logos, and its *enhypostasis* in the Logos.[10]

Barth indicates that while these two ways of affirming the same 'indissoluble bond', in statements about God and in statements about Jesus Christ, are correlated with distinct areas of theological inquiry, they are in fact mutually necessary. 'God can as little be without his humanity as his humanity can be without him, be considered or known without him, or indeed be worshipped and invoked without him.'[11] Thus for Barth the conviction I am attempting to explicate – that Jesus' history is God's own – can and should be analysed in two different ways. One is to consider this conviction in terms of what it says about God on account of his indissoluble link with Jesus Christ. I will confine my attention here to the complementary, properly christological procedure, in which the conviction is considered in terms of what it says about Jesus Christ, precisely as a particular person, on account of his indissoluble link with the being and activity by which God defines himself – that is, on account of the incarnation.

Barth's initial step in explicating the conviction that God is the ultimate subject of Jesus' history, and thus in clarifying the logical primitiveness of 'incarnation' among the predicates of Jesus Christ, is to draw attention to other aspects of Christian belief which especially clarify the fittingness or appropriateness of the conviction in question.[12] This procedure has already been at work in the summary remarks I have made on the place of the divinity of Jesus Christ in Barth's Christology. The explicative and inter-pretative connections Barth traces between Christian beliefs are often extraordinarily complex, nowhere more so than when the *explicandum* is the conviction that Jesus' history is God's own. For the present, limited purposes, the point to bear in mind is that these connections are instrumental in specifying the meaning of the conviction. The sense of the conviction that Jesus' history is God's own is specified, for example, by the perception that the cross is the climactic event of Jesus' particular life and thereby the central event (with the resurrection) of reconciliation.

> The cross was and is the crown of the life of the man Jesus because it came about conclusively in his crucifixion that He genuinely took to Himself the situation of man as it is in the judgement of God and therefore in truth, making it God's in his own person, and therefore radically altering and transform-ing it.[13]

Given that on the cross of Jesus Christ the lost human situation is 'God's in his [Jesus'] own person', the belief that Jesus' history is God's own must, on Barth's account, be construed maximalisitically. He often does this by stressing the 'identity' of Jesus' history, and therefore of Jesus himself as a particular person, with God.[14] However, statements of 'identity' in Christo-logy tend to be relatively uninformative unless accompanied by some clarifying explanation, as already seen in connection with the basic assumption that Jesus' own history is really identical with the reconciliation of the world to God.[15] So Barth seeks ways of stating the conviction that God is the ultimate subject of Jesus' history that will clarify this identity in a properly christological context, that is, in terms of what it says about Jesus Christ. One such way is indicated in a number of remarks which suggest that

Jesus' particularity, 'the way from Bethlehem to Golgotha', necessarily implies or entails the immediate presence of God as the subject of this history. 'We must not see and think man – that is, the man Jesus – if we do not immediately also see and think God. In and with the being (*Wesen*) of man the being of God immediately encounters us here [in Jesus]. In and with man we immediately find God existing here.'[16] Given Jesus' particular identity, his union with God is necessarily given as well. Strictly speaking, Barth seems to argue, 'Jesus' history is God's own' has the force of an analytic proposition.

Barth completes the initial phase of his explication of the belief that God is the ultimate subject of Jesus' history by casting that belief in negative form. Jesus Christ, 'where he is not known (*erkannt*) as this one [the Son of God] . . . can no doubt be perceived (*gekannt*) in his humanity, abstracting from him [the Son of God] as its subject, but thereby he is only misunderstood (*verkannt*).'[17] Typically couched in epistemological rather than logical terms, this negative formulation helps to clarify what is at stake for Barth in the positive explication that Jesus' particularity necessarily implies or includes his divinity. Barth's point in maintaining that Jesus' particular humanity can only be misunderstood (*verkannt*) if abstracted from the immediate presence of God is not that his history, 'the way from Bethlehem to Golgotha', is inaccessible to the public eye (including the eye of historical criticism). 'As man and as such of human essence he is also "there" for those who do not know (*erkennen*) him as the Son of God: he is therefore visible and discernible (*kennbar*) for them, and susceptible of various interpretations, like all other men.'[18] The point rests instead on the assumption that genuine knowledge of a human history or particular identity involves recognition of the subject of that history. In the case of Jesus' history or particularity, this seemingly obvious assumption implies that if one is acquainted (*gekannt*) with 'the way from Bethlehem to Golgotha', and thus with Jesus himself, and yet fails to recognize that this history is that of the Son of God, then one has failed to achieve a genuine knowledge of the history itself. Rather, the history or particularity has been misunderstood (*verkannt*), in the sense that it has not led to a recognition of its ultimate subject, a recognition integral to the knowledge of the history itself.[19] As Barth puts the point, persons acquainted only with Jesus' history, and not thereby with God himself, 'do not know (*wissen*) with whom they have to do. They call Him by His true name – Jesus of Nazareth. But they do not know to whom they give this name.'[20]

In the initial phase of his explication of the belief that God himself is the ultimate subject of Jesus' history, and thereby of the logical primitiveness of 'incarnation' among the predicates of Jesus Christ, Barth's primary aim has been clarification. To that end, he has reformulated the belief in several ways which seek to make more plain what is being affirmed in this belief, and also what is being denied. This process of clarification suggests further possibilities of explication which would proceed in ways other than reformulation alone. One such procedure, which promises potentially great explicative reward, would be to give an account of how it is that God is the ultimate subject of Jesus' history. That is, one could develop a description, or several descriptions, of what reality must be like given the belief in question. In this case, that would mean giving a description of the way in which Jesus' history is God's own, such that Jesus' history necessarily implies the immediate presence of God as its ultimate subject and cannot be appreciated without recognition of God as its subject. This is the procedure upon which Barth seizes; he wants to advance his explication of the conviction by offering an ontological description.[21] The conviction itself, of course, seems to imply an ontological affirmation: God is in fact the subject of this particular history.[22] However, Barth wants not only to make the affirmation but also to penetrate more deeply into the reality affirmed and so give a descriptive account of how the affirmation obtains. There may be many good reasons for giving such an account and it may be that such an undertaking is indispensable to theology. For the purposes here, however, the decisive issue is quite specific: it is precisely by offering an ontological description that Barth attempts further to *explicate* what the conviction affirms and denies, that is, what it means.

In another connection, the pivotal feature in Barth's ontological explication of the belief that God himself is the ultimate subject of Jesus' history has already been encountered. Summarizing the basic relation between Jesus' particularity, his significance and his divinity, Barth says that Jesus Christ as a particular person is only 'there' (*da*) in so far as God is present in him as the redeemer of all persons.[23] Jesus' own history, 'the way from Bethlehem to

Golgotha', comes to pass precisely because God is its ultimate subject. According to Barth, the 'act of divine majesty' which constitutes God's original self-determination is the *ratio essendi*, and therefore the *ratio cognoscendi*, of 'the humanly temporal being of Jesus Christ'.[24] His particular identity, in other words, exists or is real and thus is available for ostention and description, because and in so far as God wills to make it his own.[25] 'This Man exists in as much as (*weil und indem*) the Son of God is this Man – not otherwise.'[26]

There are two points Barth especially wants to underscore in this kind of remark. One is that it is precisely Jesus Christ as a particular person who exists because God wills to be the subject of a human history. 'What became and is in the divine act of the incarnation is, of course, a man. It is the man Jesus of Nazareth.'[27] By maintaining that Jesus' particular humanity (and only therein the humanity he shares with everyone else) depends for its reality upon his divinity, Barth's primary purpose is simply to offer an explication of the belief that Jesus' history, and no other, is God's own. By doing so, he is giving a partial account of incarnation attentive to the broader assumption that this, like any characterization of 'that which is significant for salvation', can only be ascribed to Jesus Christ. The other pivotal point concerns the distinctive character of Jesus' existential dependence upon God. It is not simply the case that the reality of Jesus' history depends upon God's creative will. 'The same is true', Barth notes, 'of every man and every creature, for all things need the existence of God as Creator for their own existence.'[28] God is not the subject, *per assumptionem*, of every human history and certainly not of every creaturely reality, although all are existentially dependent upon him. Yet Barth aims to explicate the conviction that God is the ultimate subject of Jesus' history by describing that history as existentially dependent upon God. In order to describe the existential dependence of Jesus' history such that God is really the subject of this history and not simply its creator, Barth takes a further step. Speaking of Jesus Christ as a particular person (*die Besonderheit Jesu Christi*), Barth says, 'his existence as man is identical with the existence of God in his Son'.[29] Jesus' history 'is there', in other words, because God bestows his own existence upon that history; God allows 'his own divine existence to be the existence of the man Jesus'.[30] This specification of Barth's basic descriptive claim seems especially well suited to explicating the belief that Jesus' history is God's own: that history belongs to God in virtue of God's own existence.[31]

This is the point, in his explication of the conviction that God is the ultimate subject of Jesus' history, at which Barth utilizes the longstanding technical distinction between the *anhypostasis* and *enhypostasis* of Jesus' particular humanity.[32] Barth uses this distinction in two different ways. One is to provide alternative formulations, in light of the history of theology, for his own ontological account of the belief that God is the ultimate subject of Jesus' history. The other is to push this explication in a new direction, by proposing a limited causal or genetic account of how God is the subject of Jesus' history.

1   Like most technical terms, *anhypostasis* and *enhypostasis* have been used in different ways, and for sometimes quite different purposes. Consequently, while the terms are ordinarily employed to make a precise distinction in some specific context, it is quite difficult, given the differing contexts of that employment, to say precisely what they mean in abstraction from some specific context.[33] The general sense of the distinction in Barth is basically that of the Protestant scholastics from whom he took it, but his explicit purpose in using it is somewhat different than theirs – to draw, in an ontological description, a maximally strong connection between Jesus Christ as a particular person and the incarnation of God in him. For Barth, Jesus' particular humanity, 'the way from Bethlehem to Golgotha', is *anhypostasis* in that 'apart from its concrete existence (*Dasein*) in God in the event of the *unio*, it has no existence of its own'.[34] Correlatively, Jesus' history is *enhypostasis*, in that 'in virtue of the *assumptio*, the human nature acquires existence (subsistence) in the existence of God, meaning in the mode of being (*hypostasis*, "person") of the Word'.[35]

Especially in its negative formulation, this technical distinction seems usefully to clarify the appropriateness of Barth's basic explicative description, which claims that Jesus' history or particular identity 'is there' because God is its subject, who imparts his own existence to it. If, as the *anhypostasis* is especially designed to deny, Jesus' history were assumed to exist or be 'there' apart from the immediate presence of God in that history, which Barth describes as God's bestowal of his own act of existence, then it is

hard to see how the initial conviction that God is the subject of
Jesus' history could be maintained. That is, if the autonomous
existence of Jesus' history is affirmed and Barth's explicative
description denied, there seems to be no way of affirming at the
ontological/descriptive level that God is immediately present in
this history, himself the subject of the 'lowliness, temptation,
suffering, rejection and death', which comes to pass there.[36] On
the contrary, it would seem that one could only affirm some lesser
kind of divine presence, which is not unique to Jesus' history, and
which does not involve the ascription of the events and patterns of
that history to God himself. Consequently, Barth attaches great
importance to affirming the *anhypostasis* and *enhypostasis* of Jesus'
particular humanity.

> We have seen what depends on it: no less than the fact that in
> Jesus Christ we do not have to do with a man into whom God
> has changed Himself; no less than the unity in which as man
> He is the Son of God, and as the Son of God man; and finally
> no less than the universal relevance and significance (*Trag-
> weite und Bedeutung*) of His existence for all other men.[37]

2   Hints of a causal or genetic aspect in Barth's ontological
explication are already visible in some of the passages to which I
have drawn attention.[38] That is, Barth says not only that Jesus
Christ as a particular person exists in virtue of the immediate
presence of God but also, as this language readily suggests, that
he comes into existence by an act in which God directly communicates his own being.[39] Prior to its union with God, Barth argues,
the humanity of Jesus Christ was a 'possibility', of a relatively
definite kind. That humanity is 'in a determinate form the concrete possibility of the existence of a single man, elected and
prepared not by itself, but (here the election and call of Israel and
Mary intervenes decisively) by God'.[40] When God assumes this
possible humanity into union with himself by sharing his own
existence with it, that possibility becomes a particular person –
Jesus Christ. 'As the Son of God made his own this one specific
(*bestimmte*) possibility of human essence (*Wesens*) and existence
(*Dasein*) and made it a reality, *this* Man *came into being*, and He, the
Son of God, became *this* Man.'[41] Once again, the usefulness of
moving to a new level of explication, this time a more causal one,

is clear in light of the conviction of which Barth is trying to give an account. Jesus' history is God's own, so that conviction emphasizes, precisely in its particularity and uniqueness. The quasi-causal aspect of Barth's explication accounts for that emphasis in an especially graphic way. A single but abstract possibility for a human history, Barth seems to argue, becomes 'Jesus of Nazareth' when God makes that possibility his own actual history. God does not simply become incarnate, his incarnation particularizes Jesus' history, that is, actively makes Jesus 'this man'. In this way, as Barth describes it, Jesus' particular identity, as such, is God's own.

By way of summary it can be seen that there are basically two stages in Barth's explication of the belief, indispensable to the logic of his Christology, that Jesus' history or particular identity is God's own. One is clarifying reformulation, often in terms of the noetic import of the belief; the other is ontological description, which tries to provide a conceptual picture of the state of affairs that the belief affirms. The latter in turn has several aspects; sometimes Barth simply aims to describe the way in which God is the ultimate subject of Jesus' history or particular identity, at other times he gives a limited causal account of how this comes to be the case. In practice, these two basic stages and their various aspects are not always clearly, and never explicitly, distinguished. Cumulatively, the various facets of Barth's overall explication yield a definite set of answers to the heuristic questions proposed at the outset.

1   The basic sense or meaning of the belief can be stated by saying that the immediate presence of God is the ground for the knowledge of Jesus' particular identity (the *ratio cognoscendi)*, *because* it is the ground for the being of Jesus' particular identity (the *ratio essendi*). Adequate knowledge of Jesus' history requires recognition that God is the ultimate subject of the human action and passion which come to pass in it, because that history 'is there' only in virtue of God's immediate presence.

2   The basic sense of the belief implies affirming that in the incarnation, God communicates his own existence to Jesus' history, thereby causing it to be that particular history. This is the

way or mode in which God is the ultimate subject of Jesus' history. This explication of 'incarnation' seems consistent with the basic procedural assumption of the first way, namely that Jesus Christ as a particular person is the ultimate criterion of all that is significant for salvation. In fulfilment of his primal decision about his own being and identity, God becomes incarnate: not simply in 'human nature' or 'a human history', but precisely by actualizing the particular history of Jesus Christ. Since his specific history and no other comes to pass when God becomes the subject of a human action and passion, 'incarnation' can be ascribed only to Jesus Christ. At the same time, the logical primitiveness of 'incarnation' or 'divinity' among the predicates of Jesus Christ has not only been retained, but has received some explication. Whenever we ascribe some feature-specific redemptive significance to Jesus Christ, God is already included in the subject of that ascription, since Jesus Christ is only 'there', as the actual subject of such characterizations, because God is immediately present in him.

Barth's account of the conviction that God is the ultimate subject of Jesus' history or particular identity, as this outline of it indicates, relies heavily upon the explicative and clarifying force of an ontological description. In his effort to specify the meaning and import of the belief, at least within an explicitly christological context, by far the greatest weight seems to be borne by an increasingly technical descriptive account of the state of affairs affirmed in that belief. There is something incongruous about this procedure, an impression which is likely to grow as the technical complexity of the description increases. The incongruity does not lie primarily in any of the host of conceptual and technical questions that might be raised about the ontological or meta-physical feasibility of his description. Barth could and does provide replies to the objections that questions of this kind might suggest, which, while they may not demonstrate that the objections are false, at least show that they are *solubilia argumenta*, without the force of necessity.[42] Indeed, assuming the need for an ontological description of the way in which God is the subject of Jesus' history and given the conceptual alternatives as he sees them, his decisions at each step of the description seem clearly defensible in light of the conviction (or, more accurately, network of convictions) of which he is trying to give an account. Neither does the incongruity lie in the fact that there seem to be ontological descriptions, quite different from Barth's, which also honour the conviction that Jesus' history is God's own. There seems to be no necessary reason why there cannot be several appropriate and complementary technical descriptions of the same reality (which does not, of course, mean that all descriptions are appropriate).

Rather, the incongruity about Barth's procedure consists simply in the enormous *explicative* weight he expects the ontological description to bear. That description is supposed to specify and elaborate the sense of this basic Christian belief.[43] But the description rapidly grows quite complex, a growth attended by a multiplication in the number of concepts and assumptions (in Barth's case, only partially articulated) needed to understand the description. Replying to relevant objections would presumably only increase the complexity of the description and its related assumptions. As a result, even the sympathetic reader is likely to sense a persistent vagueness in Barth's explication; the explicative value of the ontological description, although perhaps not inconsiderable, seems dwarfed by the amount of explanation the description itself needs. Hence the incongruity: articulating the sense of this professedly basic Christian belief, Barth begins to make the belief seem exceptionally arcane.

This incongruity suggests that it would be useful to investigate a different procedure by which the same basic belief might be explicated. It is for this purpose that I shall undertake a brief discussion of Thomas Aquinas. While he by no means abandons ontological description, Thomas shifts much of the *explicative* weight from describing the state of affairs affirmed by the belief to analysing explicitly the kinds of propositions in which the belief is affirmed.

THOMAS AQUINAS'S LOGICO-SEMANTIC EXPLICATION OF 'THIS MAN IS GOD'

I have already drawn brief attention to several features of the Christology of Thomas Aquinas. Turning now to a more detailed analysis of one aspect of his Christology, it will be useful to specify the quite limited aim of the discussion of Thomas. I am concerned with the way he uses logico-grammatical tools to help explicate basically the same christological conviction that Barth finds so central, namely (to employ a more Thomistic formulation) that whatever is rightly said of Jesus Christ as a particular person is thereby said of God. I shall, in other words, be limiting my attention to only a slice of Thomas's Christology, and at the same time to only one instance of the much wider use of logico-grammatical analysis in his theology. This will, unfortunately, leave unexplained the whole of which this slice is but a small part but it is hoped that the bearing of Thomas's approach upon the problem suggested by the analysis of Barth will still be evident.

Unlike Barth, whose explication of the conviction with which I am concerned is rather relentlessly realistic, Thomas is explicitly interested in the relation between language and reality with regard to christological affirmations. Or, to be more precise, Thomas is concerned with specifying the relation between basic, stateable convictions about Jesus Christ and technical, ontological description of the state of affairs affirmed in those convictions.[44] In order properly to locate the function of explicitly logico-grammatical analysis in Thomas's Christology, it will be useful first to outline his view of the relation between christological conviction and ontological description.

Commenting on I Cor. 2:8, 'If they had known, they would not have crucified the Lord of glory' (Vulgate), Thomas makes a brief remark which indicates with striking simplicity his basic attitude toward the function of technical ontological description in Christology. Thomas assumes that since the positive statement, 'the Lord of glory was crucified', is clearly implied by the express words of Scripture, it must be affirmed. He also gives a brief account, which is not an immediate concern here, of how this affirmation is made, that is, of how this predicate can apply to this subject. Concluding, he remarks that 'by this saying of Paul, the error of the Nestorians is brought to nothing, who said that there is one nature in Christ of God and man. Because if their opinion were correct, it could in no way be verified (*verificari*) that "the Lord of glory was crucified"'.[45] In this case, 'the Lord of glory was crucified' functions as a christological conviction of the kind with which I am concerned, where what happens in Jesus' history is ascribed to God himself. But the Nestorian ontological description of the incarnation or union of natures, as Thomas understands it, proposes different ultimate subjects for the properties or attributes of the divine and human natures. For that reason, Thomas argues, it must be false, precisely because it cannot 'verify' a conviction in which a predicate appropriate to one nature is ascribed to a subject with another nature. That is, given the shared technical vocabulary of 'person' and 'nature', the Nestorian account does not describe what reality must be like, given the affirmation that 'the Lord of glory was crucified'.[46]

This same conception of the way basic convictional affirmations govern ontological description in Christology is evinced in Thomas's comments upon another Biblical passage which he treats as a central conviction about Jesus Christ, 'The Word became flesh' (Jn. 1:14). Again arguing against 'Nestorianism', Thomas points out that 'it is impossible that one of two individuals (*singularium*), which are different in subject (*suppositum*), be predicated of the other'. For this reason, he continues, 'if in Christ the person or subject of the Word and the person or subject of the man are different, then what the Evangelist says will not be true: "The Word became flesh"'.[47] This lack of congruity with the Biblical affirmation, Thomas argues, requires that the ontological description be revised.[48] In other words, it is the way Scripture speaks about Jesus Christ which requires that, if the alternative is mere 'indwelling', the relation of humanity and divinity in Jesus Christ be described as 'hypostatic union'.

In light of these examples, the force of Thomas's general formulation of the function of ontological description with respect to christological conviction will be easier to appreciate. On Thomas's account, the central ontological description of the incarnation is that in Jesus Christ, unabridged divine and human natures are united in one person, and thereby in one 'hypostasis' and 'supposit'. The concern here is why this descriptive formulation is accepted over all the alternative uses of essentially the same terminology (primarily the logical alternatives suggested by the ancient heresies, which Thomas considers in great detail). For Thomas, the decisive reason is that 'only in this way is it possible to save (*salvari*) those things which are taught in Scripture concerning the Incarnation'.[49] Scripture does not, of course, explicitly teach this or any other ontological description of the incarnation. But, as we have seen Thomas argue, it does speak about Jesus Christ in a particular way: 'Holy Scripture attributes without distinction (*indistincte*) those things which are God's to this man, and those things which are this man's to God.'[50] The function of an ontological account of the incarnation, therefore, is to 'save' this *modus loquendi* of Scripture, to render an account of reality governed by the way Scripture speaks about Jesus Christ. This distinctive way of speaking, which for Thomas is found paradigmatically in Scripture, and secondarily in the councils and the church at large, is logically basic in a theology of incarnation; the appropriateness of any ontological description of the incarnation or 'hypostatic union' is measured by its conformity to this *modus loquendi*.

Thomas does not simply propose this relationship of priority and dependence as a general procedural observation about Christology, but specifies the basic way in which Scripture's manner of speaking stipulates a particular use of the technical terminology of 'person' (or 'hypostasis') and 'nature'. That in reality of which the properties of a nature are predicated, Thomas notes, is called the 'hypostasis' or 'supposit' of that nature.[51] Therefore, 'since with regard to Christ there is one and the same subject (*indistinctum est et unum id*) of which human and divine things are predicated, it is necessary to say that Christ is one hypostasis and supposit of human and divine nature.'[52] The aim of using the technical terminology of 'person' and 'nature', with the various complications that can attend its use, is to give a description of a specific reality, namely the incarnation of God in Jesus Christ. But the description we actually give, Thomas argues, is necessary (*necesse est dicere*) because of the way we speak (following Scripture) about Jesus Christ and, more specifically, because of a pattern of predication evinced in our speech about Jesus Christ.[53]

Thus for Thomas the proper and primary subject matter of Christology, and thereby of a theology of incarnation, is the *modus loquendi* of Scripture concerning Jesus Christ. The task of giving an ontological description of the incarnation is clearly distinguished from that of grasping the way Scripture speaks about Jesus Christ and is assigned a derivative place in a theology of incarnation. This position suggests that the relation between language and reality in Christology, or more precisely between the scriptural *modus loquendi* and ontological description, is at least two-fold. This two-fold relation is evident in both the primarily logico-grammatical and primarily descriptive sections of Thomas's Christology, as will be plain when one of the ways Thomas explicates the conviction that 'this man is God' is examined.

The character of the relation between language and reality in Thomas's Christology can be indicated by employing a distinction between the *definition* of truth (or of the 'relation of language to reality') and the *criterion* of truth. Like most medieval theologians, Thomas thinks that a proposition is true, in the final analysis, because in some sense it is 'adequate to' or 'conforms to' reality.[54] In a broad and non-technical sense, it can be said that on Thomas's account, a true proposition is one which in some way 'corresponds to reality'.[55] 'Correspondence to reality' is the definition of truth for Thomas, and this definition seems to apply in a christological context not only to what Scripture says about Jesus Christ but also to the technical description of hypostatic union which depends on and conforms to what Scripture says.[56] Since Thomas holds the ontological description to be true in this sense, there are a number of passages in his Christology which argue that, because there is in fact a union of two natures in one person or hypostasis, we (and Scripture) have a legitimate basis for speaking about Jesus Christ the way we do.

This might seem to countermand the claim that the hypostatic union must be affirmed precisely on account of Scripture's *modus loquendi*, and thereby to place ontological description, rather than this *modus loquendi* itself, at the logical heart of Christology.[57] However, the incongruity is only apparent. The ontological description of the incarnation as 'hypostatic union' fits the definition of truth, that is, it corresponds to reality. But the *criterion* of its truth, the reason it can be asserted to correspond to reality and thus to fit the definition of truth, is its relative conformity with Scripture's way of speaking about Jesus Christ. At least with regard to 'divine things' (*in divinis*, as Thomas typically puts it), those which are objects of faith in this life but not of knowledge, we do not formulate technical descriptions by directly inspecting the relevant state of affairs, but by deploying our technical descriptive language in a way which conforms to ('saves') the convictions paradigmatically stated in Scripture.[58]

In light of this distinction between the definition and the

criterion of truth, it is possible to summarize the two-fold relation
between Scripture's *modus loquendi* concerning Jesus Christ and an
ontological description of the hypostatic union as follows: (1) The
content and mode of what Scripture says about Jesus Christ are
true in that there is a state of affairs in reality which corresponds
to them, and is appropriately described, among other ways, as
'hypostatic union'. (2) This description itself is to be affirmed as
true (as corresponding to reality) because it conforms to or
coheres with the content and mode of what Scripture says about
Jesus Christ.

My interest, it will be recalled, lies in indicating how Thomas
explicates the belief (to use his formulation) that 'God is this
man', and 'this man is God'.[59] More precisely, I want to see how
Thomas accounts for these convictions in a way consistent with
the assumption that they can only apply to Jesus Christ. In order
to explicate a similar conviction, Barth appeals to a complex
description of the reality which the conviction affirms. Thomas
also has a place, as has been shown, for the kind of technical
description Barth employs. But he considers ontological description ill-suited for the specific task of explicating these convictions,
that is, of clarifying and specifying what the convictions affirm
and deny.

The reason for this deficiency lies in the character of the
relation of divinity and humanity in Jesus Christ. That relation is
'a certain unique union (*unio singularis*), beyond all the modes of
union known to us'.[60] Based upon the *modus loquendi* of Scripture, it
is possible to give reasons for affirming 'hypostatic union' as a
basically appropriate description of the way in which 'this man is
God', and also to give reasons for excluding descriptions which
clearly fail to 'save' the *modus loquendi*. But this does not mean for
Thomas that 'hypostatic union' is an adequate description of the
way in which 'this man is God'. On the contrary, he insists that it
must be regarded, its relative appropriateness notwithstanding,
as an inadequate description. Our language and understanding,
Thomas holds, are suited to giving adequate descriptions of
created reality (whether or not they actually succeed in doing so
in any particular case). The created reality which is probably most
like the hypostatic union of divinity and humanity in Jesus Christ,
Thomas usually supposes, is the union of body and soul in the
individual human person. Even this most apt example, however,

'fails to represent the [hypostatic] union, just as all human examples fail (*deficiunt*) to represent divine things'.[61] 'Hypostatic union' is a 'divine thing', that is, it is something we say about God. Like all divine things, Thomas maintains, we can give a description of it but we cannot specify the sense in which the description applies.

In order to give an account of this situation, Thomas employs a distinction, drawn from the linguistic theory of his day, between what a term signifies (the *res significata*) and the way in which it signifies (the *modus significandi*). When we speak of God, the *res significata* of our terms can apply to him, at least in some cases, because he possesses in a divine and therefore perfect way that which the term signifies (for example, perfection terms like 'good' and 'wise'). On the other hand, the *modus significandi* of the terms never applies to God, because it is suited to the description of creaturely reality rather than divine reality; we have no way of expressing what it is to be divinely 'good' and 'wise'. But we never use our terms, even in speaking about God, without introducing some mode of signification appropriate to creatures; consequently, our language about God 'fails to represent divine things'.[62]

With regard to the case at hand, all our notions of union, unity, hypostasis and so forth are informed by modes of signification suited to the various unions and subjects ('hypostases') we encounter among created things. We do not have concepts which express the mode of the divine unity, power and subsistence, which we would need, Thomas argues, if we were adequately to describe the 'hypostatic union'.[63] So, while we can affirm for good reasons that 'hypostatic union' is an appropriate description of the state of affairs in which 'this man is God', we cannot say what the description means; since it is a 'divine thing', we have no *modus significandi* for 'hypostatic union'. It is for this reason, Thomas seems to imply, that ontological descriptions of the incarnation require an ever increasing load of qualifications and thereby so quickly become complex and unwieldy.

This difficulty, as has been seen, makes Barth's technical theology of incarnation relatively unhelpful as an explication of the belief that God is the ultimate subject of Jesus' history or particular identity. Thomas's analysis of the derivative place of such technical accounts and of their ineluctable descriptive inadequacy, suggests the usefulness of an alternative kind of explication. It may be more helpful to attend explicitly to important features of the christological *modus loquendi* itself – that is, to engage in a logico-grammatical analysis of the belief that 'this man is God'.

My present interest in the logico-semantic side of Thomas's Christology is quite specific. I am concerned to clarify the 'logical primitiveness' of incarnation among characterizations of Jesus' significance. For Thomas, this is primarily a matter of explicating the logical primitiveness of 'is God' among the predicates of Jesus Christ, and thus of analysing propositions like 'this man is God'. To be sure, my specific interest is only one of the topics in Christology to which Thomas applies this kind of analysis, as a survey of the questions raised in *Summa Theologiae* III, 16 would indicate. Thomas's aim in this complex and variegated logico-grammatical analysis, taken as a whole, can be seen as one of specifying and enriching his account of the christological *modus loquendi* of Scripture. He does this by considering a number of propositions which function as paradigms or test cases and so help to define, by virtue of their coherence or incoherence with Scripture's essential *modus loquendi*, the parameters of appropriate discourse about Jesus Christ. The basic descriptive picture which 'verifies' this *modus loquendi* ('hypostatic union') is never far from Thomas's mind in these logico-grammatical discussions; the latter help to explicate that description by clarifying the criteria of its truth, namely the various aspects of Scripture's *modus loquendi* about Jesus Christ.

In the *Summa Theologiae*, Thomas begins the explicitly logico-grammatical section of his Christology with an analysis of the propositions *Deus est homo* ('God is a man', or 'this man'), and *Homo est Deus* ('A man', or 'This man' 'is God').[64] Taken together, these two propositions seem not only to be authorized by, but to summarize the basic contours of, that scriptural way of speaking in which the things of 'this man' and of 'God' are predicated of one another *indistincte*, that is, with no distinction regarding the subject of whom they are said.[65] The analysis of these propositions is not the primary place, however, where Thomas attends in detail to the logical primitiveness of 'is God' among the predicates of Jesus Christ and thereby to the function of this predicate with regard to the particularity of Jesus Christ. Rather, the principal object of Thomas's analysis of these propositions is to isolate the grammatical feature (specifically, the *modus significandi*) of the terms *Deus* and *homo* that allows them 'truly and literally' (*vere et proprie*) to be predicated of one another, namely that they are concrete rather than abstract terms.[66] In order to clarify the issue with which I am primarily concerned, Thomas uses a different method of analysis, which was known in his day as 'reduplication'.

For Thomas, a reduplicative proposition is one that is qualified by an expression like 'according as' or 'in so far as' or simply 'as'. The force of this kind of qualifying expression is to indicate 'that on account of which the predicate belongs to the subject'.[67] So, to use a few of Thomas's examples, 'a body, according as it is coloured, is visible', is a reduplication.[68] So is the statement, 'this man is curly, on account of his hair'.[69] In each case the predicate ('visible', 'curly') applies 'truly and literally' to the subject ('a body', 'this man'). The appropriateness of the predication could easily be recognized without the reduplication (for example, 'a body is visible'). But the special function of the term or phrase introduced by 'according as' or its equivalent is to specify the *respect* in which the predicate applies to the subject (or, as the case may be, a respect in which it does not apply). Because they readily help to isolate the features of a subject in virtue of which various predicates apply to that subject, reduplicative propositions are especially useful in Christology.

As I have indicated, Thomas approves the proposition, 'A man is God' (*Homo est Deus*); indeed he seems to regard it as expressing an essential feature of Scripture's way of speaking about Jesus Christ. It may therefore seem somewhat surprising at first glance when he explicitly rejects the proposition, 'Christ, as man, is God' (*Christus, secundum quod homo, est Deus*).[70] However, the point of proposing this reduplicative proposition for analysis is not to question the assertion, 'Jesus Christ is God', but to isolate the respect in which the predicate 'is God' applies to Jesus Christ. The question, then, is whether we predicate 'is God' of Jesus Christ 'in so far as he is man'. The answer to that, Thomas points out, depends in part upon whether the term *homo* in a reduplicative phrase (such as *secundum quod homo*) has the force of a predicate or of a subject. It can be taken either way, but Thomas argues that it is more natural to take it as a predicate, since 'as man' is really a kind of shorthand for 'according as he *is man*'. And a bare predicate, introduced without any qualification (like *homo* in this case), is ordinarily 'taken formally'; it indicates some formal or common feature of the subject to which it applies, in this case the very nature or essence of the subject.[71] So the question, in effect, is whether Jesus' human nature or essence, that in virtue of which he and all other human beings fit the definition of *homo*, is the respect in which we say he 'is God'.

In respect of his human nature, Thomas emphasizes, Jesus Christ does not differ from any other human being. 'That which belongs to Christ, as man, belongs to any man.'[72] It is for precisely this reason, he argues, that the proposition must be denied. According to the *modus loquendi* of Scripture, the 'things of God' are not predicated of Jesus Christ in virtue of that which he has in common with all other human beings, that is, 'in so far as he is man'. If 'is God' is applied to Jesus Christ in virtue of what he has in common with all others, it could just as readily apply to any other human being as to him. Thomas puts the point even more starkly: 'If Christ, as man, is God, it follows that every man is God – which is obviously false.'[73] However, for the same reason that Scripture's way of speaking about Jesus Christ excludes the proposition, 'Christ, as man, is God', it authorizes the obverse proposition. It is true to say, Thomas contends, that 'Christ, as *this* man, is God'.[74] This is precisely the respect in which Scripture attributes the 'things of God' to Jesus Christ. He 'is God' in virtue of that by which he differs from all other human beings, that is, in virtue of all that makes him 'this man', or what Thomas calls a 'determinate subject'.[75] Both propositions are useful in specifying Scripture's way of speaking about Jesus Christ as a particular person and about the incarnation of God; together they indicate what kind of speech is excluded and what kind is enjoined. The mutual explicative force of the two propositions is nicely summarized by Thomas in a passage from the *Scriptum super Sententiis*.

This name 'man' does not introduce a determinate subject of human nature, unless a demonstrative is added, and it belongs only to a specific subject of human nature to be God *per se*. Because of this, unless something else is added or understood, this proposition should not be accepted without qualification: 'Christ, as man, is God.'[76]

Thomas also develops an elaboration of the basic ontological description of incarnation as 'hypostatic union' along the lines suggested by this bit of logico-grammatical analysis. At least one reason for doing this, as I have pointed out, lies in Thomas's definition of truth. Since truth is most broadly defined by Thomas as the adequation or conformation of the mind to the thing and since statements which cohere with Scripture's *modus loquendi* (such as, 'Christ, as *this* man, is God') are assumed to be true in this sense, theology for Thomas should also give what I have been calling an 'ontological description' of 'the thing' to which the mind is 'conformed' by affirming such propositions.

The ontological or descriptive aspect of Thomas's Christology can indeed become rather more complex even than Barth's; here I will simply indicate quite briefly the basic direction which that development takes, as it bears on my specific interest. Jesus Christ 'is God', according to Thomas's linguistic analysis, precisely in so far as he is 'this man', a 'determinate subject'. He 'is God', therefore, in so far as he is 'Jesus', the bearer of this proper name, who is distinguished from all other persons by his 'determinate properties' and his specific location in space and time.[77] By contrast, he is not 'God' simply in virtue of that which he has in common with all other persons, considered in abstraction from the ostensible and describable features which make him 'Jesus'. To use terminology employed earlier, Jesus 'is God' as a 'particular individual', but not as a 'positive individual'.[78] This suggests a mutual internal relation or correlation between the subject 'Jesus Christ' and the predicate 'is God'. As Thomas argues, it is in respect of his particular identity or 'determinate properties' that the predicate 'is God' applies to Jesus Christ; only on that basis does it apply to the humanity which all other persons also possess. But the converse also seems to hold. If this predicate is applied in a proposition, then the determinate subject Jesus Christ must be present. Correlatively, apart from the application of the predicate 'is God', this determinate subject (*iste homo*) is not present, but only 'a man' (*homo*). Jesus Christ is 'this man', a determinate subject, just in so far as he 'is God'.

This last point is accentuated in the way Thomas develops his ontological description of 'hypostatic union'. Ontologically speaking, to recall, Jesus Christ 'is God' for Thomas in that there is in him a single hypostasis of human and divine natures, or, more precisely, in that the divine Logos is the hypostasis or ultimate subject of his particular humanity.[79] On Thomas's account, a hypostasis or person is that which exists independently or by itself (*per se*); it is that which 'subsists'.[80] Moreover, a subject in a given nature is particular or 'determinate', that is, actually ostensible and describable, on account of its subsistence or independent existence. This means that 'the individuation appropriate to human nature is personality', since 'personality' is for Thomas simply the independent existence of a human nature (or, more broadly, of any rational nature).[81] Therefore Jesus Christ is a particular or determinate subject of human nature, 'this man' and not simply 'man' or 'a man', in so far as he subsists or has independent existence. And, following the basic description of 'hypostatic union', Jesus exists independently in or through the person (or hypostasis) of the Logos.

> Not on its own account does human nature in Christ subsist separately, but it exists in another, that is in the hypostasis of the Word of God (not, indeed, like an accident in a subject, nor literally like a part in a whole, but by an inexpressible act of assumption).[82]

At this point, Thomas's ontological description is quite congruent with Barth's, despite the conceptual differences. As for Barth Jesus' history or particular identity is only 'there' because God makes it his own, so for Thomas Jesus is only 'there' as a particular or determinate subject because he exists in the person of the Word. In either case, Jesus Christ is a particular person only on account of the incarnation of God in him. As I have shown, though, Thomas reaches the point of giving an ontological description of this affirmation by a rather different route than Barth and thereby needs to rely a good deal less on such a description for explicating the basic sense and import of the affirmation.

Like Barth's, Thomas's way of explicating the belief that 'Jesus Christ is God', and correlatively the logical primitiveness of incarnation among the characterizations of Jesus' significance, can be summarized readily with reference to the questions posed at the outset.

1 The basic sense of the belief, which Thomas's method of analysis highlights, is that Jesus Christ 'is God' precisely as 'this

man', rather than simply as 'man'. Thomas gives an account of
the conviction that 'Jesus Christ is God' in which, if 'incarnation'
predicates apply at all, their grammar requires them to apply
exclusively to Jesus Christ. Thomas has not, of course, attempted
to prove that such predicates actually do apply, or that the bare
idea of incarnation requires Jesus Christ as its subject. But then it
is not, *per assumptionem*, the bare idea of incarnation which is
significant for salvation, but rather incarnation as a predicate of
Jesus Christ.

2   What must be affirmed about the bearing of 'incarnation' on
Jesus' particularity, and thereby about the logically primitive
function of 'incarnation' among the predicates of Jesus Christ, is
also cast into bold relief by Thomas's analysis. He is 'Jesus', the
determinate subject who receives any other saving predicates and
is their criterion of meaningfulness and meaning, only in so far as
he receives the predicate 'is God'. The consistency of this logically
primitive function of 'incarnation' with the first way is already
evident from the way Thomas explicates the basic sense of the
belief that 'Jesus Christ is God'. For Thomas, Jesus 'is God'
precisely as a particular person; this predicate can apply only to
him, as 'this man', and to no other sharer in our common nature.
This is just that conviction about Jesus Christ which Thomas,
Barth and Rahner all want to honour in Christology, not only with
regard to incarnation, but with regard to everything that is said of
Jesus Christ and his ultimate significance.

In light of Thomas's explication of the belief that Jesus Christ is
'God incarnate', even more clearly than Barth's, a concluding
recollection of Rahner may not be wholly out of place. For
Thomas, Jesus Christ 'is God', explicitly in virtue of that which
distinguishes him from us as a human being, rather than that
which we hold in common with him. For Rahner, it seems, Jesus
'is the absolute saviour' in so far as he is the first instance of a
general pattern which we can realize in common with him. And, I
have argued, because for Rahner the saving character of this
pattern logically depends upon its being at least potentially
common to us and him, that which distinguishes him from us as
human beings need never have a place in 'the idea of an absolute
saviour'. To be sure, this contrast does not constitute the dif-

ference between the two ways of giving a theological account of the conviction that only Jesus Christ can be the unique redeemer; it only typifies that difference. Yet at perhaps no single point is the divergence of the two ways, and the peculiar difficulty the second way will have in honouring that conviction, more striking.

NOTES

1 Karl Barth, *Church Dogmatics* (Edinburgh: 1932–68) (hereafter *CD*), IV/1, p. 553. The German original is Karl Barth, *Kirchliche Dogmatik* (Munich and Zurich: 1932–68) (hereafter *KD*), IV/1, p. 617. References to all of Barth's works will be given for both German and English editions, whenever the latter are available (see Preface). Cf. *KD*, IV/1, p. 244; *CD*, IV/1, pp. 222–3: 'Because he was a *man* as we are, he was in the situation in which he could be judged as man, as this comes upon *us*.' This implies, to use the language I have employed, that any potential characterization of redemption must be fit for application to Jesus as a particular person on account of the distinctive shape of his history. But something else is necessary for the judgement of Jesus 'as man' to be a saving event for us. 'Because he was *God's Son* and himself God, he had the competence and power to allow that to happen to him in our place. Because he was the divine *judge* who had entered our midst, he thereby had the authority – in his self-surrender to judgement in our place – to administer the divine justice of grace.' On the logical indispensability of divine 'competence', 'power' and 'authority' for the redemptive significance of Jesus' action and passion, cf. also *CD*, IV/1, p. 233, p. 236; *KD*, IV/1, p. 255, p. 259.
2 *CD*, IV/2, p. 51; *KD*, IV/2, p. 54.
3 On the notion of a feature-specific characterization of Jesus' significance, as distinguished from a feature-neutral one (of which 'incarnation' is in fact a leading instance), cf. chap. 3, pp. 89–91.
4 It would be both desirable and illuminating to investigate the particularity of Jesus Christ in Rahner's theology of incarnation as well. Some of his technical analyses of incarnation suggest a high evaluation of the conviction that Jesus' human history is God's own history, even though, in contrast to Barth and Thomas, he does not explicate this conviction with explicit attention to questions of particularity (cf., e.g., his idealist reconceptualization of the notion of hypostatic union in Karl Rahner, *Theological Investigations* (TI), tr. Cornelius Ernst et al. (20 vols, New York: 1961–83) vol. 11, pp. 180–3. This is a translation of Karl Rahner, *Schriften zur Theologie*

(SzT) (16 vols, Einsiedeln: 1954 – 84), vol. 1, pp. 201–4. See the Preface for the practice of citing these references.)

But these considerations do not find their way into the mainstream of his developed Christology, viz., his analysis and deployment of the idea of an absolute saviour. Since the notion and dogma of the incarnation of God is an indispensable but logically derivative alternative formulation of the notion of an absolute saviour (cf. chap. 2, pp. 37–9 and pp. 40–2), the particularity of Jesus Christ would presumably not be the criterion of 'significance for salvation' in a Rahnerian Christology cast primarily in terms of 'incarnation', just as it is not, if my argument is correct, in one cast in terms of 'an absolute saviour'. As a result, explicating the logical priority of 'incarnation' in such a theology is a different task from that which faces Barth and the first way; as I have indicated, it is the task of showing that 'absolute saviour', which includes 'incarnation', is maximally coherent with the general criterion of significance for salvation.

5   *S. Thomae de Aquino Summa contra Gentiles* (hereafter *SCG*), IV, 35, 13, editio Leonina manualis (Turin and Rome: 1946). Cf. also III, 2, 5, ad2. (On the method of citation for Thomas's *Summa Theologiae*, cf. chap. 2, n. 86). All translations from the Latin are my own. Cf. also on this point Barth's statement that 'the classical doctrine of the two natures speaks of the one Jesus Christ, and only of Him. And it does this *a posteriori*, with a reference to him (*im Blick auf ihn*), to the Son of God actually existing in the flesh. It does not derive from a known *a priori*, a superior possibility, but only from the given actuality, from Him Himself' (*CD*, IV/2, pp. 61 – 2; *KD*, IV/2, p. 66. Cf. also chap. 4, n. 35). On the issue of possibility and actuality in this connection, see the next point (no. 3).

6   This is also the logic, it will be recalled, of one aspect of my argument against Rahner's treatment of the idea of an 'absolute saviour'. He treats this concept as a class name, even though this is inconsistent with his own assumptions about Jesus Christ as its unique subject.

7   'Proofs (*probationes*) which are introduced against the faith are not demonstrations, but soluble arguments (*solubilia argumenta*)', I, 1, 8, r.

8   Walter Kreck, *Grundentscheidungen in Karl Barths Dogmatik: Zur Diskussion seines Verständnisses von Offenbarung und Erwählung* (Neukirchen – Vlvyn: 1978), p. 195. For several of the Barthian texts that support this remark, cf. chap. 4, n. 38.

9   This *theologoumenon* is particularly interesting as a kind of microcosm of the reorientation in Barth's theology which seems to begin with 'The Doctrine of Election' (cf. chap. 4, pp. 129–30). In his *Die christliche Dogmatik im Entwurf. Erster Band: Die Lehre vom Wort Gottes.*

Prolegomena zur christlichen Dogmatik, ed. Gerhard Sauter (Zurich: 1982) pp. 358–64, and again in *Church Dogmatics* I/2, pp. 166–71; *KD* I/2, pp. 181–7, Barth issues a ringing endorsement of a real distinction between the Logos *asarkos* and *ensarkos,* which he basically equates with an affirmaation of the *Extra Calvinisticum.* In order to uphold the sovereignty of God in the act of revelation, and the 'event' character of revelation, it is necessary, Barth maintains, to affirm that even in the incarnation (*ensarkos*), the Logos has a being and activity 'outside' the assumed humanity (*extra carnem*); 'on that account the "Extra Calvinisticum" is an indispensable Christological decision (*Bestimmung*)' (*Die christliche Dogmatik,* p. 364; cf. the more modest statement of the same point in *CD* I/2, p. 171; *KD,* I/2, p. 186).

Having made the turn to a radical theology of election, and thus to the consistent primacy of 'the name and person of Jesus Christ' for God's own being as well as our knowledge of God, this affirmation seems at best strikingly incongruous (in light, e.g., of *CD,* II/2, p. 96; *KD,* II/2, p. 103: 'It is He, Jesus, who is in the beginning with God . . . This is what is guaranteed in Jn. 1:1'). Barth does indeed emphatically reject the *logos asarkos* on these grounds, albeit without reference to his earlier endorsement (cf. *CD,* IV/1, pp. 52–3; *KD,* IV/1, pp. 54–6). Yet curiously he retains the *Extra Calvinisticum,* despite its basic similarity to the *logos asarkos,* and thus despite its apparent inconsistency with a theology governed by the primacy of the assumption that God is inseparable from 'the name of Jesus Christ' (cf. *CD,* IV/1, pp. 180–1; *KD,* IV/1, pp. 196–7). Barth proposes, of course, a modified and harmonious construction of the *Extra Calvinisticum* (cf. Eberhard Jüngel, *Barth-Studien* (Zurich–Cologne, Benzinger and Gütersloh: 1982), p. 338, n. 16). But his explicit retention of it also seems to owe something to a virtually constitutional unwillingness to disagree with the Reformed theologians of the sixteenth and seventeenth centuries when *they* disagreed with the Lutherans, an inclination no doubt exacerbated by what Barth called the 'pig-headed confessionalism' of many of his Lutheran contemporaries (cf. Eberhard Busch, *Karl Barth. His Life From Letters and Autobiographical Texts,* 2nd edn, tr. John Bowden (Philadelphia: 1976), p. 429).

10 As I will shortly consider Barth's use of this distinction in some detail, I will not explain it at this point.

11 *KD,* IV/2, pp. 112–13; *CD,* IV/2, p. 102.

12 Barth's approach here might usefully be illuminated by a comparison with the Thomistic *argumentum ex convenientia* (e.g., that for the incarnation on account of the goodness of God in III, 1, 1, r), but I will have to forego such an exploration in this context.

13 *CD*, IV/2, p. 293; *KD*, IV/2, p. 326.

14 For example, Barth says that 'in the existence of this man we have
    to reckon with the identity (*Identität*) of his action as true man with
    the action of the true God' (*CD*, IV/2, p. 99; *KD*, IV/2, p. 110). For
    related statements of the 'identity' of Jesus as a particular person
    with God, cf. *CD*, IV/2, pp. 97–8, p. 114; *KD*, IV/2, pp. 107–8, p. 127.

15 Cf. chap. 4, n. 17.

16 *KD*, III/2, p. 79; *CD*, III/2, p. 68. (As the language indicates, this
    remark comes in the context of Barth's articulation of the christo-
    logical orientation of theological anthropology.) Similarly, '[Jesus]
    is *himself* [i.e., has his particular identity], in the fact that he does the
    work of God and in this action is *one* with God' (*KD*, III/2, p. 74; *CD*,
    III/2, p. 64). Cf. also *CD*, III/2, p. 62; *KD*, III/2, p. 72.

17 *KD*, IV/2, p. 113; *CD*, IV/2, p. 102. A perhaps more striking, but
    rather less helpful remark of the same type is that 'in itself and as
    such the humanity of Jesus Christ is a predicate without a subject'
    (ibid.).

18 *KD*, IV/2, p. 100; *CD*, IV/2, p. 91. For a similar employment of the
    distinction between acquaintance (*kennen*) and recognition or
    knowledge (*erkennen*), cf. *KD*, IV/2, p. 40; *CD*, IV/2, p. 38.

19 The qualification 'ultimate' is of course crucial, since the presence
    of the divine subject in Jesus Christ does not preclude but rather
    includes and implies an independent human will and action on his
    part. 'That he does the work of God, and in this action is one with
    God, does not mean that he himself, this man as such, is extinguish-
    ed, disappears, and no longer exists. Precisely in his doing the work
    of God and thus in his unity of being (*Einssein*) with God he is on the
    contrary truly himself, this *man*' (*KD*, III/2, p. 74; *CD*, III/2, p. 64).
    An analysis of the two-fold will and action in Jesus Christ, and more
    generally of the non-oppositional relation between divine and
    human agency, is outside the scope of my present purpose.

20 *CD*, IV/2, p. 91; *KD*, IV/2, p. 100. Barth's contention that an
    apprehension of Jesus' particularity which abstracts from his
    divinity can only be a defective apprehension of Jesus himself can
    be traced back to his first dogmatic Christology. Indeed, it receives
    some of its sharpest formulations there, as a warrant for the claim
    that the notion of a 'merely historical' knowledge of Jesus Christ is
    in fact incoherent. 'From the same concrete identity [viz., 'of the
    reality of the humanity of Christ with the reality of the Word of
    God'] it follows that any *Jesus cult*, any worship of the human nature
    or the historical appearance of Christ *as such* is impossible, because
    it has no object' (*Die christliche Dogmatik*, p. 357; cf. p. 353). Indeed,
    such worship is here characterized as 'the divinization of nothing'
    (*Die christliche Dogmatik*, p. 358). For the initial version of these

formulations in Barth's first lectures on dogmatics, cf. '*Unterricht in der christlichen Religion*', *Erster Band: Prolegomena*, ed. Hannelotte Reiffin (Zurich: 1985), p. 194. On this issue cf. also *CD*, I/1, pp. 404–6; *KD*, I/1, pp. 424 – 6; *CD*, I/2, pp. 136–8; *KD*, I/2, pp. 150 – 1.

21 By 'ontological' or 'technical' description here, I mean primarily a description which (a) is supposed to be true, in the sense that it obtains in reality, and (b) uses concepts that can be applied, although perhaps not in a univocal sense, to realities other than the one being described. 'Two natures are united in one person', for example, often has been treated as an ontological description, in basically this sense, of the state of affairs in which 'the Word became flesh'. Cf. below, n. 47.

22 Barth appears to take this entirely for granted, and so does not explicitly distinguish, as I have done, between clarifying the belief and giving an ontological account of it. The two are indeed intermingled, sometimes inextricably so, in Barth's text.

23 Cf. chap. 4, n. 41. Jüngel puts Barth's point neatly. 'The true man Jesus is there only in the concrete coexistence of God and man in one and the same history' (Jüngel, *Barth-Studien*, p. 242).

24 *CD*, IV/2, p. 37; *KD*, IV/2, p. 39.

25 At just this point, it should be noted, the internal relation between Christology and the doctrine of God is especially clear in Barth. The radical presupposition of Jesus' particular humanity is God's self-election, i.e., his decision to bear this name.

26 *CD*, I/2, p. 151; *KD*, I/2, p. 164. Cf. *KD*, I/2, p. 165; *CD*, I/2, p. 151: 'God himself in person is the subject of a real human being and doing. And precisely in this way, in that God is its subject, and not otherwise, is this being and doing real.' Like much of the more technical material in Barth's Christology, this assertion of the existential dependence of Jesus' particularity upon the incarnation of God in him first appears in the *Die christliche Dogmatik*. 'The reality of the humanity, the flesh and the historicity of God the reconciler stands and falls with the reality of his act among us, with the reality of the Word spoken to us and received by us' (*Die christliche Dogmatik*, p. 352). Cf. also '*Unterricht in der christlichen Religion*', p. 183.

27 *CD*, IV/2, pp. 47–8; *KD*, IV/2, p. 51.

28 *CD*, IV/2, p. 90; *KD*, IV/2, p. 99.

29 Ibid.

30 *CD*, IV/2, p. 51; *KD*, IV/2, p. 55. Cf. *CD*, IV/2, p. 41; *KD*, IV/2, p. 44; *CD*, I/2, p. 136; *KD*, I/2, p. 150.

31 Barth never discusses the position he takes here as a topic in its own right but introduces it only in the explicative connection I have just outlined. The position is amplified somewhat, as will be seen, when Barth takes up the *anhypostasis* and *enhypostasis* of the humanity of

Jesus Christ. By making no significant distinction between discussion of Jesus Christ's 'act of existence' and of the *anhypostasis/enhypostasis*, Barth follows the lead of Protestant scholasticism, from which almost all of the technical material in his Christology derives.

By contrast, the 'act of existence' in Jesus Christ was extensively discussed as a distinct topic in medieval and renaissance scholasticism, especially after Thomas Aquinas, under the rubric 'Whether in Christ there is only one act of existence (*esse*)?' (III, 17, 2). Although it is worked out in much greater detail, Thomas's position on the issue is essentially the same as Barth's: 'the eternal existence (*esse aeternum*) of the Son of God . . . becomes the existence of this man, in so far as human nature is assumed by the Son of God into a unity of person' (III, 17, 2, ad2): On the *esse* of Jesus Christ as *increatum*, cf. III, 16, 10, ad3; III, 2, 6, ad2. For a detailed discussion of the relevant Thomistic texts and subsequent interpretations, cf. A. Patfoort, *L'unité d'être dans le Christ d'après S. Thomas. A la croisée de l'ontologie et de la christologie* (Paris: 1964). For a succinct and vigorous argument that Thomas's stated position on this matter should be taken entirely at face value (a legion of commentators notwithstanding), cf. Etienne Gilson, 'L'esse du Verbe incarné selon Saint Thomas d'Aquin', *Archives d'histoire doctrinale et littéraire du Moyen Age*, 43 (1968), pp. 23–37. Given the source, Gilson's remark about the long history of dispute on this topic in Catholic theology is worth pondering. 'The contours of this controversy are vague, and their sterility is confirmed' (p. 37).

32 Apparently this distinction first enters Barth's theology in the '*Unterricht in der christlichen Religion*', p. 193, and is discussed in some detail in *Die christliche Dogmatik*, pp. 352–3. His appeal to it is a result of his initial encounter with the theology of Protestant Orthodoxy, via the compilations of Heppe and Schmid, during the years of his first teaching appointment in Gottingen (cf. Busch, *Karl Barth*, pp. 153–4). It is retained, with no basic change in definition, in the *Church Dogmatics*. Cf. the explicit discussions in *CD*, I/2, pp. 163–5; *KD*, I/2, pp. 178–80; *CD*, III/2, p. 70; *KD*, III/2, p. 81; *CD*, IV/2, pp. 49–50, 91; *KD*, IV/2, pp. 52–3, 100.

33 I can give a brief indication of the difficulty. The terminology was introduced by Leontius of Byzantium around the middle of the sixth century, but *not* the actual position which was later typically associated with that terminology, especially in the West (cf. John Meyendorff, *Christ in Eastern Christian Thought* (St Vladimir's Seminary Press: 1975), pp. 67–8). In medieval scholasticism after the middle of the thirteenth century, the typical position is affirmed with varying degrees of clarity (especially when, as with Thomas Aquinas, John of Damascus is known in translation), but the termi-

nology is absent (cf., e.g., III, 2, 2, ad3). Only in Protestant scholasticism, it seems, is the typical position, together with the by now ancient terminology, affirmed for the first time in the West.

34 *CD*, I/2, p. 163; *KD*, I/2, p. 178.

35 *CD*, I/2, p. 163; *KD*, I/2, p. 178. Barth regards the following remark from the *Leiden Synopsis* as a particularly good brief statement of the relation between these two complementary concepts. 'That flesh [i.e., the humanity of Jesus Christ] has no subsistence of its own outside the Son of God [*anhypostasis*], but is sustained and borne by and in him [*enhypostasis*]'. Cited ibid., and *CD*, III/2, p. 70; *KD*, III/2, p. 81.

36 *CD*, IV/3, p. 40; *KD*, IV/3, p. 42. This is not to say, of course, that Barth's is the only ontological description which could be consistent with this conviction but rather that, unlike the alternative he discusses, it actually is consistent.

37 *CD*, IV/2, p. 49; *KD*, IV/2, p. 53.

38 Cf. especially above, n. 27. Here again Barth does not explicitly make the distinction I am using, i.e., between ontological description and causal explanation.

39 This distinction between Jesus' humanity 'being' and 'coming into being' has a clear parallel in traditional discussions which typically distinguish between the *unio* of Jesus' humanity to the person of the Logos, and an *assumptio*, a divine act in which that humanity becomes united to the Logos (cf. Thomas Aquinas, III, 2, 8; 3, 4). Barth also speaks explicitly of assumption as well as union.

40 *KD*, IV/2, p. 52; *CD*, IV/2, p. 48. Barth elsewhere characterizes this possibility as that of 'the first Son of Mary' (*CD*, I/2, p. 149; *KD*, I/2, p. 164).

41 *CD*, I/2, p. 150; *KD*, I/2, p. 164 (emphasis from the German). Cf. *CD*, I/2, p. 149; *KD*, I/2, p. 164: 'The Word appropriated this possibility to Himself as His own, and He realized it as such when He became Jesus.'

42 If our primary concern were with the relative merit of Barth's technical description, this last point would, of course, have to be argued in detail. Such an argument is undertaken, in a way almost wholly focused on ontological description, in Hans Stickelberger, *Ipsa assumptione creatur: Karl Barths Rückgriff auf die klassische Christologie und die Frage nach der Selbständigkeit des Menschen*, (Berne: 1979).

43 This project, I should stress, is distinguishable from and secondary to (at least for Barth and Thomas), that of locating a specific belief in the spectrum of Christian beliefs and articulating its *convenientia*. I have very briefly indicated Barth's way of doing the latter with respect to the belief that Jesus' history is God's own; cf. above, p. 162 and pp. 168–9.

44 This should not be taken to imply that for Thomas (or, indeed, for Barth) the only use, or even necessarily the primary use, of basic convictional statements about Jesus Christ (e.g., 'this man is God' is to make an affirmation about reality. I am only assuming that for Thomas such an affirmation is frequently and in various contexts included in the use of such statements and that theology must therefore, among its other responsibilities, give some account of the state of affairs being affirmed. A full treatment of this issue in Thomas would require a separate study, but the following remarks will provide some backing for my assumption, at least in a christological context.

45 *In I Corinthios* (caput) 2, (lectio) 2, no. 92. *S. Thomae Aquinatis Super Epistolas S. Pauli Lectura*, vol. 1, ed. Raphael Cai (Turin and Rome: 1953). 'One nature' (*unam naturam*) here seems an obvious mistake, as the context clearly calls for 'two persons'. Since there is not yet a critical edition of Thomas's commentaries on Paul, it is impossible to tell whether the mistake goes back to Thomas himself or not; it is in either case not decisive for the purposes here. In his frequent discussions of 'Nestorianism', Thomas always associates that label with the view that 'in Christ the human person is a distinct person from the person of the Word', which seems to be the sense of this *lectio* on I Cor. as well. *Quaestio Disputata de Unione Verbi Incarnati* [hereafter *de Unione*] 1, r. *S. Thomae Aquinatis Quaestiones Disputatae*, vol. 2, ed. P. Bazzi, et al. (Turin and Rome: 1965).

46 Thomas also characterizes the function of ontological description in Christology as 'verifying' convictional affirmations with regard to the creedal statements that in Jesus Christ, God was born, crucified and died. In a similar *reductio* against 'Nestorianism', Thomas argues that 'if there were another ultimate subject (*hypostasis*) in Christ beyond the subject of the Word, it would follow that those things which belong to this man would be verified of someone other than the Word, e.g., to be born of the Virgin, to suffer, to be crucified and buried' (III, 2, 3, r). On the need for a vigorous affirmation, in accordance with Scripture and the logic of its statements about Jesus Christ, that 'God died' on the cross of Christ, cf. *SCG*, IV, 34, 11–14.

47 *In Ioannem* 1, 7, no. 170. *S. Thomas Aquinatis Super Evangelium S. Ioannis Lectura*, ed. Raphael Cai (Turin and Rome: 1952). Similarly, cf. *Quodlibetum* IX, 2, 1, r.

48 In the same vein, cf. *In Romanos*, 1, 2, no. 35, *Super Epistolas S. Pauli*, vol. 1. When Paul says that God's own Son has come to be in the flesh (cf. Rom. 1:3), 'this way of speaking (*modus loquendi*) would have no place if this union had been accomplished only in the manner of indwelling'.

49 *SCG*, IV, 39, 1. For a similar, although rather more polyvalent

remark regarding the status of technical trinitarian language, cf. I, 32, 1, ad2.

50 *SCG*, IV, 39, 1. This means that there can be only one subject for what we say of 'God' and 'this man'. 'It is necessary that it be one and the same of which both are said' (ibid.).

51 *SCG*, IV, 39, 2. 'That in the genus of substance of which natural properties are predicated, as befits the nature in question (*secundum naturam propriam*), is the hypostasis and supposit of that nature'. A 'person' is simply a 'hypostasis' or 'supposit' of a rational nature. Cf. I, 29, 2, r; III, 2, 3, r.

52 *SCG*, IV, 39, 2.

53 It is important to stress, as I have noted in passing, that Thomas's argument here is not that the *terminology* of 'two natures united in one person' is necessary, but that *given* this terminology (which no one in his day contested), a specific deployment of it is necessary. He might have argued for the necessity of this terminology in technical description on other grounds (e.g., its use in the language of the ancient Creeds and Councils; cf. e.g., III, 2, 1, sc; 2, 2, sc), but he does not explicitly do so.

54 Cf. I, 16, 1, r: 'Truth is in the mind in so far as the mind is conformed (*conformatus*) to the thing understood'; 'truth is the adequation (*adaequatio*) of the thing and the mind'. The qualification 'in some sense' is essential, as the discussion of the *modi significandi* of christological discourse will shortly make more clear.

55 There are, of course, technical notions of correspondence (e.g., those favoured by logical positivists) which might not be compatible with Thomas's notion of *adeaquatio*, especially if the latter were interpreted in a transcendental fashion (as, e.g., Rahner does).

56 So, for example, Thomas argues that the Nestorians cannot consistently assert a 'communication of names' in Jesus Christ, and yet *deny* that 'union in hypostasis and supposit' is an appropriate description of the reality of the incarnation. Denying the hypostatic union, the Nestorians assert, as Thomas sees it, a union 'according to the communication of names, for example when we say that this man is God and the Son of God. It is obvious, however, that [this procedure] implies an accidental union' (III, 2, 6, r).

57 For example, immediately following the passage in which he argues that the necessity of affirming the hypostatic union is based upon the necessity of speaking about Jesus Christ in a certain way (cf. above, n. 52), Thomas makes a seemingly contrary assertion. 'In this way [viz., given the hypostatic union], divine things will be truly and properly said of that man, on account of the fact that "man" introduces a supposit not only of human nature, but also of divine' (*SCG*, IV, 39, 2).

58 In this the structure of theology is parallel to the structure of faith, the direct and immediate object of which is propositions; the reality believed is the object of faith only indirectly, as mediated by propositions (fundamentally, biblical and creedal ones). Cf. II-II, 1, 2, r. I am not implying here, it should be added, that Barth holds a fundamentally different view. His insistence that the particular identity of Jesus Christ is accessible to us only in its narrative depiction, for example, would seem to preclude the idea that we formulate technical descriptions of aspects of the biblical world by some kind of direct inspection. However, at least in the sections of his Christology with which I am concerned here, he does not distinguish, even for heuristic purposes, between saving the *modus loquendi* of Scripture and giving a description of reality.

59 For these ways of stating the basic conviction with which I am concerned, cf. III, 16, 1–2.

60 *de Unione*, 1, r. Cf. *de Rationibus Fidei contra Saracenos, Graecos, et Armenos*, 6, no. 983 (hereafter *de Rationibus*). 'Since the efficacy of the divine power cannot be comprehended by the human intellect, God can be united to the creature in a higher way (*sublimiori modo*) than the human intellect is able to grasp. Therefore, we say that God is united to human nature in Christ in a certain incomprehensible and inexpressible way.' *S. Thomas Aquinatis Opuscula Theologica*, vol. 1, ed. Raymond Verrardo (Turin and Rome: 1954). Cf. also *SCG*, IV, 41, 8.

61 *de Rationibus*, 6, no. 984. J. H. Walgrave points out that Thomas in fact uses several creaturely models to help characterize the hypostatic union. At least in the *Summa Theologiae*, Thomas seems to find the union of an integral part to its whole ('the hand of Socrates'; cf. III, 2, 2, ad3) to be the most apt of these, rather than the union of body and soul. But, Walgrave argues (as I also do), neither any one of these models, nor all of them together, enables us adequately to conceive the hypostatic union. For Thomas, when we are trying to give an account of divine things, 'we may improperly describe them with the aid of philosophical models, which may illustrate some aspects of them, without however giving us a proper concept of them. Therefore [the models] are to be prudently applied under various corrections' (J. H. Walgrave, 'The Use of Philosophy in the Theology of Thomas Aquinas', in *Aquinas and Problems of His Time*, ed. G. Verbeke and D. Verhelst (The Hague: 1976), p. 190).

62 Cf. previous note. As a brief summary of Thomas's argument, cf. *Scriptum super Sententiis* (hereafter *In Sent.*) I, 22, 1, 2, r: 'It is to be noted therefore, that when names are applied by us [to God], who do not know (*cognoscimus*) God except from created things, they always fail (*deficiunt*) to represent divine things with respect to the mode of signification, because they signify the divine perfections in

the way in which they are participated by creatures.' *S. Thomae Aquinatis Scriptum super Sententiis magistri Petri Lombardi*, ed. P. Mandonnet and M. F. Moos (4 vols, Paris: 1929–47). For a more detailed general account of the distinction and its theological use, cf. I, 13, 3, r. The logico-grammatical distinction between *res significata* and *modus significandi* is an important analytic tool for Thomas; he uses it frequently in his theology, especially in his trinitarian and christological discussions.

For the present purposes, this cursory sketch of the issue will have to suffice. Jan Pinborg has given a detailed and highly informative account of how the notion of *modus significandi* developed, during and immediately after Thomas's time, into the basis of a sophisticated linguistic theory. Cf. Pinborg's *Die Entwicklung der Sprachtheorie im Mittelalter* (Munster Westphalen: 1967); also his article 'Speculative Grammar', *The Cambridge History of Later Medieval Philosophy*, ed. Norman Kretzmann, Anthony Kenny and Jan Pinborg (Cambridge: 1982), pp. 254–69. For some brief but penetrating remarks on Thomas's own place in the history of this development and the fundamental difference between his use of *modus significandi* and that of the later linguistic theorists, cf. *Die Entwicklung*, pp. 39–40, pp. 44–5. David. B. Burrell, *Aquinas: God and Action* (Notre Dame, IN: 1979), shows in convincing detail the importance and function of the concept of *modus significandi* in Thomas's treatment of language about God (cf. pp. 8 – 10, 62 – 5), although his discussion is informed by the relevant historical research only in a very general way. Cf. also the article of M. D. Chenu, 'Grammaire et théologie aux XIIe et XIIIe Siècles', *Archives d'histoire doctrinale et littéraire du moyen age*, 10 (1935–6), pp. 5–28, which anticipates (if only *en passant*) the kind of argument about Thomas's 'agnosticisme grammatical' (p. 26) which Burrell will develop in great detail.

63 On our inability to have a *modus significandi* specifically for the divine unity and consequently for the hypostatic union founded upon it, cf. *de Unione*, 1, r and III, 2, 9. On the divine unity in distinction from 'numerical unity', cf. I, 11, 1–2; 30, 3.

64 III, 16, 1 and 2, respectively. Although I cannot go into the matter here, it should be noted that for Thomas, the affirmation, 'God is this man', is consistent with his radical understanding of creation *ex nihilo*, according to which God is of a wholly different order from the created world, such that God and the world cannot be parts of a whole, nor can they properly be compared. This issue surfaces christologically when Thomas argues that the incarnation did not take place 'in a nature', and so does not imply that 'divinity is humanity'. For a logico-grammatical analysis of this point, cf. III, 16, 5; for the related ontological analysis, cf. III, 2, 1.

65   Cf. *SCG*, IV, 39, 1–2.

66   Cf. III, 16, 1, r: 'A name signifying a given nature concretely may be truly and literally predicated of any subject of that nature, just as "a man" may be truly and literally predicated of Socrates and Plato.' According to Scripture's way of speaking, however (cf. III, 16, 1, sc), God is a subject of human nature. Therefore the concrete name "man" can be truly predicated of the name "God"'. On the difference between concrete terms (like 'man' and 'white') and abstract terms (like 'humanity' and 'whiteness') as a difference in *modus significandi*, cf. I, 39, 5, r; III, 16, 5, adl.

67   *In Sent.*, III, 10, 1, 1, r (no. 23): 'That which is reduplicated in a proposition by the fact that I say "according as" (*secundum quod*) is that on account of which (*per quod*) the predicate belongs to the subject.' As this remark indicates, the Latin phrase *secundum quod* ('according as') is for Thomas the most typical means of forming a reduplicative proposition. *Secundum quod* was regarded in medieval logic as one of the *syncategoremata*, which for Thomas means a term or phrase which does not itself predicate anything of a subject, but 'bears on the order of the predicate to the subject' (I, 31, 3, r.) On the *syncategoremata*, cf. Norman Kretzman, 'Syncategoremata, sophismata, exponibilia', in *Cambridge History of Later Medieval Philosophy*, pp. 211–45. Reduplicative propositions using *secundum quod* are a frequent topic of analysis in Thomas's Christology; cf., e.g., III, 22, 3, adl; 46, 12; 49, 1, adl; 50, 1, adl. The presence of such propositions in medieval Christology goes back at least as far as Anselm's *Epistola de Incarnatione Verbi*, ed. F. S. Schmidt, vol. 2: *S. Anselmi Opera Omnia*, (Edinburgh: 1946), p. 29, l. 11, although in Anselm they have not yet become an explicit subject of analysis.

68   III, 16, 10, ob2. Cf. *In Sent.*, III, 10, 1, 1, r (no. 24), where Thomas gives several examples of different kinds of reduplication and offers a classification of them.

69   Cf. *SCG*, IV, 48, 3.

70   Cf. III, 16, 11; *In Sent.*, III, 10, 1, 1, i.

71   For Thomas's argument that 'man' in the reduplicative phrase 'as man' should be taken as a predicate, and thus as introducing a nature or essence, cf. III, 16, 10, r. 'It should be noted that a name placed in reduplication is more properly taken for the nature than for the subject, since it has the force of a predicate, which is taken formally. For the phrase "Christ as man" is the same as if it were said, "Christ, according as he is man"'. On the predicate as that which is 'taken formally', cf. III, 16, 7, ad4.

72   III, 16, 11, sc.

73   III, 16, 11, sc.

74   Cf. III, 16, 11, ad2. 'When one says "this man", the demonstrative

pronoun refers the name "man" to the subject. And therefore "Christ, as this man, is God", is true, rather than "Christ, as man, is God."' For a more detailed discussion of this proposition, cf. *In Sent.*, III, 10, 1, 1, ii.

75 For Barth, of course, what makes Jesus Christ 'this man' is his 'history'.

76 *In Sent.*, III, 10, 1, 1, i, sol. (no. 27): for a somewhat different medieval logico-grammatical argument with the same aim as Thomas's, i.e., to show how 'incarnation' can be understood in such a way that, as *per assumptionem*, it applies only to Jesus Christ, cf. Anselm, *de Incarnatione Verbi*, 11 (*Opera*, vol. 2, pp. 28–30, especially 29, ll. 26–9.)

77 Cf. III, 17, 1, r. 'This name "Peter" or "Jesus" introduces one possessing human nature in a distinct way, i.e., under determinate individual properties.' On Thomas's conception of a 'proper name' as that which designates the distinct individual, cf. I, 33, 2, r. On spatio-temporal location ('ostensibility') as an irreducible aspect of individuation, cf. III, 77, 2; *In Boethii de Trinitate*, 4, 2.

78 Cf. chap. 2, pp. 44–6.

79 Cf. III, 2, 2, r: 'Because the Word has a human nature united to himself, although the human nature is not part of his divine nature, it follows that the union was accomplished in the person, not the nature, of the Word.' On the basic coherence of this description of 'hypostatic union' with the logical form of propositions like 'This man is God', cf. above, nn. 47, 50.

80 Cf. III, 16, 12, ad3: 'Just as "person" signifies something complete and subsisting by itself in rational nature, so "hypostasis", "subject" and "thing in a nature" (*res naturae*) signify something subsisting by itself in the genus of substance as a whole.' Cf. also III, 2, 2, ad3. On 'person' as equivalent to 'hypostasis', cf. above, n. 51.

81 *SCG*, IV, 41, 5. Cf. also III, 16, 12, ad2. On 'personality' as equivalent to 'the independent existence of a rational nature', cf. III, 2, 2, ad3: 'Not every individual in the genus of substance, even in rational nature, is a person, but only that which exists independently.'

82 *de Unione*, 2, r. Cf. *de Unione*, 3, ad5; III, 2, 2, ad3.

6

Concluding Note

At the outset of this study, I said that if the overall christological strategy pursued by Rahner were ultimately unsuccessful, then a genuinely fundamental decision would be called for, not only about method in Christology, but about the basic aims of Christology. And so it seems. Rahner carries out the strategy I have called the second way with extraordinary care and no small measure of intellectual panache. Yet, as I have argued in my analysis of his Christology, there seems to be no way to make this overall method or strategy consistent with the assumption that Jesus Christ is the sole and unique ascriptive subject of whatever is conceived to have 'ultimate' or 'saving' significance. Hence the choice: one can have either a christological method like Rahner's, or a christological assumption like Rahner's, but it seems impossible to have both. It would be quite consistent, of course, to accept Rahner's methodological premise alone and to develop a Christology (or the working equivalent of one) which explicitly recognizes that on this basis, there can be no attempt to ascribe the function of 'that which is ultimately significant' uniquely to Jesus Christ. I have instead accepted Rahner's christological assumption and tried to indicate the outlines of a christological method for displaying the meaningfulness of redemption (or its functional equivalent) which is consistent with this assumption. My analysis of Barth and (in a much more limited way) of Thomas Aquinas suggests that there is an overriding logical requirement for such a method: it must define the function of 'ultimate' or 'saving' significance in such a way that Jesus Christ as a particular person is logically indispensable to the definition. But here too, there is explicit recognition that a decision has been made. For a Christology which follows what I have called the first way, there can be no

recourse to characterizations of 'that which is ultimately significant' in purely general terms, and hence only indirect and mediated links between the description and experience of redemption
(or its equivalent) through Jesus Christ, and other descriptions
and experiences of that which has the function of 'ultimate
significance' in human life.

The continuing appeal of the second way probably rests to a
significant degree on the promise of avoiding this decision, and
thereby of retaining at least a modicum of the cultural (especially
high-cultural) weight Christianity carried in an earlier day. But
there appears to be no way of avoiding this decision. And, since
one is inclined to suppose that inconsistency cannot at length
endure, it seems that a method like Barth's, rather than one like
Rahner's, holds the greater promise for a Christology committed
to the conviction that Jesus Christ as a particular person is
uniquely and ultimately significant.

Bibliography

Anselm, *Epistola de Incarnatione Verbi*, ed. F. S. Schmidt (Edinburgh; Thomas Nelson: 1946), vol. 2: *S. Anselmi. Opera Omnia.*

Assenmacher, Johannes, *Die Geschichte des Individuationsprinzips in der Scholastik* (Leipzig, Felix Meiner: 1926).

Backes, Ignaz, *Die Christologie des hl. Thomas v. Aquin und die griechischen Kirchenväter* (Paderborn: Ferdinand Schöningh Verlag: 1931).

Balthasar, Hans Urs von, *Karl Barth. Darstellung und Deutung seiner Theologie*, 2nd edn (Cologne, Verlag Jakob Hegner: 1957).

Barth, Karl, *Anselm: Fides Quaerens Intellectum. Anselm's Proof of the Existence of God in the Context of His Theological Scheme*, tr. Ian W. Robertson (London, SCM Press: 1960).

—— *Church Dogmatics* (4 vols, 13 parts), tr. G. W. Bromily, et al. (Edinburgh, T and T Clark: 1956–75).

—— 'Der Glaube and den persönlichen Gott', *Zeitschrift für Theologie und Kirche*, 24 (1914), pp. 21–32; pp. 65–95.

—— *Die christliche Dogmatik im Entwurf. Erster Band: Die Lehre vom Wort Gottes. Prolegomena zur christlichen Dogmatik*, ed. Gerhard Sauter (Zurich, Theologischer Verlag: 1982).

—— *Ethics*, tr. Geoffrey W. Bromily (New York, NY, Seabury: 1981).

—— 'Extra Nos – Pro Nobis – In Nobis', in *Hören und Handeln. Festschrift für Ernst Wolf zum 60 Geburtstag*, ed. Helmut Gollwitzer and Helmut Traub (Munich, Chr. Kaiser Verlag: 1962, pp. 15–27).

—— *Kirchliche Dogmatik* (4 vols, 13 parts) (Munich: Chr. Kaiser Verlag and Zollikon-Zürich, Evangelischer Verlag: 1932–68).

—— '*Unterricht in der christlichen Religion*', *Erster Band: Prolegomena*, ed. Hannelotte Reiffin (Zurich, Theologischer Verlag: 1985).

Borchert, Ernst, *Der Einfluss des Nominalismus auf die Christologie der Spätscholastik. Nach dem Traktat de communicatione idiomatum des Nicholaus Oresme* (Munster, Aschendorffsche Verlagsbuchhandlung: 1940).

Bouillard, Henri, *Karl Barth* (3 vols) (Paris, Aubier: 1957).

Burrell, David, *Aquinas: God and Action* (Notre Dame, IN, Notre Dame University Press: 1979).

Busch, Eberhard, *Karl Barth. His Life From Letters and Autobiographical Texts*, 2nd edn, tr. John Bowden (Philadelphia, PA: Fortress Press: 1976).

Carr, Anne, *The Theological Method of Karl Rahner* (Missoula, MO, Scholars Press: 1977).

Chenu, M.-D. 'Grammaire et théologie aux XIIe et XIIIe siècles', *Archives d'histoire doctrinale et littéraire du moyen age*, 10 (1935–36), pp. 5–28.

Clayton, John Powell, 'Is Jesus Necessary for Christology?: An Antinomy in Tillich's Theological Method', in *Christ Faith and History. Cambridge Studies in Christology*, ed. S. W. Sykes and J. P. Clayton (Cambridge, Cambridge University Press: 1972), pp. 147–63.

Frei, Hans W., 'An Afterword: Eberhard Busch's Biography of Karl Barth', in *Karl Barth in Re-View. Posthumous Works Reviewed and Assessed.* ed. H.-Martin Rumscheidt (Pittsburg, Pickwick Press: 1981).

—— *The Eclipse of Bibilical Narrative* (New Haven, CN, Yale University Press: 1974).

—— *The Identity of Jesus Christ. The Hermeneutical Bases of Dogmatic Theology* (Philadelphia, PA, Fortress Press: 1974).

—— 'Niebuhr's Theological Background', in *Faith and Ethics. The Theology of H. Richard Niebuhr*, ed. Paul Ramsey (New York, NY, Harper and Row: 1957), pp. 9–64.

Gilson, Etienne, 'L'*esse* du verbe incarné selon saint Thomas d'Aquin', *Archives d'histoire doctrinale et littéraire du moyen age*, 43 (1968), pp. 23– 37.

Hirsch, Emanuel, *Geschichte der neuern evangelischen Theologie* 4th edn (5 vols) (Gütersloh, Bertelsman Verlag: 1968).

Jüngel, Eberhard, *Barth-Studien* (Zurich-Cologne, Benziger and Gütersloh, Gütersloher Verlagshaus Mohn: 1982).

Kant, Immanuel, *Critique of Pure Reason*, 2nd edn rev., tr. Norman Kemp Smith (London, Macmillan: 1933).

—— *Religion Within the Limits of Reason Alone*, tr. Theodore M. Greene and Hoyt H. Hudson (New York, NY, Harper and Row: 1960).

Kelsey, David H., *The Uses of Scripture in Recent Theology* (Philadelphia, PA., Fortress Press: 1975).

Kreck, Walter, *Grundentscheidungen in Karl Barths Dogmatik: Zur Diskussion seines Verständnisses von Offenbarung und Erwählung* (Neukirchen-Vluyn: Neukirchener Verlag: 1978).

Kretzmann, Norman. 'Syncategoremata, sophismata, exponibilia', in *The Cambridge History of Later Medieval Philosophy*, ed. Norman Kretzmann, Anthony Kenny and Jan Pinsborg (Cambridge, Cambridge University Press: 1982), pp. 211–45.

Landgraf, Artur Michael, *Dogmengeschichte der Frühscholastik*, Part 2: *Die Lehre von Christus*, vol. 1 (Regensburg, Verlag Friedrich Pustet: 1953).

Lessing, Gotthold, *Lessing's Theological Writings*, tr. and ed. Henry Chadwick (Stanford, CA, Stanford University Press: 1972).

Lindbeck, George A., *'Fides ex auditu* and the Salvation of Non-Christians', in *The Gospel and the Ambiguity of the Church*, ed. Vilmos Vajta (Philadelphia, PA, Fortress Press: 1974), pp. 92–123.

—— *The Nature of Doctrine. Religion and Theology in a Postliberal Age* (Philadelphia, PA, Westminster Press: 1984).

Locke, John, *The Reasonableness of Christianity*, ed. I. T. Ramsey (Stanford, CA, Stanford University Press: 1958).

Loux, Michael J. (ed.), *Universals and Particulars: Readings in Ontology*, rev. edn (Notre Dame In, University of Notre Dame Press: 1976).

Meyendorff, John, *Christ in Eastern Christian Thought* (St Vladimir's Seminary Press: 1975).

Morris, Thomas V., 'St. Thomas on the Identity and Unity of the Person of Christ: A Problem of Reference in Christological Discourse', *Scottish Journal of Theology*, 35 (1982), pp. 419–430.

Pannenberg, Wolfhart, *Jesus – God and Man*, 2nd edn, tr. Lewis S. Wilkens and Duane A. Priebe (Philadelphia, PA., Westminster Press: 1977).

Patfoort, A., *L'unité d'être dans le Christ d'après St. Thomas. A la croisée de l'ontologie et de la christologie* (Paris, Desclée: 1964).

Pinborg, Jan. *Die Entwicklung der Sprachtheorie im Mittelalter.* (Munster Westphalen, Aschendorffsche Verlagsbuchhandlung: 1967).

—— 'Speculative Grammar', in *The Cambridge History of Later Medieval Philosophy*, ed. Norman Kretzmann, Anthony Kenny and Jan Pinsborg (Cambridge, Cambridge University Press: 1982), pp. 254–69.

Principe, Walter H., 'St. Thomas on the Habitus-Theory of the Incarnation', in *St. Thomas Aquinas 1274–1974: Commemorative Studies*, ed. Armand A. Maurer, vol. 1 (Toronto, Pontifical Institute of Medieval Studies: 1974), pp. 381–418.

—— *The Theology of the Hypostatic Union in the Early 13th Century* (4 vols) (Toronto, Pontifical Institute of Medieval Studies: 1963–75).

Rahner, Karl, 'Death', in *Sacramentum Mundi. An Encyclopedia of Theology*, ed. Karl Rahner et al., vol. 2 (New York, NY, Herder and Herder: 1969), p. 58, cols 2–62, col. 1.

—— *Foundations of Christian Faith: An Introduction to the Idea of Christianity*, tr. William V. Dych (New York, NY, Seabury: 1978).

—— *Grundkurs des Glaubens. Einführung in der Begriff des Christentums* (Freiburg, Herder: 1976).

—— *Hörer des Wortes. Zur Grundlegung einer Religionsphilosophie*, 2nd edn, rev. ed. J. B. Metz (Munich, Kösel-Verlag: 1963).

—— *Ich Glaube an Jesus Christus* (Einsiedeln, Benziger Verlag: 1968).

—— *Im Gespräch*, vol. 1, ed. Paul Imhof and Hubert Biallowons (Munich, Kösel-Verlag: 1982).

—— 'Jesus Christ, IV: History of Dogma and Theology', in *Sacramentum*

Mundi. An Encyclopedia of Theology, ed. Karl Rahner et al. (New York, NY, Herder and Herder: 1969), vol. 3, p.192, col. 2–209, col. 2.

—— *Mission and Grace*, vol. 1, tr. Cecily Hastings (London, Sheed and Ward: 1963).

—— 'Observations on the Concept of Revelation', in *Revelation and Tradition*, ed. Karl Rahner and Joseph Ratzinger, tr. W. J. O'Hara (London, Burns and Oates: 1966), pp. 9–25.

—— *Schriften zur Theologie*, 16 vols (Einsiedeln, Benziger Verlag: 1954–84).

—— *Spirit in the World* (London, Sheed and Ward: 1979).

—— *Theological Investigations*, 20 vols, tr. Cornelius Ernst et al. (New York, NY, Seabury and Crossroads: 1961 – 83).

—— 'Transcendental Theology', in *Sacramentum Mundi. An Encyclopedia of Theology*, ed. Karl Rahner et al. (New York, NY, Herder and Herder: 1969), vol. 6, 287, cols 1–289, col. 2.

Russell, Bertrand, *Introduction to Mathematical Philosophy* (London, Allen and Unwin: 1919).

Schellevis, Leendert, *De betekenis van Jezus' mensheid. Een onderzoek naar de christologie van Karl Rahner (mit einer Zusammenfassung in deutscher Sprache)* (Utrecht, Drukkerij Elinkwijk BV: n.d.).

Schleiermacher, Friedrich, *The Christian Faith*, 2nd edn, tr. H. R. Mackintosh and J. S. Stewart (Philadelphia, PA, Fortress Press: 1976).

Sparn, Walter, '"Extra Internum": Die christologische Revision der Prädestinationslehre in Karl Barths Erwählungslehre', in *Die Realisierung der Freiheit. Beiträge zur Kritik der Theologie Barths*, ed. Trutz Rendtorff (Gutersloh, Gerd Mohn: 1975), pp. 44–75.

Stephan, Horst, *Geschichte der deutschen evangelischen Theologie seit dem deutschen Idealismus*, 2nd edn, rev., ed. Martin Schmidt (Berlin, Alfred Töpelmann: 1960).

Stickelberger, Hans, *Ipsa assumptione creatur: Karl Barths Rückgriff auf die klassische Christologie und die Frage nach der Selbständigkeit des Menschen*, (Berne, Peter Lang: 1979).

Strawson, P. F., *Individuals. An Essay in Descriptive Metaphysics* (London, Methuen: 1959).

—— *Subject and Predicate in Logic and Grammar* (London, Methuen: 1974).

Thomas Aquinas, *de Rationibus Fidei contra Saracenos, Graecos, et Armenos*, ed. Raymond Verrardo, vol. 1: *Opuscula Theologica* (Turin and Rome, Marietti: 1954).

—— *Expositio super librum Boethii de Trinitate*, ed. Bruno Decker (Leiden, Brill: 1955).

—— *Lectura in I Corinthios*, ed. Raphael Cai, vol. 1: *Super Epistolas S. Pauli Lectura* (Turin and Rome, Marietti: 1953).

—— *Lectura in Romanos*, ed. Raphael Cai, vol. I: *Super Epistolas S. Pauli Lectura* (Turin and Rome, Marietti: 1953).

—— *Quaestio Disputata de Unione Verbi Incarnati*, ed. P. Bazzi et al., vol. 2:

Quaestiones Disputatae (Turin and Rome, Marietti: 1965).

—— *Quaestiones Quodlibetales*, ed. Raymond Spiazzi (Turin and Rome, Marietti: 1949).

—— *Scriptum super Sententiis magistri Petri Lombardi*, 4 vols, ed. P. Mandonnet and M. F. Moos (Paris, Lethielleux: 1929–47).

—— *Summa contra Gentiles* (Turin and Rome, Marietti: 1946).

—— *Summa Theologiae*, 4 vols, ed. Peter Caramello (Turin and Rome, Marietti: 1948–52).

—— *Super Evangelium S. Ioannis Lectura*, ed. Raphael Cai (Turin and Rome, Marietti: 1952).

Weger, Karl-Heinz, *Karl Rahner. An Introduction to His Theology*, tr. David Smith (New York, NY, Seabury: 1980).

Walgrave, J. H., 'The Use of Philosophy in the Theology of Thomas Aquinas', in *Aquinas and Problems of His Time*, ed. G. Verbeke and D. Verhelst (The Hague, Martinius Nijhoff: 1976), pp. 181 – 93.

Welte, Bernhard, 'Homoousious hemin. Gedanken zum Verständnis und zur theologischen Problematik der Kategorien von Chalkedon', in *Das Konzil von Chalkedon. Geschichte und Gegenwart*, ed. Aloys Grillmeier and Heinrich Bacht, vol. 3: *Chalkedon heute* (Würtzburg, Echter-Verlag: 1954), pp. 51–80.

Index